Ab-Sa-Ra-Ka; or, Wyoming Opened

KAM-NE-BUT-SE.   ECHE-HAS-KO.   TE-SHUN-NZS.
(*Blackfoot.*)   (*Long Horse.*)   (*White Calf.*)

CROW CHIEFS.

Ab-Sa-Ra-Ka; or, Wyoming Opened

The Classic Account of a U.S. Army Officer's Wife
on the Great Plains During the Indian Wars

Margaret Irvin Carrington

Ab-Sa-Ra-Ka; or, Wyoming Opened
The Classic Account of a U.S. Army Officer's Wife on the Great Plains During the Indian Wars
by Margaret Irvin Carrington

First published under the title
Ab-Sa-Ra-Ka; or, Wyoming Opened

Leonaur is an imprint of Oakpast Ltd

Copyright in this form © 2012 Oakpast Ltd

ISBN: 978-0-85706-922-1 (hardcover)
ISBN: 978-0-85706-923-8 (softcover)

http://www.leonaur.com

Publisher's Notes

The views expressed in this book are not necessarily those of the publisher.

Contents

Prefaces	9
Prologue to First Edition	13
Absaraka, Home of the Crows	15
Absaraka Described	19
The Natural History and Climate of Absaraka	24
Organization of the Expedition to Absaraka	29
Incidents of the Platte River Travel	34
Reminiscences of Ranching, and Old Times on the Route From Leavenworth to Sedgewick	40
Union Pacific Railroad to Laramie	45
Fort Laramie Council of 1866	52
Laramie to Reno	57
Fourth of July in Absaraka	64
Location of Fort Philip Kearney	70
Arrival of Indians	75
Massacre of Louis Gazzons' Party	80
What Bridger and Beckwith Say	88
Reinforcements on the Way	90
Fort Philip Kearney and Surroundings	94

Indian Response to a National Salute	100
Hostile Sioux and Friendly Cheyennes	104
Indians All in Their War-Paint	108
Domestic, Social, and Religious Life, With the Episodes Therein Occurring	113
Indian Warfare	117
The Arrow Beats the Revolver	121
Extracts From Journal	126
Fetterman's Massacre	130
The Funeral, and Burial of Fourscore and One Victims of the Massacre	137
Comedy of Errors	141
March to Fort Reno	146
Fort Reno to Fort Caspar—Thence to the United States	152
In Memoriam	156
Omaha to Virginia City, Montana	160
Indian Affairs on the Plains—Incidents of 1865-7	167
Indian Affairs on the Plains—Incidents of 1867	177
Indian Affairs on the Plains—Incidents, 1867-1873	192
Indian Affairs on the Plains—Incidents From 1874 to 1877	204
Indian Affairs on the Plains—Incidents of 1877	221
Honour to Whom Honour	233
Appendix	237

Dedication.

With acknowledgments to Lieutenant-General Sherman, whose suggestions at Fort Kearney, in the spring of 1866, were adopted, in preserving a daily record of the events of a peculiarly eventful journey, and whose vigorous policy is as promising of the final settlement of Indian troubles and the quick completion of the Union Pacific Railroad as his "*March to the Sea*" was signal in crushing the last hope of armed rebellion, this narrative is
respectfully dedicated.

Prefaces

PREFACE TO SIXTH EDITION

Wyoming, long recognized by the Interior Department as "Absaraka," will soon be a State. Its original opening for settlement is correctly given in this volume. A full report of its mineral, agricultural, and other natural resources, made in 1866, and that of the massacre, three times called for by the United States Senate, finally appeared in 1887 in Senate Executive Document 33, Fiftieth Congress.

The Report of the Fort Phil Kearney Massacre, now in Appendix II., was long suppressed. Neither Custer, Dodge, nor Dunn had the materials for a correct historical relation. The hasty report of Major-General Philip St. George Cooke, who was promptly removed from command by Lieutenant-General Sherman, is valueless, from its ignorance of his own orders and despatches.

The conference with the Ogallalla Sioux in 1867, referred to by Custer, is given in full from the original notes in my possession.

It is time that the fostered false impressions as to Indian operations, 1866-70, be corrected by authentic records.

Henry B. Carrington,
U.S.A. (Retired).

Hyde Park, Mass., March 2, 1890.

PREFACE TO THIRD EDITION

Absaraka had indeed a tragic opening to settlement. The disaster which in 1870 robbed the army of twelve officers and two hundred and forty-seven brave men, was but the sequel to that series of encounters which first reached the world through the tragedy of 1866. It is now of even more importance to know the country which depends so much upon armed force for its settlement and the solution of the Indian controversy.

During January, 1876, General Custer said to the writer, "It will take another Phil Kearney massacre to bring Congress up to a generous support of the army." Within six months, his memory, like that of Fetterman, became monumental through a similar catastrophe. With larger experience on the frontier,—for Fetterman had none,—but with equal faith in the ability of white troops to handle a largely superior force of Indians, fearless, bravo, and a matchless rider, Custer had also the conviction that the army was expected to fight the hostile savage under all circumstances and at every opportunity.

A brief outline of events, embodying operations in that country up to the present time, will have value to all who watch our dealings with the Indians of the Northwest.

The introductory map was deemed sufficiently definite by Generals Custer and Brisbin to take with them for reference, and its present form includes the additional forts and agencies, as furnished by the favour of General Humphreys, Chief of United States Engineers.

The itinerary of Chapter 30 has permanent value. The first military occupation of that country is also accurately presented in the original text. There never was a more ill-considered impulse of the American people than that which forced the army into the Powder River and Big Horn countries in 1866, to serve the behests of irresponsible speculative emigration, regardless of the rights of tribes rightfully in possession. There never was a wilder grab for gold than the succeeding dash into the Black Hills in the face of solemn treaties.

The compensations of time bring to the surface the fruits of unsound policy, and the treaties of 1866, at Laramie—a mere sham so far as they concerned the tribes beyond—have ripened. The fruit has been gathered. Honoured dead bear witness. I stated distinctly, at the time of the massacre, that if that line should be broken up it would require four times the force to reopen it; and since then more *thousands* of troops have been wrestling with the issue than hundreds were then employed for its protection. Of the struggle for the Big Horn country an impression was embodied in one earnest paragraph:

"While there has been partial success in impromptu dashes, the Indian, now desperate and bitter, looks upon the rash white man as a sure victim no less than he does a coward, and the United States must come to the deliberate resolve to send an army equal to a fight with the Indians of the Northwest. Better to have the expense at once, than to have a lingering, provoking war, for years. It must be met, and the time is just now."

But the force was not available for that purpose, and a lingering, provoking war, for years, has followed.

There is no glory in Indian war. If too little be done, the West complains; if too much be done, the East denounces the slaughter of the red man. Justice lies between the extremes, and herein lies the merit of that Indian policy which was inaugurated during the official term of President Grant. So much of falsehood mingled with fact, and so keen was the popular scent for some scapegoat at the first public announcement of a war which had been constant for six months, that even now the public mind retains but a vague impression of the lessons of that massacre. It has indeed required another fearful tragedy to invoke an examination into the relations of the American people toward these Indian tribes, and to solve the problem whether a Christian nation will exercise patience, restrain wrong, and yet do what is right by both races.

To place a new edition of Absaraka before the public is no hasty offering for transient effect, but to give the world historical facts, many of them otherwise unnoticed, and thus aid them to appreciate the vicissitudes of frontier army life.

The writer has little change to suggest in the narrative text, although nearly ten years have elapsed since it was first written. The accompanying new matter, and notes, will enable the reader to follow other operations in the valleys of Powder, Tongue, Big Horn, and Yellowstone Rivers, while the additional map includes territory as far north as the British Possessions, and the future battlefield region, if Indians invade from Canada.

The portraits illustrate styles of Indian dress, while introducing the leading chiefs who figure in the narrative, and are known, by name, to the entire people of the United States.

It is no weak incentive to the enlargement of this record that the sacrifice of Fetterman, Brown, Custer, Bradley, and their associates, is kept in memory, while tribute is ever paid to her whose life so soon passed away after the trials of that unexpected and extreme exposure.

Henry B. Carrington

Wabash College, Crawfordsville, Ind.
May, 1878.

Prologue to First Edition

The importunity of friends, who have been interested in the journal of a summer's trip and a winter's experience on the Plains, and which, as a matter of taste, now assumes the more easy flow of narrative, has over ruled the first refusal to permit its use in more available form for their leisurely reading. Gathering many of its details from officers of the posts, from Major James Bridger, and others, and so gathering as each day's experience unfolded events of interest, there is no assumption of anything further than to express the facts so recorded just as they were impressed upon the judgment or fancy.

If, on the one hand, the recital of military preparations or movements be so inartificial as to excite the smile of the critic, or if the natural tendency to adopt the idioms and style which, every way and forever, surround the wife of an officer, shall seem so constrained as to repel the lady reader, it can only be said that we wrote, when we wrote, just as the surroundings inspired or compelled us.

In this change from the form of a journal we have adhered to its record, and preserved the integrity of the original, so as to reproduce our life as it was lived and give incidents as they transpired.

While nearly one-half of the Indian demonstrations were under our own eye, the authentic reports of others were of equal value to history; and the narrative differs little from what would be the written experience of others, except that we availed ourselves more fully of classes of facts and sources of knowledge equally open to all, and so cherished their record, as in earlier life we garnered up details of a first visit to Mammoth Cave or the Falls of Niagara.

If our statistics and statements as to Indian councils, usages, or raids, or the record of labour, casualties, and incidents, savour much of *routine*, yet through incidental form we have gathered historical facts, and thus do we present our life and the exact history of the first year of the military occupation of Absaraka.

And again; if there be a savour of whining because the soldiers were so few and support was unfurnished, it will not be taken as criticism to offend anybody, since everybody knows how small was the army, and how incapable of immediate expansion to meet the issues of the North-western frontier at the close of the war.

So, then, our friends will accept this response to their wishes, and *at least* gather instruction for their guidance when they undertake their first visit to Absaraka, Home of the Crows.

CHAPTER 1

Absaraka, Home of the Crows

Absaraka, in the language of the Crow Indians, translated, *Home of the Crows*, was once the field of their proudest successes.

The fertile basins of the Yellowstone, Big Horn, and Tongue Rivers were enlivened by the presence of their many villages; and in the early days of Bridger and Beckwith, the Crow Indians accumulated considerable wealth by a prolific trade in pelts and dressed furs, which those veteran trappers and frontiersmen delivered for them at St. Louis and other border depots for Indian commerce.

Partially girt in by the Big Horn and Panther Mountains, yet roaming at will, they were masters of a region of country which has no peer in its exhaustless game resources, and is rarely surpassed in its production of wild fruits, grasses, and cereals; while its natural scenery, made up of snowy crests, pine-clad slopes and summits, crystal waters, and luxuriant vales, certainly has no rival in our great sisterhood of States.

The Snake Indians, who roamed farther north and west, and who had even crossed lances with the Pagans and Bloods, on the confines of British America, were unable, man for man, to match their more numerous and more adventurous rivals, the Crows, and at last, in 1856, joined friendly hands with them, or at least observed a fair neutrality in the later conflicts of the Crows with their hereditary and deadly enemies, the Sioux and Northern Cheyennes.

When the Cheyennes of the Black Hills of Eastern Dakota divided their bands, and one portion went to the Red River country, while another portion left the old home, with nearly half of the remaining families, for Powder River and Tongue River valleys, the Ogillalla Sioux at last found allies to support their operations against the Crows. With a portion of the Arrapahoes, Blackfeet, and Gros Ventres of the

Prairie, popularly known as the Big Bellies, they prosecuted the war with vigour and unrelenting hatred. Breaking into the long-coveted region about which they had been testing their valour for years in fruitless forays and uncertain adventures, the Sioux, aided by their new friends, succeeded in occupying the choice valleys of the lower Big Horn and Tongue Rivers, and still held them in comparative independence when the expedition of 1866, sent to open the new route to Virginia City, forced them to accept the challenge of the *white man* for the future possession of their stolen dwelling-place.

The Crows fell back of the Yellowstone, though still operating eastward as far as the west bank of Big Horn River; and a few attempted something like local improvement, imitating the Flat Heads, who, though few of numbers, were not the less energetic, and seemed to be really desirous of gaining some affinity with the ideas and civilization of the whites.

With all these changes and the continued aggression of the Sioux, the Crows maintained their passion for their old and their favourite home. It had its peculiar virtues. At once grand and beautiful, prolific in game beyond all precedent, susceptible of culture and the development of vast mineral wealth, while offering a new avenue for travel to Montana nearly five hundred miles shorter than that by Salt Lake City, how can it be deemed strange that they looked upon that redundancy of game, that exceeding fertility, and that natural forage, as wonderfully adapted for their perpetual home and abiding-place!

The white man had given it no distinctive name, and had scarcely trespassed upon its soil. Farther west, he had occupied the Madison and Jefferson branches and the head waters of the Missouri. Flourishing towns and cities had been located, and the Indians, who had so long been driven westward, were *now* crowded *back* upon the Yellowstone and Big Horn; so that the Crows must soon renew their active antagonism with their old plunderers, or seek other fields or methods of life.

This great hunting sphere, though nameless, had a natural independence both of Montana and Dakota, while attached in part to each. All that lies east of Black Foot and Clarke's Passes had its special relation to the territory extending as far as Powder River. Somebody had indeed ventured to style this country *Wyoming*, a name which might do very well for a county of Pennsylvania, but had the least claim for application to the stolen land of the Crows.

These same Crow Indians, in addition to their natural title to the land, maintain, to this day, the proud claim *never to have killed a white man but in self-defence.* All their intercourse in 1866, and their relations in 1867, combine to show the integrity of their friendship and the truth of their protestations.

Their very enemies concede to them the rightful title to the territory so long struggled for. At a formal council held at Fort Philip Kearney in July, 1866, between Colonel Carrington and certain Cheyenne chiefs, who were then in close relations with Red Cloud and other *Ogillalla* Sioux, but desirous of breaking loose from the tie, that they might receive protection from the whites, the following question was addressed to Black Horse:

"*Why do the Sioux and Cheyennes claim the land which belongs to the Crows?*"

Black Horse, The Wolf that Lies Down, Red Arm, and Dull Knife promptly answered:

"*The Sioux helped us. We stole the hunting-grounds of the Crows because they were the best. The white man is along the great waters, and we wanted more room. We fight the Crows, because they will not take half and give us peace with the other half.*"

Absaraka is therefore in fact, as the Crows have fondly named that whole region (absurdly styled "Wyoming by some), the "Home of the Crows."

Bound to it by sacred legends; endeared as it is by years of occupation and wasting conflicts for its repossession; pressed by the whites from the west, and now approached from the east, yet restricted to the use of the Upper Yellowstone and west bank of the Big Horn Rivers, the Crows still maintain their rightful title, and ask of the white man that he acknowledge it.

No less firmly do they maintain inviolate their solemn faith once pledged to the white man, and they look to his advent, in sufficient numbers, as the signal of their own deliverance and the destruction of their old enemies the Sioux.

Ready to co-operate with the whites—*kindly disposed toward the new road*—beginning to appreciate the fate of the red man who shall oppose the progress of civilization and frontier settlement, they regard with something like hope the strong arm of that progress, and stand ready to perpetuate their own life by a just conformity to its reasonable demands.

There is another fact which appeals strongly to other sentiments than those that favour simple justice.

Among all the tribes of the Northwest, the Crow Indian stands *first* in manliness and physical perfection.

While they alone have the title to negotiate the right of way for the New Virginia City road, independently of its *occupation* by the Sioux and their allies, they also have pride of race and nation. *They can be trusted as friends within its boundaries* whenever they are treated with the consideration they deserve. Would white men do more?

The Crows lost possession by robbery. Their enemies have become the white man's enemy. Their enemies have ignored treaty obligations, nave despised all terms of compromise or honourable warfare, and defy the Crows and white man alike.

To the Crow, therefore, should be tendered support and friendship. Whatever the result as to the possession of the soil, it is as wicked to give it to the Sioux, for fear of his enmity, as it is to rob the Crows, if they wish to retain or jointly enjoy it.

Above all, the land should bear its true name, and thus give to posterity *some* index to its past history and the issues and struggles which have preceded its use by the white man. Let it be known, whether as Territory, State, or Indian Reservation, as Absaraka, Home of the Crows.

Herein, honour is rendered to noble red men, for such these are! *Herein*, justice is done to the Crow nation, which has hardly been less honourable and true to their friendship than the Naragansetts, the Delawares, and the Pawnees. *Herein*, shall be established a memorial name that will connect with the last supremacy of the red man a tribute to those who were truly worthy; and past injustice shall be partially atoned for, in giving to the Crow Indians this perpetual recognition in the land of Absaraka, the Home of the Crows.

Chapter 2

Absaraka Described

This land of the largest liberty for the red man and the chase is as varied in surface and general features as it is attractive to the various tribes that have contended for its possession.

Nearly all maps, and even the experience of Major James Bridger, the chief guide of the expedition of 1866, and that of Mr. Brannan, an assistant guide, who was with General Connor in 1865, so far as he advanced in the valley of Tongue River, fail to furnish such data as to afford an adequate judgment of this region and its capacity for future development.

All guides and scouts very naturally fix their attention upon points where water and grazing can be found by emigrants *in transitu*; but they do not as often generalize the result of these varied adventures, and fix the relations of diverse soils and geographical features to the purposes of advancing civilization and general settlement.

And yet, as the army and people have been released from the engrossing interests of a great domestic war, and the failure of the Laramie treaty of 1866, with its immediate succession of hostilities to every foot of progress over the route claimed to have been guaranteed by that treaty, have turned the attention of the national Congress and the national army to this new field of fight, it will be found that no portion of the public domain, heretofore almost *terra-incognita*, will challenge a greater public favour when its elements of value are known.

Not that it will prove a paradise for mere adventurers who aspire after good and sudden riches at the expense of the substantial development of the lands they traverse and prospect; but this idea is founded upon the basis of actual settlement, and the ultimate adoption of Absaraka into the great family of American States.

And yet, it is true that even the adventurer will find a field of promise. Every creek, from Clear Fork to the Upper Yellowstone, gives gold colour, and there is no doubt that patient, well-directed labour will realize fair returns. Certain it is, that but for the Indian hostilities—engendered partly by bad faith exercised toward some of their bands; partly by excessive intimacy, degrading to both the white and red man, and resulting in the ultimate vengeance of the latter when he learns the drift of such intimacy; partly by failure to support the Indians who deserve support; and especially by failure to punish those who were incorrigibly wicked and ugly—the new route, so short, and in the main so fruitful in supplies for the emigrant, would become a favourite with all travellers to Eastern and Lower Montana.

Of course it has its supposed rivals. Salt Lake City, so beautiful in location, with its shaded avenues, its ever-flowing fountains, and lavish soil, cannot cheerfully spare from its markets the long trains which have made the circuit by its route; and everybody who owns a light-draught steamer will willingly transport from St. Louis, Nebraska City, or Omaha, as many passengers as the capacity of his cabin or the stage of river moisture will permit; but the mathematical difficulty of making the hypotenuse of an acute angled triangle greater than the sum of the sides is a never-failing embarrassment to either party, and the question of distance remains as nature established it.

The honest stranger who seeks a home in Lower Montana, and a short reliable route to Bozeman City, the Gallatin Valley, and Jefferson City, and the agricultural or mineral districts of that region, desires more definite information of the land to which his thoughts turn; and not only the people of Nebraska, Iowa, Minnesota, Illinois, and Indiana, but those of more eastern States, are pushing their trains across the plains, looking in vain, as they have long looked, for some definite details of the route they are to traverse.

It is not always convenient, each day, for the emigrant to depend upon some transient *ranchero* or squatter for information aa to the next grass, timber, or water along the route; and it is therefore of practical value for the traveller to have a definite outline of the country before furnishing such details as specify the route, with its history, resources, and supplies.

The *geographical* outline of Absaraka is special and full of interest.

The general course of the Big Horn Mountains is from southeast to northwest, until it reaches the Big Horn River, when the direction changes westward; but the Big Horn Mountains proper die out before reaching the Upper Yellowstone River and Clark's and Blackfoot

Passes, yet only a short distance from the former.

At the lower or south-eastern terminus, the range doubles back upon itself to the southwest, in form not unlike a Big Horn or cornucopia, and gives significance to its name, although the "Big Horn" of the mountain sheep is credited as source of the title.

Of course it is presumed that the reader has gained some knowledge of the course of the Platte, and entertains at least general ideas of the routes to Salt Lake City by way of Denver, Fort Bridger, or Forts Laramie and Caspar.

While this narrative will embrace directions for the traveller, even from the South Platte, and especially after the journey leaves the line of the Union Pacific Railroad, with all the definiteness needed for daily practical use, it does not require, in this general description of Absaraka, that those elements should be noticed at present.

Omitting, therefore, all branches of the Big Cheyenne, and all tributaries of either Fork of the Platte, the general survey begins with Powder River.

Powder River, which is a muddy stream, comes from the southern side of the Big Horn Mountains and a south-western source, and therefore is not a part of the great aggregate of bright channels that combine to feed the Missouri River from the Big Horn range proper. True it is, that it may be held responsible for their subsequent discolouration, and it does help the Missouri to no little portion of that final burden of deposit and gravity which so unfavourably appeals to the first taste of the traveller from the East; but this is *its mission*, and simply vindicates its own character, as do similar currents in the aggregate of the great flow of human life.

The Big Horn range of the Rocky Mountains possesses two distinct and marked features. There is, first, a central or backbone range, which culminates in perpetual snow, where Cloud Peak grandly rises as the chief of all its proud summits, falling off slowly and patiently toward the southern valleys that are soon confronted by similar ranges of the Wind River Mountains beyond.

The second range is north of the first, and after clearly leaving the loftier sweep, it presents nearly a perpendicular face to the north, except where the earnest torrents have cut deep gorges, and thus forced their way to the main tributaries of the Missouri.

Between these ranges, and varying in breadth from twelve to twenty-five miles, are fine hunting-grounds, abounding in noble orchards, wild fruits and grasses, as well as the choicest game for the huntsman.

This special tract is hardly a true plateau, as are the more uniform offsets of the *Tierre Calients* of the Mexican ranges; but with all its vicinity to perpetual snow, there are gentle slopes which possess peculiar loveliness and many elements of future value. With this general outline in mind, let the traveller start from Fort Reno on Powder River.

He is in the midst of a sterile country, a sage desert. Before him rise the snow-clad mountains, but he has weary miles to travel before he gets the real value of their benignant expenditure of clear cold water upon the vales below.

A march of twenty-six miles brings him to Crazy Woman's Fork. This river, ever flowing, is also ever muddy, having received its largest contingent of supply from the same yellow source as Powder River. Six miles northwest, and following the sweep of the Big Horn northern range, and some six to eight miles outside its general base, a new country opens. Sage brush and cactus, which for nearly two hundred miles have so largely monopolized the soil, rapidly disappear. The change is beautiful as it is sudden. One narrow divide only is crossed, and the transition is like the quick turn of the kaleidoscope, which retains indeed the outline, but supplies new combinations and new tints for every object the light illuminates.

Twenty-three miles from Crazy Woman's Fork, the bright, noisy, and transparent waters, and the rich valley of Clear Fork are reached:—so swift that mules and horses have difficulty in crossing; so clear that every fish and pebble is well defined; and so cool that ice in midsummer is no object of desire, this same Clear Fork introduces the series of natural charms that have endeared the country to the savage, and will in the future have equal beauty for those who seek homes in a new and hitherto undeveloped land.

Clear Fork is a genuine flow from the Big Horn Mountains, and is a type of many others no less constant, pure, and valuable. It is partly snow derived, and partly the sum of innumerable springs.

Rock Creek comes next, with far less pretension, but similar in character.

After passing Lake Smedt,—the great nursing haunt for ducks, wild geese, and brant, and which bears the name of Father De Smedt, who, as a Catholic priest, has ministered to the spiritual and social wants of the north-western tribes for many years,—and only fourteen miles from Clear Fork, the traveller comes suddenly upon the two Piney Forks of Clear Fork of Powder River.

Here exhaustless supplies of pine and all affiliated trees gather about the mountain sides and crawl down even to the islands of the larger fork, where access is easy and convenient; while the abundant game, the local supremacy of the situation and its relations to the predominating lodge trails of the country, have made this immediate region the theatre of active Indian hostilities from the time of its first occupation.

Peno Creek, Goose Creek, Tongue River, Rotten Grass Creek, Little Big Horn, and Big Horn Rivers succeed, each with bright tributaries; and so, stream succeeds stream as far as the great mountain gates through which the traveller enters the rich Gallatin Valley and finds himself in Montana proper.

Nearly parallel, but distant from twelve to twenty-five miles northward from the Big Horn range, are *Mauvais Terres*, or "Bad Lands," whose conical hills and irregular outlines present all the desolate features of old volcanic *debris*; and when seen from some commanding point, appear to be hopelessly barren of good, either to man or beast.

And yet, all the rivers above named, and many others, boldly cut their way through these obstructions, and gather upon their borders rich fringes of vegetation and many elements of future development and profit.

The valleys of these streams greatly vary in width and scope; that of the Big Horn ranging from fifteen to twenty miles, and that of Tongue River covering nearly twice that area after it receives the contributions of Goose Creek and its other mountain feeders.

The region of country embraced within this outline, including the Upper Yellowstone and all east of Black Foot and Clark Passes, grasps more area of land than most of the large States or Territories; and with all its natural connections with Montana and Dakota, possesses an individual *status* that must eventually give it independence of each.

CHAPTER 3

The Natural History and Climate of Absaraka

The agricultural features of Absaraka have had incidental notice, but not sufficiently to advise a stranger of their real merit.

Wild wheat and oats abound in all the main valleys; both are grateful to stock, and sustain them well. The grasses are very heavy, so that in the summer of 1866 they were almost too resistant for easy use of machinery, and so thick that a horse could not be trotted rapidly in the bottom lands of Goose Creek and Tongue River.

Grasshoppers now and then made a visit, coming in clouds, like the drifting smoke of a prairie fire; but *they* failed to destroy the great grass region. Still they are no insignificant enemy, and a literal statement of their dense masses, put in the most guarded manner, would seem like the tale of a Munchausen or Gulliver. They cover a blade of grass until it bends to the earth. They cover horse and rider, ruthlessly dashing at every exposed part of the face or breast. They pass over with a rush, like the night roar of the cascades of the Pineys; and they shield the eye so that you can look the sun in the face as though a light flirt of snow had crossed its disk. And yet they are so subject to the mastery of the mountain winds, whose currents are as constant as they are fickle, that they quickly change their place of labour and again renew it in other fields of freshness and beauty.

The soil of the valleys is, in the main, a rich, deep loam, well adapted for vegetables, and in that climate for cereals; but alternate late and early frosts seem combined to refuse to *corn* a fair chance with other grain, while on the other hand barley, so grateful to mules, could seek no better region for its best development.

While rain, other than the dripping skirts of some mountain shower, is rare as diamonds, the numberless dashing streams, tributary to the great flows, present such ready means of irrigation that small labour and expense would apply them to all desired uses. Besides this, the deep snows of the winter season long leave the effects of their fertilizing agency, and when the autumn has turned all general vegetation from green to brown, the side hills will still be spotted with verdant places, where the lingering snow had last struggled, as if to contend with the summer's sun, for mastery of the grass it had gifted with such precocious life and protracted vigour.

Of wild fruit there is great variety. Raspberries, strawberries, gooseberries, red currants, plums, cherries, and rock grapes are among the number. The cottonwood-trees are often festooned with the vine of the hop, which here gives forth its product in such profusion and perfection, as will find no rival in the cultivated acres of Eastern New York.

The pine and hemlock, the spruce and balsam, the Cottonwood and ash, and willow are some of the trees which are ready of access and ample in supply for the demands of generations.

The climate is invigorating and healthful. *There is no dew*; and sickness is so rare, that for days in succession, during the constant labour and exposure of 1866, no soldiers attended the stated daily *sick* call, and the hospital itself was monopolized by cases of surgery only.

The summer temperature rarely exceeds ninety, and the nights are always cool and refreshing. Few take cold; and from July 15th, 1866, to January 15th, 1867, the barometer changed from fair, or very dry, only at the advent of winds sweeping from the snow mountains, and at one storm of mixed rain and snow, near the date of the autumnal equinox.

The field of natural history is rich beyond all precedent. The vicinity of Piney Forks and Tongue River is in the very heart of the game country. It is, as between several tribes, a semi-neutral and general hunting-ground. It is a great thoroughfare for migration to and from the Arkansas, and the hills in front and rear of Fort Philip Kearney are seamed and scarred by countless trails, where the Indian ponies have dragged lodge poles in their periodical or other changes of habitation and hunting.

The antipathy of the Indian to its occupation by the white man is very intense and bitter. The rattle of the mower, the whistle of the steam sawmill, the felling of timber, the quick rise of stockade and substantial warehouses and quarters, are such sure signs of permanent possession, that they lose no opportunity to steal or kill when they can do so with comparative impunity. Yet the game still clings to its favourite haunts, and the Indian must press upon the steps of the white man or lose all hope of future independence. Herds of elk proudly stand with erect antlers, as if charmed by the morning music of garrison guard parade, or as if curious to understand this strange inroad upon their long secluded parks of pleasure. The mountain sheep look down from the beetling crags that skirt the perpendicular northern face of the Big Horn Mountains, and yield to no rival their claims to excellence for food. The black and white tail deer and the antelope are ever present; while the hare and the rabbit, the sage hen and prairie chicken, are nearly trodden down before they yield to the intrusion of the stranger.

Brant, wild geese and ducks multiply and people the waters of Lake Smedt, and are found in nearly the same profusion all along the streams under the Big Horn Mountains; while the grizzly and cinnamon bear, not unseldom, give up their lives and their rich material for the table, when, in the pursuit of wild plums and other fruit, they are crossed by the hunter and are dropped by his rifle. Last, and largest, and numberless, the buffalo, with tens of thousands in a herd, sweep back and forth, filling the valleys as far as the eye can reach, and adding their weight and numbers to the other substantial claims of the red man to entitle this same Absaraka, "*Their last and best hunting-grounds.*"

The Big Horn River and its branches, as well as the streams beyond, are plentifully supplied with trout, the mountain pike, and other valuable fish, and thus complete the complement of supplies with which the country is so generously provided.

Innumerable wolves do indeed pierce the night air with their howls; but like the beaver, whose dams incumber all the smaller streams, and the otter, they are forced to yield their winter covering for those nice coats and caps, those mitts and blankets and leggings, which make men glad when zero is often reached, or the mercury calmly congeals in the bulb.

And yet, with the intervals of extreme cold and protracted snow, there is comparatively little suffering, unless from scurvy, when antiscorbutics are scarce, or men are careless, and rheumatism attends peculiar exposure. The dry snows, when in real earnest, penetrate every crevice, and drift about every obstruction. Valleys and gulches are filled, and travel is tedious or in abeyance; but the winter has its pleasures no less than the summer, and but for the hostility of the red man, the upper garrisons of that line would hardly exchange their posts for any other on the frontier.

The mineral field imparts some of its peculiar contributions to the stores of Absaraka. Gold colour is given in nearly all the streams, as already once indicated. Whether the sources of those streams will ever equal Montana precedents, must remain for the hard labour or good chance of the adventurer, or the skill and patience of some enterprising *savant*, to determine. The Black Hills, east of Fort Reno, have indications that promise rich returns of labour, and the Lower Powder River has been left unoccupied by miners only because of the hostility of Buffalo Tongue and other Indians who infest its valley. The few excursions of a geological and scientific character, made in 1866, were almost always restricted in range and results by the exposure involved, and the absolute impossibility of procuring escort from small and hard worked commands. Small samples of lead and silver were found, but these and gold will have to be worked for. Neither will often be stumbled upon by treasure seekers; neither will they roll their offerings to the feet of idlers to solicit the appropriation of their pounds and ounces.

Coal is exhaustless. It can be found all along the route from Powder River to the Upper Yellowstone, and the red buttes which dot the country for miles northward are grand repositories of the same article. Lignite and the lower grades of wood coal are the prevailing type; but a vein was opened close to Fort Philip Kearney, soon after its establishment, in 1866, which was advantageously used in welding of iron, and will prove no less valuable for winter fires.

Limestone is attainable from the mountain, although somewhat difficult of transportation at present. Clay is abundant, and of such quality as to make a firm plaster coating upon simple exposure to the sun.

While the discolouration of the red buttes has been traced to the presence of iron, and it is also found in many of the sands, no ores have yet been exposed, nor have indications been made of its presence in any available supply. All other building materials are plentiful, and the tall pines furnish clear lumber of any required length or breadth, without a knot or blemish to mar their uniformity or beauty. Where some Indian fire has spread and struck a forest, so as to benumb its growth, the house builder finds his sound dry timber, which readily takes the plane and a handsome finish, and the perfection of its seasoning in that dry atmosphere is a work of short duration.

The magnetic variation at Fort Phil Kearney is 19° 20', and its altitude over six thousand feet above the level of the sea; while half as high again above it rises Cloud Peak, completing the landscape and crowning all with its purity and beauty.

CHAPTER 4

Organization of the Expedition to Absaraka

Fort Kearney, Nebraska, was the rendezvous where the first expedition was organized for the permanent occupation of Absaraka. With little positive information of the country to be occupied, we had the assurance that it was a precious region to the Indian; the most direct route for emigration to Montana; and then, there was the pressure of public opinion at the West in favour of the early establishment of the route, under the sanction of military authority, and its corresponding guarantees of troops and the support of connected posts.

Maps were consulted in vain for something definite in the way of description, and everybody's book which said anything about the Indian of the Rocky Mountains was eagerly read and carefully digested, from the adventures of Lewis and Clarke to the last newspaper correspondent from the Plains.

Then we had the foreshadowings of the long-heralded Laramie council to be held in May, when all the Indians of the disputed region were to assemble, and where, after the inevitable smoking and talking, a solemn peace was to be established and ratified, and a genuine right of way was to be secured to the modern land of Ophir.

Then began preparations for the march. Reports were conflicting as to whether the climate belonged truly to the frigid or temperate zone; whether the land was prolific in vegetation, or barren and worthless.

A winter's march from Fort Leavenworth to Fort Kearney in 1865, when the mercury was twelve degrees below zero and two feet of snow was first to be shovelled aside before a tent could be pitched—when the prairie winds penetrated every garment, and drifting snows often blinded any advance—was deemed a sufficient experience to decide the ladies to undertake the journey and risk the issues of a Rocky Mountain winter.

It was a little drawback to the perfection of plans for housekeeping that the only post on a line of more than seven hundred miles was to be abandoned, and that all the posts in the new command were to be built far from civilization and supplies, and in time for winter use; but seeming banishment did not discourage, after the purpose was settled to go on.

The general plan had been outlined by General Pope, who had large experience in Indian affairs, and had in view the exact relations of the new route to advancing emigration, the quickest communication with Montana, and the probability of a peaceful occupation through the agency of the Laramie council.

Northwest of Fort Laramie, one hundred and sixty-seven miles distant, was Fort Reno, formerly Fort Connor, named after General Connor, who marched to Tongue River in 1865, and returned safely, after meeting ample opposition to discourage a farther advance. This was to be moved about forty miles west, to be rebuilt for a four-company post, and two additional forts were to be constructed—one on or near the Big Horn River, and the second on or near the Upper Yellowstone. To this duty the 2nd Battalion of the 18th U. S. Infantry had been assigned, under the command of Colonel Carrington of that regiment, who was also designated as district commander, with headquarters at the *new* Fort Reno. The battalion numbered at that time just about two hundred and twenty men, many of whom were veterans having less than a year to serve, but, with the band and clerks, making an aggregate of nearly two hundred and sixty who were preparing for the trip.

General Dodge, who then commanded the United States forces in Kansas and the territories, and whose map is the only intelligible map of that country, actively interested himself in the expected movement, and within a week after he received application for a steam sawmill, had purchased and started it on its journey. The Interior Department furnished maps. The Smithsonian gave *its* contributions. Professors Silliman and Dana, of Yale College, supplied standard English and American works upon the various departments of natural science; while *transit, level*, and other instruments for surveys, observations, and such other duty as would aid in the exploration and development of a new country, were also provided.

A strange medley was that outfit, and its catalogue, to which something was constantly added, opened our eyes to a clearer view of the fact that we were to live a pioneer life, and begin a new career at the very foundation of border experience.

Tools of all kinds were of course to be gathered together. Thus, there were mowing machines, and shingle and brick machines, doors, sash, glass, nails, locks, and every conceivable article that can enter into house-building. Future blacksmiths, wheelwrights, painters, harness-makers, and carpenters, who were to be hunted up out of the command, had to be provided with the implements of their craft. All contingencies had to be anticipated, so that the day of arrival in the new country should be the day of commencement, and there should then be no delay to wait for anything from the United States.

Meanwhile, the Laramie contributors to the public press were swelling the numbers of the Indians who already were or soon would be at the conference, some estimating the number as high as twenty and even thirty thousand. Certainly there were indications that the Indians were really intending to visit that post and deliberate upon surrender of the coveted route.

The death of the young daughter of "Spotted Tail," and her burial at Laramie with religious rites and many complimentary services, had brought that chief into closer relations of friendship, and messengers had been sent far and wide to bid Cheyennes and Arrapahoes, as well as Sioux, to the grave discussion.

The contingency that the Indians who occupied the territory in question might stay away, and then fight the expedition, was so remote in the assurance of a treaty, that it was hardly considered, except that it induced a request for a short delay, until the arrival of recruits who were already enlisted and on the way from New York.

The band donned additional equipments, and drilled with the Spencer carbine, and these same arms afterward proved of infinite value; while the afternoon and evening music of the band lightened the labour and sweetened the privations of our partial exile.

While still waiting for recruits, General Sherman visited the post, entering into the spirit and plans of the expedition with his usual energy and skill. At his suggestion some of the ladies began their daily journal of events, and thus laid the basis for the conversion of *one* into this narrative for the eyes of friends who could not share the trip.

On the 13th of May the recruits arrived, and were distributed among the companies to *learn to be soldiers.* With them came the

3rd Battalion, Company F of the 1st Battalion, and recruits for the whole regiment, thus swelling the marching command to nearly two thousand men. But the routes to Salt Lake City were to be guarded, both the direct mail line and the northern road by Forts Laramie and Caspar, so that the eight companies of the 2nd Battalion remained as the fixed detail for the Mountain District.

There was no cavalry, but as the outgoing volunteer regiments were to leave their horses at Laramie, and we were to have two hundred to mount infantry until cavalry could be furnished, the interesting experiment of determining how many could ride a horse was initiated. Fortunately, two volunteer cavalry regiments passed by, on the way home for muster-out, and the two hundred horses were procured at once. This was doubly agreeable to officers and men, as it transpired that, on arrival at Laramie, the volunteers had preferred to ride to the Missouri River on horseback rather than to *walk*, and there were not horses enough to replace a few that died on the road.

As memory reverts back, it now seems fortunate in another aspect, as otherwise there would have been no horses for couriers or pickets, and the expedition might have experienced even more difficulties than it did encounter in communicating with the United States and the positions occupied. So cavalry was *improvised*. Men got upon the horses, and the majority actually made the first trip to water without being dismounted. Some men were embarrassed when the long Springfield rifle was put on the horse with them, but both man and horse soon learned how it was to be done.

At length all things were declared ready. Rocking chairs and sewing chairs, churns and washing machines, with a bountiful supply of canned fruits, were duly stored inside or outside of army wagons; while turkeys and chickens, and one brace of swine, added a specially domestic cast to some of the establishments prepared for the journey. Thanks to a defective flue, which set fire to our house, burning it, with all the contents of the attic, a few days before we left—some *best chairs*, bedsteads, and mattresses (all properly packed), with a half hundred beef tongues, some potatoes and selected groceries, were prematurely consumed; but as this was only an incident very possible in army life, the fun of the affair made up for its losses.

The last thing done looked a little warlike: the magazine was opened and all the ammunition that could be spared from the fort was drawn out and loaded in wagons; but its comparatively meagre supply gave little annoyance, as Laramie would be expected to furnish the deficit in case any further fighting material should be required in the way of powder and lead. Then we had the news that a battalion of the 13th Infantry had been ordered to build a new post at the foot of the Northern Black Hills, while two companies were to keep open the road thence to Fort Reno, thus giving fair assurance that the Indians of that location and Powder River valley would be watched and held to their own theatre of action in case the Laramie council should fail to establish a peace on the Plains.

The expedition had the following organization: District Commander, Colonel H. B. Carrington, 18th U. S. Infantry; Assistant Adjutant-General, Brevt. Captain Frederick Phisterer, Adjutant 18th U. S. Infantry; Chief Quartermaster, Lieutenant Frederick II. Brown, Quartermaster 18th U. S. Infantry; Chief Surgeon, Brevt. Major S. M. Horton, Assistant Surgeon U. S. A.; Acting Assistant Surgeons, Dr. H. M. Matthews, Dr. B. N. McCleary, and Dr. H. Baalan; Battalion Commander, Brevt. Major H. Raymond, 2nd Battalion; Mounted Infantry, Captain T. Ten Eyck, 18th U. S. Infantry; Battalion Adjutant, Brevt. Captain Wm. H. Bisbee, 2nd Battalion. The additional officers were Captain and Brevt. Lieutenant Colonel N. C. Kinney, Captain J. L. Proctor, Captain T. B. Burrows, Lieutenant J. J. Adair, Lieutenant Thaddeus P. Kirtland, Lieutenant Isaac D'Isay.

As chief guide. Major James Bridger had been selected, assisted by H. Williams, who had been a guide to several expeditions to the Republican during the winter of 1865-6; and thus organized, the command was ready.

Chapter 5

Incidents of the Platte River Travel

Few days on the plains are more bright and promising, notwithstanding such a cloud of dust as the plains only can supply, than was the nineteenth day of May, *A.D.* 1866.

Two hundred and twenty-six mule-teams, besides ambulances, were the outfit, and the band of over thirty pieces regaled us with just the right music, until the column passed Kearney City, popularly known to travellers as "*Dobey (Adobe)* Town."

The march was along the Platte River, whose quicksand and fickle currents have been the bane of travellers since Lewis and Clarke abused it and Colonel Bonneville crossed it. Alkaline and muddy,— sometimes disappearing under the sandy bed, so that a footman can cross from shore to shore without seeing water, and again flowing even with its banks; sometimes surfeiting the south channel, under the pressure of a strong north wind, and again, within the same sun, rolling back so as to foil the calculations of some traveller who crossed in the morning, expecting an equally safe crossing at night,— it has no disputant to oppose its claim to be the most unaccountably contrary and ridiculous river the world ever saw.

But in our course along the Platte in 1866, we had, such as it was, all the water we wished. One day was much like another day, with the same march at the earliest dawn, the same adventures with rattlesnakes, the same pursuit of wild flowers, the same inopportune thunderstorms, the same routine of guard mounting at sunset, the same evening music from the band, and the same sound slumber. Recurring Sabbaths gave us our only intervals of rest; and the fact that at Fort Reno we overtook trains which started before us, but marched *daily*, is a substantial testimony, concurrent with all intelligent experience, that the observance of the Lord's day is indispensable alike to man and beast. On such occasions Lieutenants Adair, Kirtland, and D'Isay, occasionally joined by Mr. Phisterer, tenor, helped to make something like true melody from the sweet Sabbath bell sent us by the Sabbath school of Rev. Mr. Dimmick, of Omaha, before our departure from Kearney.

Fort McPherson, then consisting of shabby log-cabins, but now a beautiful and well-built post, was passed on the 24th of May, the only halt being to seek additional ammunition and take along an idle sawmill not needed at that post. On the 29th we camped near the Old California Crossing, and received a call from Col. Otis and some gentlemen of the Peace Commission, who, with agreeable presents for the red men, were on their way to the Laramie council. About dark the news was brought that nearly three hundred Indians had crossed the Platte nearby for a hunt on the Republican, having permission to be absent from Laramie until other bands came in and the commission should formally assemble.

"Old Little Dog," whose son burned Julesburg in 1864, came into camp and made complaint that some one of our soldiers had entered his lodge and stolen his rifle. After a somewhat curious observation of the performance of the band and special admiration of the bell-chimes, and upon being assured that his gun should be found and returned to him, he sprang upon the bare back of his pony with all the elasticity of youth and *more* than the skill of our mounted infantry, and galloped swiftly away. He had the appearance of being very old, but his agility and address in his intercourse with that pony were decidedly suggestive of the probable skill and activity of the young warriors of his nation.

Fort Sedgwick, near the so-called city of Julesburg, was reached on the 30th of May. This city, though burned by Little Dog, had been rebuilt, so as to number nearly a dozen houses and stores, and a year later, in 1867, another Julesburg, of canvas and portable frame buildings, dwellings, shops, hotels, refectories, and *recreatories*, had sprung up on the north side of the river, as an accompaniment to the progress of the Union Pacific Railroad, boasting its three thousand inhabitants, all of them determined to remain there until they could do as well or better elsewhere farther on. The water and soil of the new location were not equal to those of the Wabash, Scioto, or Connecticut River valleys: but, on the other hand, in neither of these old-fashion regions could a wall tent rent at one hundred dollars per day; neither could a piece of canvas, sufficiently large to cover a billiard table, command its thousand dollars per week.

But in 1866 we stopped three days, out of respect for the Platte. This delay was somewhat relieved by shopping calls upon the post sutler, Mr. Adams, nephew of Mr. Stanton, Secretary of War, while the troops were drawing supplies or caulking and fitting out a large flat-boat, which, procured from Denver, was at the fort, nearly half a mile from the element for which its inventor had designed it.

After caulking, this apparatus had to be conveyed to the water; a double cable had to be sprung across the river, and science was summoned to do its best to adapt its heavy draught to the quicksand, shoals, and currents of the ubiquitous Platte. Two hundred men made quick work, and when the science of the learned was appalled at the magnitude of the undertaking, the common sense and practical skill of Captain Ten Eyck, an old surveyor and lumberman, solved all problems and crossed the craft safely. Twenty yoke of cattle drew the first cable over, when mules struggled in vain to start it; and Mrs. Lieutenant Bisbee and Jean were the first family passengers after the ferry was actually established.

But the natural contrariness of the Platte, although so signally rebuked by the passage of a *real* boat, and permitting its current to aid in its flight, was never more conspicuously developed than when it really seemed to under- stand that the object of that boat was to get wagons, teams, and stores to the north bank in safety, and thereby circumvent its ugly temper. Although the river had been examined for miles to see if there was not some available ford, before shipcraft and navigation were resorted to, no sooner did that boat attempt its mission in real earnest with prospect of success than this identical Platte River fell more than afoot. Then could be seen navigation under difficulties. New eddies, spiteful currents, and outcropping bars, with desperate quicksand and the constantly varying depth of water, in turn caught it, and stopped it, and turned it, until the gallant crew actually leaped overboard. Then, partly kept out of the river bottom by a grasp upon the gunwale, and partly kept in progress by hand-over-hand along the cable, those intrepid mariners crossed that boat once again in less than four hours by the watch.

The prospect of spending until the autumn fall of water in completing the transit, aroused a fresh spirit of enterprise and developed new expedients. The slight fall of water had been carefully gauged, and, unknown to the water sprite who was plainly in league with the Sioux of *Absaraka*, and therefore opposed to our further advance, a great array of timber was procured; wagons were unloaded; false beds or frames were prepared; half loads replaced full loads, and a bold push was made to defy all elements of evil. To be sure, the lead mules would be swimming, the middle team pulling, the wheel team floundering, and the wagon would be rolling in quicksand; but the expedient of double teams always left some one or more span on the earth's surface, to pull on or push on the others.

It was crossing the Platte in more ways than one; for we did it in very spite of that natural forlornness of disposition which so undeniably approximates the natural depravity of man. Enough to say that the Platte was crossed. A few mules got their ears under water, to drown from innate stubbornness. A few harness were cut to save others. Some riders had to tow the lead team with ropes; and enough whipping was applied for a week of ordinary travel. Water *would* melt sugar and cake the flour, and now and then a stray knapsack or haversack floated down the current; *but, the Platte was crossed!*

Before the consummation of this achievement, which the innovations of the railroad will prevent us from renewing, there was a social entertainment in camp not to be forgotten.

It was the last reunion of the officers of the 18th Infantry. The bill before Congress proposing to add two companies to each battalion, and thus make of each a new regiment, was already *fait accomplit*; and a regiment that alone had filled its twenty-four companies within a year after its organization in 1861, and which had received into its ranks over five thousand men, was finally to separate and prepare for new relations and new titles.

The young officers, full of regrets, but as full of life and devotion to the general comfort as ever, arranged a farewell concert of "Ironclad Minstrels," under the supervision of Majors Van Voast and Burt. Hospital tents were unloaded and united in one grand pavilion. Camp stools and chairs from baggage wagons, or the fort, were brought into requisition, and a grand concert was the result.

It is an old army fashion to enliven the monotony of frontier life by extemporized opera, charades, readings, and the miniature drama; and the illustrations on this occasion were excellent. The string band gave us a splendid orchestra, and the violins and violoncello, the clarionets and the flute, the French horns and the trumpet, the trombone and the tuba, alternately supplied the solo, or replenished the chorus, as the bones and banjo called for their interference. Faces only were unfamiliar; and the fifteen or twenty sergeants and soldiers, who, with fine voices, perfect harmony, and the usual *bon-mots* of Ethiopian minstrelsy, entertained the lovers of, now and then, a little sport, did as full justice to their music as they had effectually transformed themselves from Caucasian to African by the pervasive laws of burnt cork.

Then came the parting at the colonel's tent. A part of the command were to march two days longer with headquarters, while others were to leave the next morning for other fields of duty.

Captain Neil, Mrs. Neil, and Miss Bella had already occupied post headquarters at Fort Sedgwick. Captain Kellogg, Mrs. Kellogg, and little Harry, who, with Harry and Jimmy Carrington, had raced ponies daily on the march from Kearney, were also detached with Lieutenant Wilcox and two companies, and practical separation began.

Army life alone has these peculiar separations. Bound closely in social intimacies, separated from the affinities of active life in the States, the fleeting friendships of garrison or camp life are full of fraternal endearments, both in sickness and health, that go very far, when gentlemen *are* gentlemen and ladies *are* ladies, to atone for banishment and public service far from the courtesies and amenities of civil life. Hence, when tender relations *are* established and congenial spirits meet, it is painful to sunder those ties.

Then the *esprit de corps* of families becomes hardly less sacred than that which unites officers when the ideal of army pride is attained, and each regards the honour of another as dear as his own, and jealousies and backbitings sink to the level of their own intrinsic meanness. Exceptions only prove how essential is such a law for social life in the army, and those who violate its behests, alone are degraded and suffer. No caste of rank invades their social life, neither does the parade-ground entrench upon the parlour; yet the proprieties and courtesies of good society everywhere affirm their prerogatives and give delight-someness to the relations of all.

So pleasant was the parting at Sedgwick, even with its sadness; and long will that evening recall to the old 18th its participation on that occasion when so long a goodbye was begun.

Two days of marching from Fort Sedgwick brought us to Louis' Ranch at the upper crossing of Lodge Pole Creek. *Now*, the Union Pacific Railroad has passed that point, and from Cheyenne begins its borings for the waters of the Pacific. The South Platte was left at Sedgwick. The first day's march is seventeen miles to Lodge Pole Creek, and the second is eighteen miles to Louis' Ranch. Here we spent another social evening with those of the third battalion under

Major Lewis, a true man and perfect soldier, whose destination was Camp Douglass, by way of Lodge Pole Creek Cañon, and so on to the pleasant land of Deseret and Salt Lake City. Here also we parted with Mrs. McClintick and Mrs. Burt and their husbands, and Mrs. Burt's sister, Miss Reynolds, thus still more reducing our coterie of ladies, and still farther separating us from the associations of the march and old times at home.

CHAPTER 6

Reminiscences of Ranching, and Old Times on the Route From Leavenworth to Sedgewick

Up to Louis' Ranch all styles of being, and the very routes of travel have changed. This very Pacific Railroad, with its swift pulse, drives everything along, and its chief engineer, General Dodge, seems to attempt the annihilation of time and space, with the same indefatigable spirit as that with which he won the thanks of everybody at old Kearney in aiding their efficient outfit for the Plains; and Superintendent Durant is tireless as he is successful. But the change from 1865, and even from 1866, when our narrative gathers its chief contributions, is marked. *Then*, no railroad stretched its hard arms after the traveller or emigrant; and the report of its coming was like the prophecies of some madmen who think that New York City will soon travel westward, to absorb the prerogatives and location of Rocky Mountain custom and commerce.

Before this railroad began its journey, travellers from Leavenworth varied their days' marches, as few will be able to do again. There was first a rough ride to the "Nine Mile Station," with its uncomfortable stone house. Then came, in turn, the crossing of the Acheson and Pike's Peak Railroad; Kinnekuck, on the Big Grasshopper, beyond Grenada, where the "*kickapoo*" Indians were buying and begging; Big Muddy; Ash Point; Big Blue, with Simpson's capital Yankee store of notions; Rock Creek; Big Sandy; Little Blue River, with its perpetual Indian alarms and occasional depredations; Little Blue Station; Spring Creek; Pawnee Ranch; Sand Hill Station; and Valley City, or "Dog Town," only nine miles from Fort Kearney.

Valley City was then ambitious and enterprising; but, in 1867, our friend Haney was the sole resident; and Hook, the old caterer for Fort Kearney, had gone farther west to establish his fortunes in some larger field of usefulness and profit. We saw him at McPherson, in June, when on his winding way, and the papers say he is mayor or alderman in the proud city—Cheyenne.

In those days, Kearney City was a busy mart of trade, and future south side railroads will restore its business. Plattsmouth and Nebraska City sent many an outfit of loaded wagons. Ox-teams and mule-teams, and teams with horses, and horses with saddles, brought many new visitors, who lunched, bartered, and journeyed on. Here, Piper and Robinson, Brown and Linnell, Michel, Thomas, Dr. Brashure, Talbot, the veteran officer, and a host of others devoted their time to the well-being of all who lingered at their doors; but it was after Kearney was passed, that the glory of legitimate ranching began. McLean and the genial Sydenham, our Fort Kearney postmaster; Gallagher; Pat Mallalley; Dan Smith; Gilman, a man of business, straightforward and worthy, and Coles, were a few who ministered to our comfort on the way to McPherson.

Then came Fitchies, Burkes, Morrows, Bakers, Browns, Beauvais, and Valentines, all accommodating and excellent. We stop to speak of Jack Morrow, the prince of ranchmen, and the king of good fellows. *He* is a ranchman indeed! Fortune has showered her favours about his life's journey and prosperity dwelleth within his walls. Keen in business, generous, and *"hail fellow"* his career, on the *South* Platte, has become temporarily restricted; but, with his indomitable spirit, no sooner did that Union Pacific Railroad shoot by his ranch, on the northern shore, than he moved ranch and all across its quicksand and waters, and went on his usual course as if nothing new had come along. A two-storey frame, one of the best on the Plains, went *down*, *over*, and *up* again, as if the *genii* of Aladdin's lamp had been assigned to special duty in his behalf, and Jack was himself again.

But ranchmen are westward bound. Soon, they will be known no more forever! The Pacific will stop them on *this* continent, and further than that, the future historian must write of their struggles and their triumphs. It would be just like Jack Morrow to go to Alaska, run a ferry across Behring Straits, and open a ranch for Americans and Russians who choose that route of travel from America to Europe. A tribute to the memory of ranchmen and a record of their styles and methods on the Plains is simple justice to the history of the nineteenth century. Already they are not as they were! Nebraska, one of the latest and one of the best of new States when its development shall ripen, has entertained and profited some of their best, as well as those not so ambitious or genteel.

From Fort Leavenworth to Fort Kearney, from Kearney to McPherson, from McPherson to Sedgewick, nearly all ranches have been abandoned, or the occupants only linger for the protection of their lives and property. They have had their comforts and discomforts, and among them we met some of the best and bravest and the biggest hearted men of any race or people.

To some, who have never tarried at a ranch, it will not come amiss to introduce a few samples which our experience impressed upon the memory.

Ranches alike provide for man and beast, and are arranged for their special care and protection. A large yard is surrounded by a stockade paling, with stabling, feed troughs, and hayricks, with here and there loop-holes for the rifle. In places of imminent peril from Indian attacks, such as Valentine's, Baker's, or Louis's, the wall of the upper stories and every angle of house or stable has its outlets for tiring upon an approaching foe. The log or *adobe* house, which provides for the master as well as the corral provides for his beast, is often small; but, like an eastern omnibus or street car, is unlimited in accommodations for all who seek its shelter.

Let the readers of this narrative enter with us into a few sample ranches of our actual and literal experience, for illustration of their social capacity and things as they *were*, and let them envy the life of *an officer's wife on the Plains*,

Just at dark, one bitter November afternoon in 1865, when drifting snows obscured all advance, we "*struck a ranch.*" It had but one storey, was long and narrow, and was divided into three apartments, each having a front window and door. Two Acheson coaches, respectively bound east and west, with the California and Salt Lake City mails, were in front, looking as if they had stood there for six months, through accumulating snow; and yet they were only waiting for their drivers and forlorn passengers to thaw and feed, and for the stock to do the same. Room *number one,* as well as room *number two,* had a substantial *earth* floor.

The former, about ten by twelve feet square, had quite a plain plank counter, and upon shelves behind could be seen the names of Mr. Drake, Mr. Kelly, Log Cabin, Bourbon, and others, equally euphonious, designed to represent certain bottled products, which for a considerable sum of money were susceptible of transfer on proper demand. Some were labelled Gin, which never saw *juniper*; some were labelled Rye, which never knew that cereal; and some were simply labelled Whisky, which were modest high wines and water, with very little of the water,—at least, so said those gentlemen who tried experiments of analysis for scientific purposes. Nutmegs, peppermint, navy tobacco, clay pipes, salaratus, baking powder, bologna, and ready-made clothing, with rows of canned fruits, furnished a large part of the invoice of the shelves; while black snake whips, tin cups, camp kettles, and frying-pans hung in profusion overhead. This room was well patronized, and in a half frozen state we rushed for its brilliant candle-light, waiting for further notice of our future disposition.

Being introduced to room *number two*, we found passengers, stage drivers and the teamsters of a passing train, apparently surfeited with supplies drawn from room number one, and huddled about a table, where two big platters of bacon and cabbage, with tin cups smoking with coffee, were being disposed of as supper. The conversation of the party (for the wife of the host had been sent to the States) related mainly to a recent Indian depredation on the Little Blue, and what each one would have done if he had been there at the eventful crisis. The language had a medley of positive terms, which in New England would be *profane*; and the prospect ahead drove us to inquiries as to the shelter of room *number three*.

But, finding that ourself and children and Mrs. Neil and daughter could not agreeably share its board floor with ten or twelve characters whose social habits seemed only adapted to room number one, we threw ourselves upon the courtesy of Adjutant Phisterer and Quartermaster Brown, who soon had the snow shovelled aside, our tents pitched, a piece of the corral carefully chopped for the camp stove, and all arrangements made for hot coffee, and a good wrapping up, either to sleep or freeze. We slept, *and* survived!

Another ranch was approached, when the storm compelled a full day's stop. The mules could not, or would not go on, and the drivers could neither see nor drive. The upsetting of our ambulance, and being borne by strong men a half mile through drifts is still painfully remembered, as well as the wonderful fact that while our head was nearly broken, our basket of eggs accomplished the upset without injury. Fortunately a ranch with its usual palisade and stabling was near.

The kind lady proprietress gave us her own family room; only reserving one-half for herself, her husband, and children, by the interposition of a small suspended comfort, while ample ventilation was insured between the unchinked logs, where *no* comfort was. To our jests, and especially the whimsicalities of Quartermaster Brown, an inveterate punster, always full of good cheer, who hazarded the rather profane jest that, "in his opinion, it would be hard work for the Angel Gabriel to make his trumpet reach that country,"—the old lady replied: "Well, you are the jolliest set of folks I ever saw out here:—don't see how in mercy you can laugh, and go on so!"

When Mrs. Neil asked if there were Indians about, another, with more heroism, replied that "*she* had *heard* so much about Indians, and been half scared out of her senses so many times, that she had jest about made up *her* mind that she wouldn't believe nothing more, until she was s*kulped!*" Mrs. Neil, with quick discernment, took a lounge near the fireplace, while the colonel and Lieutenants Phisterer and Brown took to a shed nearby: but during the night the California coach came down, and its half-frozen passengers rushed for the fire. The lounge was the first object of seizure; alas, for Mrs. Neil, who was only relieved from her discomfort, by loss of rest, and the banishment of strangers, until she was able to escape, and share with us the family room, *par excellence*, of the house. Our *bill* was four dollars each!

A third ranch had its front store-room and its kitchen. Voices of men, who were ranged on the earth, like rows of pins, disturbed sleep, and the kitchen stove nearly burned our blankets, while its steaming incense no less shocked our senses; but we actually slept,—everybody was good natured, and some fresh pork and new eggs for breakfast, with a cup of our own coffee, sent us on our way rejoicing.

Louis' Ranch, near the present Sydney Station, is quite a fort, and the outhouses and stables are advanced like bastions, so that enfilading fire can be had in all directions.

Such were some of the ranches of 1865.

CHAPTER 7

Union Pacific Railroad to Laramie

On the sixth day of June we continued our march. The first day was a severe and trying one, and will always be disagreeable to emigrants with loaded trains until Yankee skill shall perfect what has already been begun in the search after water. The ridge or divide which is first crossed is fully twenty-eight miles to the first water or timber. On the summit there is evidence of Anglo Saxon pluck, which was evidently designed to be the accompaniment of a future central ranch. About midway between Lodge Pole Creek and Mud Springs, a well had been begun, nearly twenty feet across and two hundred feet deep, without reaching water. The road across the divide is smooth and broad; but our first trip was in the hottest part of June, with the mercury at 101° above zero, and the infantry suffered intensely. Buffalo gnats flitted wickedly about, attacking neck and ears and every other accessible or exposed part of the body, and a *sirocco*-like wind drove the dust in our way as if determined either to petrify or melt us.

The command halted for ten minutes every hour, and officers and men alike put handkerchiefs on the head and neck to secure all the protection possible; yet there was no alternative but to undergo and *go on*. The ambulances soon filled with the lame and sun-struck, and every vacant space in the wagons was similarly occupied. No trees relieved the dismal monotony, and every halt brought into requisition the services of our patient surgeons. The tedious day at length spent itself, and we encamped at Mud Springs, just in time to receive the full benefit of a thunderstorm and small tornado, which grappled sternly with our canvas, and for a time threatened to unroof as well as drown us.

At Mud Springs are both wood and water, but neither are abundant. In midsummer, the dry sandy bed of the stream shows only here and there a few small pools; but the shovel will soon start it, and any train will find a full supply by patient labour for an hour. It is always possible to procure buffalo chips enough to boil coffee and supply fuel for a camp oven, so that scarcity of timber in the immediate vicinity of water is not a serious embarrassment until snows cover the ground. Most trains wisely take some wood from camp to camp, and a little more permanency to this indispensable station on the route will insure supplies for sale to trains. A few log-cabins that have been the quarters of a mail guard and relay of mules, with a sergeant's party in charge, duly represent the dignity of the United States; but no one will voluntarily remain longer than to secure rest from the fatigue of the long journey of the previous day.

The march of June 7th was only ten miles to Pumpkin Creek, which flows past Court-house Rock. This stream is ever flowing, and abundance of timber can be found in the *cañon* nearby. The rock itself is mainly composed of sand, hard pan, and clay, so that it is easily chopped with the hatchet, and thus steps are made for those who have the nerve and patience to climb to its top, nearly six hundred feet above the water of the creek. A few of our party accomplished the feat, Adjutant Phisterer taking the lead. The ascent is quite easy, but peculiar. The notches receive the toes and about half the foot, and the hands grasp the gaps above to support the body and keep its gravity within the line of danger.

The return trip is not so pleasant, as the heels take the place of the toes and the back rests upon the bluff itself, just as the body was inclined forward during the ascent. The view from the summit is very fine; and far off to the northwest looms up the equally singular proportions of Chimney Rock. Centuries of exposure have evidently wrought their changes upon the great face of Court-house Rock, and constant waste is now so rapidly changing its proportions that, even in 1867, it had lost some of that boldness of definition which in 1866, and for years before, had made it such a noted landmark to the traveller.

The old road and the telegraph route deflect to the right about six miles before reaching the rock: but the present route saves nearly five miles of distance and is more readily made, although somewhat more rolling and sandy.

The sketch of Court-house Rock will preserve its outline and present character; but, like all other odd and wild things in that region, it will soon become the prey of innovation and the mastery of Time.

Court-House Rock—from the East

Chimney Rock—from the East

The mounted infantry pitched their tents in the basin of the *cañon*, a short distance from the beautiful grove of cottonwood that lies at the very base of the rock, and the novel scenery made an afternoon pass pleasantly.

Twelve miles farther on we find Brown's ranch on the North Platte, and five miles more brings the traveller to Chimney Rock. While substantially the same material as Court-house Rock, it derives its name from a singular shaft which springs from the apex of a true cone, and is nearly three hundred and eighty feet high. It stands about five hundred feet from the bluff of which it was once a portion, and close to the level at which the cone leaves the general surface of the plain there is a stratum of true limestone, six feet in depth, interspersed with fossils indicating its origin, and closely resembling that of the quarries of Central Ohio. Chimney Bock is fast gathering about it the debris of waste, and will soon lose the bold outline and marked symmetry of its present proportions. It is now much more beautiful than when Fremont visited it, and is worn to such a fine delineation that it seems that the first summer's storm or winter's blast must topple it from its base and destroy it utterly.

Fifteen miles farther on we passed Terry's ranch, opposite Fortification Rocks, and approached Scott's Bluffs. These are also of mixed clay and sand, plentifully supplied with fossils, and throw a spur across the Platte basin so as to compel the traveller to leave the river and make a long detour to the south, or to pass through the bluffs themselves. This passage is by a tortuous gorge where wagons can seldom pass each other; and at times the drifting snows or sands almost obscure the high walls and battlements that rise several hundred feet on either side. Cedar-trees climb to their very summit and crop out in every canon; and although these seem to the unpracticed eye like little shrubs clinging to the cliffs, the enterprising visitor who climbs to their nestling-place finds them to be full-grown trees of large diameter and proportionate height.

Fortification Rocks were so named in 1866; and at sunset the terraces and bastions, the pinnacles and turrets are quite a good embodiment of one's natural idea of old-time fortifications on a grand and comprehensive scale.

Almost immediately after leaving the Bluffs, and at the foot of the descent, after the gorge is passed, we find Fort Mitchell. This is a sub-post of Laramie of peculiar style and compactness. The walls of the quarters are also the outlines of the fort itself, and the four sides of the rectangle are respectively the quarters of officers, soldiers, and horses, and the warehouse of supplies. Windows open into the little court or parade-ground; and bedrooms, as well as all other apartments, are loop-holed for defence.

June 12th. We marched twenty-one miles to Cold Spring or Cold Creek, which is a beautiful stream, thirty feet wide, emptying into the south channel of the North Platte.

As the Ottawa and St. Lawrence, or the Missouri and Mississippi retain their distinctive characteristics for many miles after their nominal union, so when Cold Creek strikes the south arm of the North Platte, it does not mingle with its muddy current, but each occupies its own half of the swollen stream, and so runs on its race.

A novel incident, valuable to mention for the information of other travellers, occurred shortly before sunset, which resulted in a bountiful supply of fine fresh fish for all who desired them. Sergeant Barnes took up the idea that he would fish at the junction of the two streams, and actually hooked a fine mountain pike. The news soon spread, and the soldiers gathered from all directions. For want of proper tackle a seine was extemporized. Gunny sacks were sewn together, mule shoes were fastened to the bottom for dead weight, and quartermaster's hay forks were borrowed to guide the net.

Then a strong party waded in neck deep, and with one end of this seine held firmly to shore, made a half circle with the remainder, bringing it all back to land. To the great amazement of spectators and actors, just where the eddies, at the meeting of the two rivers, struggled to keep by themselves, there was a fine school of pike. A few hauls soon landed over a hundred, varying in weight from one to four pounds. Their hard white meat was excellent, and made amends for the ridiculous stupidity of the fish and the simplicity of their method of capture. They evidently were unaccustomed to visits from the white man, or could not see his approach through the turbid waters of their neighbour Platte until too late for escape.

Up to this time we had invariably found sufficient grass for all stock, and the Platte was always at hand for water.

The next day the troops forded this beautiful creek about half a mile from its mouth, and after eighteen mile's march we encamped above Jules Coffee's ranch, four miles east of Laramie. Here two of our best sergeants were drowned, being carried away by the current while bathing.

Just about sunset, "Standing Elk"—a fine specimen of the Brulè Sioux, and who, in company with "Spotted Tail," "Two Strike," and "Swift Bear," again visited us at McPherson in 1867—called to pay his respects, receive a present of tobacco, and have a talk. He asked us where we were going, and was very frankly told the destination of the command. He then told us that:

> A treaty was being talked about at Laramie with a great many Indians, some of whom belonged in the country to which we were going; but that the fighting men of those bands had not come in, and would not; but that we would have to fight them, as they would not sell their hunting-grounds to the white men for a road.

He exhibited all indications of sincere friendship, and said that he and Spotted Tail would sign the treaty and would always be "friends." His pledge, thus given for both, and renewed at Fort McPherson in June, 1867, and often afterward, was fully redeemed, and our first interview with the Indians of the Northwest was both the assurance of the friendship of some, and the bitter animosity and opposition of many. It was proof that the careful marching, guarding of trains, and precautions against annoyance or intercourse with Indians had been judicious, and was equally suggestive of like prudence as the expedition advanced. Thus far, with the exception of Little Dog's rifle, which had been duly returned, not an Indian had suffered from injury at the hands of the command, and those who had visited the various camps had been kindly treated, and parted as friends.

HE-HA-KA-A-NA-ZIN
STANDING ELK—DACOTAH SIOUX

CHAPTER 8

Fort Laramie Council of 1866

Fort Laramie was the centre of important interests to the people of the West in June, 1866, and subsequent events show how important were the negotiations then begun, and how disastrous and costly have been the consequences of that false security as to the animus and purposes of the Indians of the Northwest which pervaded the country until the beginning of the year 1867.

The Peace Commission was in session. It was accredited from the highest sources and had in charge great interests. The proposed general peace with the Sioux, the Arrapahoes, and the Cheyennes, and their anticipated surrender of the right of way to Virginia City, by Powder Run and along the Big Horn mountains—our very route—were matters of personal interest, independent of the difficulties that would be in the way of successfully building new forts and fighting Indians with a command that was barely sufficient to do its expected work on the basis of a permanent and reliable peace.

General Cooke had closed a published circular with the emphatic and cheering assurance that "there *must* be peace," and from leaving Fort Kearney all pains had been taken to avoid collision with Indian hunting parties who were on their way to Laramie, or who were moving to and fro in anticipation of such a visit when the council was really ready.

Our trains were habitually formed in a hollow square or corral, upon reaching camping grounds, to insure the safety of stock at night, while pickets and mounted parties carefully guarded all animals on herd as soon as they were turned loose. The strictest discipline was enforced, and nothing was left undone that the energy and ambition of the officers could accomplish to instruct new recruits and prepare them for the labour and possible conflicts that the future might unfold.

No bartering with Indians was permitted under any circumstances; but all Indians who really wished an interview had the privilege of visiting headquarters, and there received kind attention and some little gifts, like tobacco or old garments, but *never* arms, powder, or whisky.

Our camp near Laramie was therefore located close enough for business, but far enough away to prevent the mingling of the troops and Indians for any purposes—thus avoiding the possibility of collisions growing out of trades in furs, beads, and other articles, in which the Indian is generally the unlucky one, and often exhibits his disappointment by becoming revengeful and wicked.

The next day, June 14th, wagons were sent to the fort for one hundred thousand rounds of rifle ammunition, and to perfect the arrangement for supplies for the upper posts to be built in the new district. Unfortunately there happened to be at the fort not a single thousand rounds for infantry arms such as are used in the army; so it was assumed that we should have a happy journey, a happy peace, and a happy future. Twenty-six wagons of additional provisions were ready, with the single drawback that drivers had to be furnished from the command; but this nice economy had the effect, practically, to put that number of soldiers *hors de combat*, in case of any trouble requiring soldiers, and thus disposed of some of the best of our men. Major Bridger told us that he had seen kegs of powder distributed to the Indians and carried away on their ponies; but this gave no concern, as there was none for *us*.

The next day came shopping, which busied our little coterie of ladies, and it certainly had claims to novelty in its associations and incidents.

The long counter of Messrs. Bullock and Ward was a scene of seeming confusion not surpassed in any popular, overcrowded store of Omaha itself. Indians, dressed and half dressed and undressed; squaws, dressed to the same degree of completeness as their noble lords; *papooses*, absolutely nude, slightly not nude, or wrapped in calico, buckskin, or furs, mingled with soldiers of the garrison, teamsters, emigrants, speculators, half breeds, and interpreters. *Here*, cups of rice, sugar, coffee, or flour were being emptied into the looped-up skirts or blanket of a squaw; and *there*, some tall warrior was grimacing delightfully as he grasped and sucked his long sticks of peppermint candy. Bright shawls, red squaw cloth, brilliant calicoes, and flashing ribbons passed over the same counter with knives and tobacco, brass nails and glass beads, and that endless catalogue of articles which belong to the legitimate border traffic. The room was redolent of cheese and herring, and "*heap of smoke;*" while the *debris* of mounched crackers lying loose under foot furnished both nutriment and employment for little bits of Indians too big to ride on mamma's back, and too little to reach the good things on counter or shelves.

The "*Wash ta-la!*" ("*very good*") mingled with "*Wan-nee-chee!*" a very significant "*no good*," whether predicated of person or thing; and the whole scene was a lovely episode, illustrating the habits of the noble red man in the mart of trade. Of course, all these Indians were thinking sharply, and many gave words to thought, so that an unsophisticated stranger might well doubt whether Bedlam or Babel were the better prototype of the tongues in use. The Cheyenne supplemented his words with active and expressive gestures, while the Sioux amply used his tongue as well as arms and fingers.

To all, however, whether white man, half-breed, or Indian, Mr. Bullock, a Virginia gentleman of the old school, to whose hospitality and delicate courtesy we were even more indebted in 1867, gave kind and patient attention, and his clerks seemed equally ready and capable, talking Sioux, Cheyenne, or English just as each case came to hand.

Outside everything was characteristic of the existing state of affairs, not to say prophetic of the future; and literal truth, in all its details, would furnish unrivalled scenes for stereoscopic views of Indian character and characteristics.

The council chamber was of course the first object of interest to us ladies after the shopping had been completed; and while the gentlemen were busy at quartermaster and commissary details, the ladies visited *it*. Pine boards had been arranged as benches in front of one set of quarters, and over these boards were once fresh evergreens. There was a unique and perfect simplicity in the arrangement, and such considerate *abandon* of all state and ceremony that no Indian need feel that he was kept at an awful distance, or must approach the agents of the Great Father with solemn awe or grave obeisance.

Under the eaves of all buildings, by doorsteps and porches, and generally everywhere, were twos, threes, or larger groups of hungry, masticating Indians of all sizes, sexes and conditions, covered with every conceivable degree of superficial clothing or adornment, with the special element of cleanliness just as critically wanting as is usual among the Indians of the Northwest.

During a long journey we had anticipated with more or less pleasure an attendance upon some of the deliberations, and it was understood that the colonel had, without success, requested authority to remain at Laramie during the treaty, in order to become acquainted with the Indians and learn both their disposition and decision as to the new route we were to travel and occupy. But he hurried everybody up, kept his men to the camp, and our stay was cut down to the actual necessities of a marching command. Besides this, it seemed that during the little time we did stop *some* Indians had been sent for *other* Indians, and the Indians who actually held possession of the route in dispute were not on hand when they were wanted.

"The Man afraid of his Horses" and "Red Cloud" made no secret of their opposition, and the latter, with all his fighting men, withdrew from all association with the treaty-makers, and in a very few days quite decidedly developed his hate and his schemes of mischief.

There being nothing to see therefore but loafing Indians, and great work to be done in preparation for winter and securing defensive positions before the rising war-cloud should break, we were all as eager to move on as the colonel was persistent in hurrying us forward. Some of the chiefs, however, were seen by the officers, and when they knew that the command was going to the Powder River country in advance of any treaty agreement, they gave unequivocal demonstrations of their dislike. One pleasant intimation was given that "in two moons the command would not have a hoof left." Another with great impressiveness thus explained his crude ideas: "Great Father sends us presents and wants new road, but white chief goes with soldiers to *steal* road before Indian say yes or no!" Some of us called *this* good logic.

Just as the troops left, one of the commissioners came to our ambulance and advised that very little dependence should be placed upon the result of the deliberations so far as the new road was concerned, for a messenger sent out to the Indians had been whipped and sent back with contempt. This was the conviction of all of us; still the ladies kept up good heart, and as they could not well go back, concluded to go on, but agreed to limit their riding on horseback to the vicinity of the train.

On the 17th of June, though it was the Sabbath, we passed Laramie, and camped at the Nine Mile Ranch, on the Platte. "We bade farewell to Laramie with great composure and no regrets. Its North Platte and Laramie Rivers, its Laramie Peak, nearly sixty miles distant, and its adventitious charms as the locality of the Laramie treaty sum up all its attractions. As at elegantly built Leavenworth, so at Laramie, water is hauled from the rivers, and a respectable fire would be ignorant of water in about a minute after it began.

This post was neglected, as were all frontier stations, during the war; being occupied by changing garrisons, whose jack-knives and bayonets, so useful in their proper sphere, had pretty much used up the pine and plaster wherever those appendages were ornamental or useful; while the parade-ground was as barren and ignorant of sod as the great highway to Salt Lake City itself. General Dandy, the post quartermaster, with his good taste and skill, had, in 1866, originated a perfect plan to secure an exhaustless supply of water, at reasonable cost, and should his successor carry his plans into effect, much can be done to redeem the forlornness of the station.

Laramie has been a profitable place for traders, and not a few ranchmen and citizens have squaw wives, and a large Indian traffic; but with some exceptions, it was to us the most inhospitable and barren post on our trip. It was then a four-company post, but was reinforced during the autumn, thus giving rise to the report of General Sanborn, special Indian commissioner, afterward published, that, "in 1866, at Fort Laramie, when all was peace, there were twelve companies of regular troops; while at Fort Philip Kearney, where all was war, only four companies were *allowed*."

Fortunately, this garrison proved ample for the defence of Fort Laramie, and the post was still safe on our return in 1867.

CHAPTER 9

Laramie to Reno

On the 18th of June, at three o'clock a.m., the bugle call started us from "Nine Mile Ranch," and we were at last directly *en route* for our new home, passing the Dry Branch of Warm Spring, Bitter Cottonwood Creek, and, after a march of sixteen miles, camped on "Little Bitter Cottonwood," where there was an ample supply of timber, water, and grass.

June 19th. After eighteen miles of advance we came to the most remarkable defile through which the Platte urges its way in its passage from the Rocky Mountains. The river, which along the line of the march from Laramie had coursed through a prairie-like bottom, here suddenly makes a short curve of half a circle to the right, then, after passing for a few hundred feet between precipitous cliffs, suddenly turns to the left by another short curve, nearly resuming the direction of its original north-western course, and again running through the prairie as before it sought its peculiar hiding-place.

The eastern face of this gorge is perpendicular, and nearly four hundred feet in height. On either side of the entrance are conical summits, of even greater elevation, which stand like sturdy sentinels, but having many natural terraces, on which are placed long lines of cedars as true and uniform in method as if the subject of systematic arrangement. The one on the right is basaltic, and as truly significant of its volcanic origin as are the Palisades of the Hudson, or East and West Rocks, near New Haven, Connecticut; and no part of the great wall which hems in the Niagara River, below the falls, has more stern and prison-like proportions.

One or two of the ladies, with Adjutant Phisterer and Dr. Horton, went around the first curve, quite within the gorge, to hunt for agates and try the effect of pistol shots, the echoes of which were startling and many times repeated. The deep, dark waters are closely pent in and shaded by these confines, so as never to enjoy the sunlight; but all of us enjoyed the sublimity and grandeur of this wonderful natural curiosity. Old Major Bridger, in his peculiarly quaint and sensible way, dropped the sentiment: "Better not go *fur*. There is *Injuns* enough lying under wolf skins, or skulking on them cliffs, I warrant! They follow ye always. They've seen ye, every day, and when ye don't see any of 'em about, is just the time to look out for their devilment." The experience of the next morning confirmed his suspicions.

As this was the last camp before the final crossing of the Platte and entrance upon the territory of the Mountain District, it was named Camp Phisterer, in honour of Adjutant Phisterer, who selected the site, and was most conspicuous in all that contributed to the pleasure or progress of the march.

June 20th. Nine miles of travel brought us to Bridger's Ferry. Here we learned that Indians had, on the previous morning, made a descent upon the stock of Mr. Mills, the proprietor of the Ferry Ranch, although his wife was a Sioux, and, besides his half-breed children, an Indian lived with him in his employ. This Indian had promptly pursued and recovered part of the stock, which they undoubtedly supposed belonged to emigrants. This Indian said that the marauders were "Bad Faces," of Red Cloud's band, and that we would certainly have trouble if men or animals were permitted to stray from the command. Major Bridger and Mr. Brannan were of the same opinion; and both claimed, as they had at Laramie, that we were advancing directly in the face of hostilities; and Major Bridger went so far as to affirm that the presents which were made to Indians at Laramie were given to positive enemies, or to those who had no influence at all over the warlike bands of the Big Horn and Powder River country.

Our next movement was to cross the North Platte. The beef herd was forced into the deep, swift current, and compelled to swim, and as a hundred men on the south bank kept them from returning, all were safely drifted across. The train and command crossed in the ferry-boat, which ingeniously works its own way to and fro by such adjustment of cables and pulleys, and such adaptations to the current, that the round trip was made in about eleven minutes.

The march of June 22nd was sixteen miles, finding wood, water, and grass in abundance.

CAMP PHISTERER CAÑON
NORTH PLATTE RIVER, D.T.

EAST VIEW OF NORTH PLATTE, 4 MILES EAST OF
MOUTH OF SAGE CREEK.
The road has crossed the ridge of sand-hills,
reaching point nearly opposite Fort Fetterman

The march of the 23rd was fifteen miles, with ample supplies of all kinds at our camp on the North Platte, near the mouth of Sage Creek. In the morning we turned northward from the Platte, passing over the red buttes and lofty sand hills and rocky ridges which rise at least live hundred feet above the valley, and these proved in a few places to be very difficult for the more heavily loaded wagons. Occasionally the windings of the river are seen far beneath, and when the road has completed its circuit, and returning descends to the river, the panorama is exceedingly beautiful.

The river can be traced backward for miles in all its course, bordered on the north by the bluffs just crossed, and on the south by the nearly level plains, which, with slight modification, extend as far west as Platte bridge, at Fort Caspar. Near this point a new fort is being erected, with the certainty that Fort Caspar will soon be abandoned or treated as an immaterial position on the route.

Just before reaching the basin, where the Fort Reno road turns northward, following Sage Creek, and the northern Mormon road passes westward toward Salt Lake City, we found an extemporized shed of boards, where Louis Gazzons (French Pete), with his Sioux wife and half-breed children, were opening their merchandise to catch travel over the new route. Here the inevitable display of canned fruits, liquors, tobacco, beads, cutlery, crackers, and cheese were modestly conspicuous, and the good-hearted trader decidedly congratulated himself that he had the first stock of goods on the route to the land of game and gold. Little did he anticipate the doom that awaited him. Mrs. Dr. Horton was the recipient of a young antelope from Louis, and for months after we were well settled at Phil Kearney, this antelope, a spotted fawn, and two colts of Captain Ten Eyck, had each evening a spirited scamper on the parade-ground, until Indians stole the ponies and the antelope poisoned himself by the substitution of fresh paint for his usual treat of sweet milk.

French Pete will be remembered as the first citizen killed during that campaign, and especially as his long course of trade and intimacy with the Indians seemed to promise, at least for himself and family, some considerable favour if not entire immunity at their hands.

June 24th. Marched fourteen miles; camped at the head of Sage Creek; found water, but used sage brush and buffalo chips for fuel. Tufts of buffalo grass were scattered between the sage brush and cactus, so that the herds found forage without any considerable departure from the camp.

June 25th. Marched fifteen miles, and camped on the South Fork of the Cheyenne, where there is plenty of grass and timber; but the great body of the water, in extremely dry weather, passes under the sand and needs slight digging to start it to the surface and secure an abundant supply. At the middle of this day's march, just at the summit of the divide, there is the best view of Laramie Peak, showing its peculiar formation, where cone after cone rises gradually until a central shoot overtops them all.

June 26th. Was enlivened by a successful attempt to open a shorter route to Wind River, avoiding Humphrey's old camp; and after a march of twenty miles we found wood, grass, and water, besides realizing a gain of over five miles in the general line of travel.

June 27th. Marched twenty-one miles, to the Dry Branch of Powder River, finding wood, grass, and water, though the grass was largely intermingled with the inevitable sage brush and cactus. Early in the morning we obtained our first view of the Big Horn Mountains, at a distance of eighty miles, and it was indeed magnificent. The sun so shone as to fall with full blaze upon the southern and south-eastern sides as they rose toward Cloud Peak, which is nine thousand feet above the level of the sea, and the whole range so closely blended with the sky as to leave it in doubt whether all was not a mass of bright cloud; while many, even with the aid of a glass, insisted that they were immense gleaming sand hills, with no snow at all.

In half an hour the air itself was invigorated by the currents from the snow banks; and even at that distance shawls became necessary, the ambulance side curtains were closed, and it seemed as if a November day was to succeed the summer's morning. In front, and a little to the northeast, could be seen the four columns of Pumpkin Buttes, nearly twenty-three miles east of Fort Reno. These buttes are landmarks for the traveller from all directions, and nearly seven hundred feet high. East of them lie the Black Hills of Dakota, and the once talked of direct route from Sioux City to Reno and Virginia City, which has been referred to in connection with the pamphlet of Colonel Sawyer published by the government.

July 28th. Passed Buffalo Springs, and down the Dry Fork of Powder River, sixteen miles, and over one divide, to Fort Reno.

The road, from early morning, was in the very bed of the stream, which, but a few inches deep, was constantly crossed by the train, and being bordered by abrupt ledges of lignite, clay, and sand, is surely indicative of an abundance, if not a surfeit, of water during the thaws of spring; while, for nearly twelve miles, the traveller is hemmed in and confined to this narrow basin, subject to constant exposure and annoyance from Indian attacks. The grass is poor, but wood and water are abundant. Many cottonwood-trees have been felled by travellers and Indians for the bark with which to feed both mules and horses; but this leaves a supply of dry wood equal to the increasing demand.

Our first view of Fort Reno was most unprepossessing; but, expecting it to be abandoned, its ugliness and barrenness did not so decidedly shock the sensibilities as if it had been gazed upon as a permanent home, or even a transient dwelling-place. We passed through more than a mile of river bottom, densely studded with large Cottonwood trees, and after fording Powder River, encamped just south of the fort, glad to have accomplished more than five hundred miles of our journey with such substantial success.

Before long, some enterprising post commander will recommend the final demolition of the fort, or shrewd emigrants will avoid it, by carrying out the feasible project for a short cut-off under the Big Horn Mountains, which was partially inaugurated in 1866, and which affords abundant supplies of grass, as well as an equal amount of timber with the present location.

So we were finally at Powder River. We had known some such hot days as are never found in the Eastern or Middle States; had drank water that had small virtue beyond its name and moisture; had used sage brush and buffalo chips for variety of fuel; but, so far, were all right and even fast seeing the country. The cactus, which annoys a horse as much as it does the pedestrian, had partly compensated for its thorns and sting by the beauty of its blossoms; and the prolific sage brush had imparted odour as well as fuel, and thus regaled the sense while it heated our coffee.

The wild tulip, larkspur, sweet pea, convolvulus, and a vine, closely resembling the Mexican plant, were among the flora that were abundant, and these, with others, were duly pressed for future care and admiration. The Indian potato and wild onion were gathered constantly by the men, and both are valuable when antiscorbutics are scarce and salt pork most abundant.

The march which brought us to Reno closed up all possibility of meeting any resident traders; and indeed, with the exception of the fort itself, there was then not a resident white man between Bridger's Ferry and Bozeman City, Montana. We were about to pass the last log-cabin, and realize practically the experience of pioneers and test our own capacity for building, keeping house, and living in the land of Absaraka! Single trains of emigrants had passed through the country. Bozeman had made one trip and had succeeded admirably in the selection of his route, and our sterling friend Bridger had a head full of maps and trails and ideas, all of the utmost value to the objects of the expedition. So we stopped at Reno, to prepare for the next, and final advance!

LARAMIE PEAK—FROM THE NORTH,
5900 FEET ABOVE SEA LEVEL.

CHAPTER 10

Fourth of July in Absaraka

Fort Reno was first located in 1865, under the name of Fort Connor.

Absolute sterility excludes all elements of vegetable beauty or production. The single redeeming feature is the fact that the river bottom for miles in either direction is abundantly supplied with timber, so that emigrants will always find the material for fuel or building: but the same old sage brush and cactus persistently monopolize the soil for miles, and Powder River itself, flowing from the south side of the Big Horn Mountains, is muddy and so strongly alkaline as to be prejudicial to both man and beast.

In June, 1866, Fort Reno was an open post, except that the warehouses and stables had a rough stockade. Officers' and men's quarters, guard-house and magazine, were on the open plain. Being nearly one hundred and forty feet above the river, the water was brought up in wagons, and no effective effort had been made to seek for better water than that of the river, although, after our second day in camp, a spring of clear water was discovered, by the enterprise of the mounted command, immediately under the bluff. Subsequently it was decided to retain the post as part of the district command. New buildings were erected, the parade was inclosed, suitable bastions and block-houses were built, and a substantial stone magazine was completed under the immediate direction of Captain Proctor.

At the date of our arrival the garrison consisted of two companies of the 5th United States Volunteers, who were simply waiting to be relieved before proceeding eastward to be mustered out of service. A company of Winnebago Indians had been at the fort, and we passed them near Laramie on the 17th of June. Many of them wished to go back with us, but there was no existing authority to employ them, and it was generally understood and distinctly affirmed by Major Bridger that some of the Sioux at Laramie expressly demanded, as a condition of their own consent to peace, that these Indians should leave the country. If this be true, it was sharp in the Sioux, for the service lost its best scouts, and no depredations had taken place about Reno while it was known that they were there.

Upon the first alarm these Winnebagoes would spring to their ponies, with rifle and lariat, regardless of rations or clothing, and, with one good whoop, disappear in pursuit. Being deadly enemies of the Sioux, it is not to be wondered that the latter should wish them out of the country; but until peace could be absolutely realized, it would have been no prejudice to that line of operations, as events transpired, to have had a few soldiers who knew the Indian styles of warfare, and were up to their tricks.

Nevertheless, the Winnebagoes departed, and their substitutes were not provided. So, as we began to live in Absaraka, we began to learn contemporaneous history.

Our camp at Fort Reno was adapted to the location. The mounted infantry were at the base of the hill, for ready access to water. Brevet Major Haymond's command was on the river's bank above, just over a slight rise, but out of sight from the fort. Headquarters tents were near the flag-staff, which had been located with view to some future expansion of the post for the accommodation of twelve companies. After a night's rest, everybody seemed busy. Three emigrant trains were in the river bottom waiting for the colonel's instructions as to their advance westward; and we were quite surprised to find that the lady travellers with those trains had no fear of Indians, and did not believe there were any had Indians on the route. One train captain told us ladies we never would see an Indian unless he came to beg for sugar, flour, or tobacco. This was all very gratifying, as this captain had been many years on the Plains, and said "he couldn't be scared worth a continental."

About ten o'clock the ladies went to the sutler's store of Messrs. Smith and Leighton to do some shopping. Suddenly a breathless messenger rushed in with the cry of "*Indian*," and said, as intelligibly as he could, that the sutlers' horses and mules were all gone. Sure enough, upon going to the door, the horses and mules were galloping up the hills across the river, while a party of Indians were following, throwing out flankers to keep the stock in the desired direction, and evidently bending their course toward the Pumpkin Buttes. No doubt they had been eager observers of our progress, just as Major Bridger said, and no less watched the emigrants. Probably they supposed the small headquarters camp, with its large corral of wagons, was that of emigrants. At all events, they crossed the river through the timber, taking advantage of a deep ravine, and struck the herd suddenly without loss to themselves, yet passing two or three of our herds, which were under guard, without venturing an attack.

At this unexpected message all became activity. The colonel was entering the door as the messenger gave the alarm. The bugle brought the mounted men to the saddle and Brevet Major Haymond and Lieutenant Adair led eighty men in pursuit. It was excessively provoking to see the coolness of those Indians as they favoured their ponies in bad places and seemed to calculate exactly how long they could take things easy and when they must hurry; but they had not long to tarry, and soon were pressing their plunder at the top of their speed.

Before the return of the party the next day, they had ridden nearly seventy miles, passing along the Pumpkin Buttes, but failed to recapture any of the stolen stock. *But* they brought in an Indian pony which the Indians abandoned when closely pressed; and this same pony was loaded with favours recently procured at Laramie. Among the variety were navy tobacco, brown sugar, a cavalry stable frock, calico dress-patterns, and other articles, which from their style and condition showed that they had not long since been taken from shelves or packages.

Indeed, the opinion expressed by everybody was afterward confirmed from Laramie, and it was thus early understood that the Indians who received presents at that post had immediately violated their obligations and commenced a new career of robbery and war.

Ten days were spent at Reno in arrangements to distribute the battalion, in reloading wagons, and relieving the companies of the 5th U. S. Volunteers. The mercury rose to 113° in the shade; wagon tyres began to break or fall off, and there was no charcoal (so Mr. Brown said) for welding and putting them in order. The warehouse was full of old supplies, and these had to be invoiced and distributed, while the quantity was twice or three times a complement for all the wagons of the command.

Business was hurried, and it was decided to leave Captain Proctor and Lieutenant Kirtland with one company to guard the stores in depot until trains could be sent back for them and the fort could be dismantled.

Meanwhile the Fourth of July came in its proper annual course, and the usual salute was fired, under the charge of Major Henry Almstedt, paymaster, an old artillery officer, and a welcome visitor at all times, especially just then, when a few things more were to be bought before launching out in that wilderness, where, except Messrs. Beal and Hughes, our sutlers, there was nothing of civilization to be had.

At length, on the morning of July 9th, at 4 o'clock, the command started. Its organization was a matter of interest to us ladies, as there were but three wives of officers left after the parting at Lodge Pole Creek, and new partings were to be anticipated, to complete the constant series which began at Fort Sedgwick.

Brevet Major Haymond, with two companies, had been assigned to the post on the Upper Yellowstone; Brevet Lieutenant-Colonel Kinney, with two companies, had been assigned to the post on the Big Horn River; and Captain Ten Eyck had been given command of the post at district headquarters, new Fort Reno, to which the change of post was to be made. By a mail received before starting, we learned from the officers that the order for a battalion of the 13th U. S. Infantry, to operate from Fort Reno eastward, had been countermanded, and thus we had no rivals to compete for the honours of opening, protecting, and defending the new route and territory of Absaraka. The news gave us women a little scare, which the officers did not condescend to notice; but they, no doubt, were all labouring under the infatuation that the second battalion, with its fresh recruits, could do *perfectly* what under ordinary circumstances would have required two or three regiments to accomplish.

An order was posted at the sutler's store, telling emigrants how to corral their trains, how to deal with or not deal with Indians, and how to procure authority for proceeding beyond the post; and it is a singular fact that every reported disaster to emigrant or other train during 1866 would have been avoided, had the terms of that order been reasonably complied with.

We started westward July 9th, 1866.

The twenty-six miles to Crazy Woman's Fork, in the blazing sun, was a severe trial. It was fully night before camp was well established, and the next morning revealed the fact that half of our transportation was disabled, although inspected daily and repaired according to all the means at hand.

Crazy "Woman's Fork has been described in general terms. The stream, just at the crossing, makes a sharp turn, giving two separate fords, but having quite a steep ledge or bank on the east side as the traveller enters its basin, but on the west gradually rising to the summit of the divide between its waters and those of Clear Creek.

Inspection was made, timber was cut, a charcoal pit was fashioned and fired, and every available blacksmith was put at work.

One means of repair was resorted to which was supposed to be as novel as it was effective. Gunny sacks were cut in strips and thoroughly soaked in water. These strips were tacked on so nicely that when secured with the heated tires they not only withstood the summer's use, but even in the winter of 1867 some of those wagons were doing excellent service without additional repair. Of course this would only answer where tyres were unbroken; neither could it be afforded that all the corn should be emptied, except as the expenditure of the journey should permit, and thus allow an accumulation of those empty.

On the morning of the 12th, the companies that were to build "New Fort Reno" marched with headquarters to select and occupy its site. The four companies destined for the more distant posts were left to perfect repairs and follow as soon as possible. Our first camp was at Clear Fork, just at noon, and its perfect beauty and completeness of natural supplies have been anticipated in the general description of this portion of Absaraka. Little episodes, of course, occurred here, as they did elsewhere. With Mrs. Horton and Mrs. Bisbee the splendid sunset was watched with real pleasure. Our camp chairs were near the tents on the banks of the creek. A chance interruption of our meditations led to the agreeable information that we were sitting just over three valuable rattlesnakes, which an orderly was kind enough to find and mangle to death. We sat no more by the brink of Clear Fork, but dreamed of rattlesnakes until the bugle sounded the reveille the next day.

On Friday the 13th we had our next indication of Indians. A few were seen upon a high hill to the left; and after passing Rock Creek, close under a commanding ridge, our attention was called to two small pieces of cracker-box planted by the roadside, on which were notes in pencil, stating that two trains had been attacked on the previous Tuesday and Friday, and that some of the stock of each had been driven off.

These were trains that were in advance of our expected arrival, but gained greater distance than they expected, through our detention at Crazy Woman's Fork.

At 11 o'clock a.m., July 13th, we had passed Lake Smedt and were in camp on Big Piney Fork, just east of the crossing of the Virginia City road, and about four miles from the Big Horn Mountains. At last, we had the prospect of finding a home, and Cloud Peak seemed to look down upon us with a cheerful face as the sunlight made his features glow and glisten.

CHAPTER 11

Location of Fort Philip Kearney

The headquarters camp of the expedition of 1866 was organized on the 13th of July of that year with special care, and greatly to the annoyance of teamsters, as the colonel had the corral formed three times until it was sufficiently compact and trim to suit him.

At 1 o'clock he was off with a small party to visit the surroundings as far back as the mountains, and seven miles westward, to determine the most eligible site for the post. A beautiful plateau had been passed just before the command halted, which seemed particularly inviting; but as Major Bridger and Mr. Brannan had both urged that the valleys of Goose Creek and Tongue River should be first visited, no decision was announced.

On the morning of July 14th, at 5 o'clock, Colonel Carrington, Adjutant Phisterer, Quartermaster Brown, Captain Ten Eyck, Guide Brannan, and Jack Stead, interpreter, with a mounted escort, left for a reconnoissance of the region of country which had such an exalted and widespread reputation as being the richest, loveliest, and grandest of all the lands of Absaraka, *viz..* Tongue River valley.

Brevet Captain Adair was officer of the day, and all was unusually quiet in camp until nearly 9 o'clock, when it was found that some men had deserted to seek the gold mines of Montana. A detail started in pursuit. They returned before noon with the tidings that they had been stopped by a band of Indians, were refused permission to go on, and were instructed to return at once with a message to the white chief, that he must take his soldiers out of the country.

This party had met that same travelling ranch of Louis Gazzons about seven miles out, and a young man in his employ as teamster, who had been discharged by Lieutenant Brown at Fort Reno, had been impressed by the Indians to see that their message was correctly delivered and an answer returned.

This lad brought peremptory orders for the white men to decide for peace or war, and if they wanted peace, to return at once to Powder River. They promised not to trouble the old post, but declared that they would not let soldiers go over the road which had never been given to the whites, neither would they let them stay and build forts. These Indians were reported to be Ogillalla Sioux, under Red Cloud as their principal leader, and they had been negotiating for several days with certain bands of Cheyennes, with whom Louis Gazzons was trading, to induce them to join on the war-path and obstruct the road and all travel upon it. French Pete had already traded for a great many skins, and was preparing to visit the camp to sell as many as he could to the officers and men of the command.

The absence of the colonel induced Mr. Adair to detain the messenger in the guard tent, and shortly after an Indian messenger approached, but quickly retreated when he found that he was not promptly joined by the white man sent in advance. A demand had also been made that the white chief, in company with Jack Stead, whom they knew at Laramie, and whose wife was a Cheyenne squaw, should go and visit their village and settle the question of peace or war.

Shortly after 6 o'clock in the afternoon, and after an absence of thirteen hours, the colonel's party came in, having found two brush *tepahs* (*tepees* or lodges), where there were signs of recent occupation by Indians; but as the detachment had crossed buttes and ridges nearer the mountains for the purpose of testing Major Bridger's recommendation that a new and shorter road should be opened to Tongue River valley, they met neither Cheyenne nor Sioux.

After due examination, the prisoner was sent back, in company with Jack, to invite the principal chief and some of his braves to come into camp, when the sun was overhead, after two sleeps (at noon of Monday the 17th), and promising that they should be kindly entertained and allowed to depart in safety.

Jack returned the following night and reported that the Indians, having been alarmed by the protracted absence of their messenger, had moved off to Tongue River, nearly thirty miles, under apprehensions of an attack, but he followed their trail, delivered his message, and secured their pledge to make the proposed visit.

The reconnoissance of the day had settled the location of the fort, as Tongue River valley was not only more remote from *pine* timber, too far from Powder River, and less advantageous as a position, but *its* selection would have left to the Indians the control of the trails about Piney's and Peno, and thus given them the very gate to Tongue River valley itself; while the abundance of grass, pure water, choice timber, and wild grain in the immediate vicinity of the site selected, left no necessity for those elements to be sought elsewhere.

Accordingly, early next morning, July 15th, although Sunday, the camp, which had been temporarily on the low ground where the underbrush of the creek and dense cottonwood might afford shelter to an enemy, was abandoned, and the plateau before referred to was occupied.

Very early in the morning, the colonel and Captain Ten Eyck, with the pioneer party, had staked out the dimensions of the future post, according to plans and drawings matured at old Fort Kearney in the spring; while, to secure at the very outset a handsome and permanent parade-ground, the long train of wagons was repeatedly driven about the designated rectangle, four hundred feet square, and officers, teamsters, and soldiers, alike were forbidden to cross, except by designated avenues, while a mowing machine soon cut the grass and gave the start to the present, (as at time of first publication), beautiful lawn of the Fort Phil Kearney *plaza*.

The tents were pitched along the streets appropriate to the respective building sites of officers' and soldiers' quarters, warehouses, sutler's store, band quarters, and guardhouse; while the established general and picket guards, with the artillery parked on the parade, soon imparted form, comeliness, and system to the whole.

By 12 o'clock a stranger might have supposed the camp to have been a fixture for weeks.

We had one episode while moving: Black George ran in, in great haste, to tell missis that it was snowing, *sure*; while other reports were, that the grass of Peno valley had been fired by the Indians, and the smoke was already sweeping down upon us. All proved to be a complimentary visit from grasshoppers as large as locusts, and for a time it seemed as if wagon-covers and tents were all to be eaten up in just about five minutes. In vain were turkeys and chickens let loose against the destroyers: the whole camp hummed with the rustle of their wings as they filed themselves on the blades of grass and became familiar generally. A kind wind from the mountains came along in the afternoon, and they left as suddenly as they arrived.

The scout of Friday afternoon had determined available points for ready acquisition of building timber, and, while Engineer J. B. Gregory was soon at work trying to put in shape and operation a horse-power sawmill until the steam mills should arrive, the whole garrison was broken into details for ditching, chopping, hauling, hewing, and such other varied duty as loomed up like a vast burden, to be overcome before winter should overtake us.

Neither was the undertaking a light one, as the district headquarters would at once become a partial depot, and supplies for a whole year had been estimated for, before the command left old Kearney.

Subsequent events confirmed the wisdom of this immediate and incessant labour; for when cold weather actually developed its power there were no surplus quarters, and the eventual, constant hostilities no less demonstrated the value of the defence and the whole arrangement of the post.

Thus, Monday morning was as busy in progress as Sunday had been necessarily occupied in location and occupation of the site.

It was deemed wise also to secure something like shape and a tenable position before the expected interview with the Indians, so as to give our visitors as good an impression as possible of our purposes and determination to *remain*.

As the diagram and map (p. 97 and p.132), furnished illustrate the plan and surroundings of Fort Philip Kearney so far as completed on the 1st of January, 1867, no further comment need be made than to say that, with all the prophecies and liabilities that the soldiers would desert for gold leads or diggings, it was found that their almost universal impulse was cheerfully to take hold of every duty and put the work through.

The fact that gold colour had been found in the creek the very first day, perhaps combined with doubt as to the safety of deserting only to run the gantlet of hostile tribes, may have stimulated labour; but never did a command apply themselves more diligently to real hard work and exacting guard duty, nor did men ever exhibit more ready obedience and willing self-sacrifice, in order to carry out the plans requiring their co-operation in execution.

To be sure, there was little kicking and cuffing and cursing administered, after the theory of some, that this is the *acme* of all discipline, and that soldiers are like cattle, to be worked by the whip and the yell; and instances of *such* discipline were publicly reprimanded and corrected, but no work, however tedious, no exposure, however protracted, no order, however sudden or urgent, failed to find willing and spirited response. Obedience was unquestioning and immediate; justice was equal and certain, and it was well understood that the colonel hated the popular theory of oaths and blows, while none the less positive in the enforcement of law. Fort Philip Kearney will be a monument of the spirit and skill of companies A, C, H, and E, 2nd Battalion, 18th U. S. Infantry, now the 27th Regiment; and its own soldiers need not fear that any rivals will do more or better work, or do it under more adverse circumstances than was *their* mission in the summer and fall of the year of grace 1866.

CHAPTER 12

Arrival of Indians

At twelve o'clock, June 16th, a few Indians appeared on the hills, and after showing a white flag and receiving assurance of welcome, about forty, including the squaws of chiefs and warriors, approached the camp and bivouacked on the level ground in front. Meanwhile, hospital tents had been arranged for this first interview with the inhabitants of Absaraka.

A table covered with the national flag was placed across one tent, chairs were placed behind and at the ends for officers of the garrison, while other seats were placed in front for visitors.

Trunks were opened, epaulettes and dress hats were overhauled, so that whatever a full dress and a little ceremony could do by way of reaching the peculiar taste of the Indian for dignity and finery, was done. The band of the 18th played without, as the principal chiefs were brought across the parade-ground to the tents and introduced to their seats by Mr. Adair. The Cheyennes came in full state, with their best varieties of costume, ornament, and arms; though there was occasionally a departure from even the Indian originality in apparel. One very tall warrior, with richly wrought *moccasins* and a fancy breechcloth, had no other covering for his person than a large gay umbrella, which, as his pony galloped briskly up, had far more of the grotesque and ludicrous in its associations than it had of the warlike and fearful.

Some were bare to the waist, others had only the limbs bare. Some wore elaborate necklaces of grizzly bears' claws, shells, and continuous rings, bead-adorned *moccasins*, leggings, tobacco pouches, medicine bags, and knife scabbards, as well as armlets, earrings, and medals.

The larger silver medals included, one each, of the administrations and bore the medallion heads and names of Jefferson, Madison, and Jackson. These medals had evidently belonged to their fathers who had visited Washington, or had been the trophies of the field or trade.

Those who claimed pre-eminence among the land were "Black Horse," "Red Arm," "Little Moon," "Pretty Bear," "The Rabbit that Jumps," "The Wolf that Lies Down," "The Man that Stands alone on the Ground," and "Dull Knife."

As these were the Indians who had sent the message of the 14th, or were in their company, the question of their inclination and temper was one of no little interest to all.

The formal assurance of the Laramie Peace Commission before its adjournment, that satisfactory peace had been made with the Ogillalla and Brulè Sioux, and that the Arrapahoes and Cheyennes had only to come in for their presents, inspired some hope that possibly the reception of this first band encountered, might result in substantial advantage beyond the mere range of the band itself.

As the front of the canvas was open, the ladies gathered in the headquarters tent close by, parted its folds and enjoyed a dress-circle view of the whole performance. As pipes passed and the inevitable "*how*," the rising up, and the shaking of hands were interludes between all solemn declarations, as well as the prelude to a new speech, or the approval of something good that had been said, the scene seemed just about as intelligible as a rapidly-acted pantomime would be to a perfect stranger to the stage.

The red-sandstone pipe had its frequent replenishing before a single "*how*" indicated that either visitor wished to make himself heard. The scene was peculiar.

In front of them all, and to the left of the table, sitting on a low seat, with elbows on his knees and chin buried in his hands, sat the noted James Bridger, whose forty-four years upon the frontier had made him as keen and suspicious of Indians as any Indian himself could be of another. The old man, already somewhat bowed by age, after long residence among the Crows as a friend and favourite chief, and having incurred the bitter hatred of the Cheyennes and Sioux alike, knew full well that *his* scalp ("Big Throat's") would be the proudest trophy they could bear to their solemn feasts; and there he sat, or crouched, as watchful as though old times had come again, and he was once more to mingle in the light, or renew the ordeal of his many hair-breadth escapes and spirited adventures. Many stories are told of his past history, and he is charged with many of his own manufacture. He is said to have seen a diamond in the Rocky Mountains, by the light of which he travelled thirty miles one stormy night, and to have informed some inquisitive travellers that Scott's Bluffs, nearly four hundred feet high, now stand where there was a deep valley when he first visited that country.

When inquired of as to these statements, he quietly intimated that there was no harm in fooling people who pumped him for information and would not even say "*thank ye*." Once he was wealthy, and his silver operations in Colorado might have been very lucrative; but he was the victim of misplaced confidence, and was always restless when not on the plains. To us, he was invariably straightforward, truthful, and reliable. His sagacity, knowledge of woodcraft, and knowledge of the Indian was wonderful, and his heart was warm and his feelings tender wherever he confided or made a friend. An instance of this will close the sketch of one who will soon pass away, the last of the first pioneers of the Rocky Mountains.

He cannot read, but enjoys reading. He was charmed by Shakespeare; but doubted the Bible story of Samson's tying foxes by the tails, and with firebrands burning the wheat of the Philistines. At last he sent for a good copy of Shakespeare's plays, and would hear them read until midnight with unfeigned pleasure. The murder of the two princes in the Tower startled him to indignation. He desired it to be read a second and a third time. Upon positive conviction that the text was properly read to him, he burned the whole set, convinced that "Shakespeare must have had a bad heart and been as de—h mean as a Sioux, to have written such scoundrelism as that." But to return to the council.

linear Major Bridger stood Jack Stead, the interpreter. Born in England, early a runaway sailor boy, afterward a seaman upon the Peacock when it was wrecked near the mouth of Columbia River; then traversing the Rocky Mountains as one of the first messengers to report the Mormon preparations to resist the United States, and the renewal of Indian hostilities, the same year; with hair and eyes black as an Indian's, and a face nearly as tawny from hardship and exposure; a good shot, and skilled in woodcraft; with a Cheyenne wife; fond of big stories and much whisky; but a fair interpreter when mastered and held to duty; and watchful as Bridger himself to take care of his scalp,—Jack Stead was the first to break the silence and announce that Black Horse wanted to talk.

Adjutant Phisterer, called by the Indians "Roman, or Crooked Nose," acted as recorder of the council, keeping full notes of the conference; and few were the diaries or letters home that did not embody the history of our first visit from Indians, and repeat some of their expressions of purpose or desire.

Neither did the Indian advocate appear to disadvantage, as the exponent of his rights and wants. Erect and earnest, he cast off the buffalo robe that had been gathered about his shoulders and in his folded arms, and while it now hung loosely from his girdle, stepped halfway toward the table and began.

With fire in his eye, and such spirit in his gesture as if he were striking a blow for his life or the life of his nation; with cadence changeful, now rising in tone, so as to sound far and wide over the garrison, and again sinking so as to seem as if he were communing with his own spirit rather than feeling for a response from the mind of another, the Cheyenne chief stood there to represent his people, to question the plans of the white chief, and solemnly advise him of the issue that was forced upon the red man. It was an occasion when all idea of the red man as the mere wild beast to be slaughtered, quickly vanished in a prompt sympathy with his condition, and no less inspired an earnest purpose, so far as possible, to harmonize the intrusion upon his grand hunting domain with his best possible well-being in the future.

Other chiefs followed "Black Horse," in harangues of varied length and vigour; and all agreed that they preferred to accept protection and become the friends of the whites. They came to represent one hundred and seventy-six lodges, and had been hunting on Goose Creek and Tongue River, when they met Red Cloud; but said that one hundred and twenty-five of their young men were absent with "Bob Tail," having gone to the Arkansas on the war-path and hunt. They had quarrelled with another band of Cheyennes, who lived near the Black Hills east of Powder River; and said there was a third band south of the Republican hostile to the whites. Two of the chiefs had with them Camanche wives whom they had married in excursions to the south.

They gave the history of a portion of our march, and stated correctly, what Red Cloud had assured them, that half of the white soldiers were left back at Crazy Woman's Fork. They said that Red Cloud told them, the morning before the messenger was sent to the camp, that white soldiers from Laramie would be at Piney Fork before the sun was overhead in the heavens; that the white chief sent soldiers from Reno after Indians who stole horses and mules; but the white soldiers did not get them back.

They also stated that the Sioux were having a sun-dance, insisting that the Cheyennes must make common cause with them and drive the white man back to Powder River; that some of Red Cloud's men had already gone back to interrupt travel on the road; that they had left their squaws in the village with thirty of their old men, and were afraid the Sioux would rob them in their absence if they should stay too long in the white man's camp; but that if they could have provisions, they would make a strong peace, and let a hundred of their young men, whose return would be in two days, go with the white soldiers against the Sioux.

Before the council broke up. Brevet Major Haymond arrived with his four companies and went into camp northwest of the fort near the river crossing.

The Indians became very restless as the afternoon progressed, and at last bade goodbye; receiving papers indicative of their good behaviour, and entering into an agreement to leave the line of road and go upon or south of the upper plateau of the Big Horn Mountains. They afterward visited Fort Caspar, behaving well, and no doubt observed their obligations as best they could.

The presents given consisted of some second-hand clothing of the officers, twenty pounds of tobacco, a dinner of army rations, and enough flour, bacon, sugar and coffee to give them a meal in their village and convince the absent of their kind treatment. They left with apparently cordial good feeling, and the understanding that they were not to approach emigrant trains even to beg; but might go to Laramie, or other military posts when hungry, as long as they remained the friends of the whites.

There is no evidence that any of these chiefs have violated their pledges.

CHAPTER 13

Massacre of Louis Gazzons' Party

At five o'clock a.m., July 17th, the herds of Brevet Major Haymond were surprised, the Indians crawling within the picket, and with great sagacity starting Wagonmaster Hill's bell mare first, so as to secure all in company. Major Haymond, with one orderly, started in pursuit, as we afterward learned, although no information was given at the post until two hours after. He left orders, we heard, for the mounted men to saddle and follow. The party thus pursuing in haste was ultimately surrounded by several hundred Indians, and when a messenger was sent in with report of the condition of affairs, two companies of infantry and fifty mounted men, with ammunition, rations, wagons, and ambulances, were at once started to the relief.

But very soon sad reports came from Peno valley, only a few miles over Lodge Trail Ridge. The casualties of the command had been two men killed and three wounded; and, more painful than all, was the report of the massacre on the road of Louis Gazzons and most of his party.

Brevet Major Haymond, finding the Indians so numerous and the ground impracticable for the use of his men, while the Indians were not only perfectly at home, but specially watchful of stragglers and fully versed in that style of warfare, fell back toward the post. On the retreat he came up with the wagons of French Pete, which had already started for camp. About the plundered wagons lay the mutilated remains of his party, with the exception that his wife, a Sioux woman, with her five children, had been able to hide in the brush until the arrival of the troops furnished an escort to headquarters.

Six men lay dead and mutilated upon the road. Such was the first lesson to the expedition of the kind of peace to be expected for the future. Henry Arrison, of St. Louis, partner of Gazzons, was among the number. The cattle, wagons, and goods that the Indians had not broken open, for want of time, were brought to the post and taken charge of by Mr. John W. Hugus, administrator, on behalf of the widow, creditors, and friends of the deceased.

The Sioux wife of Gazzons said that the Cheyennes had traded largely and pleasantly with Pete, and that the chiefs who had visited the post on the 16th were with them until midnight, smoking and trading; that during the evening some of the Sioux chiefs came up from Tongue River valley and asked Black Horse what the white man said to them, and whether the white chief was going back to Powder River. To this Black Horse answered "that the white chief would not go back, but his soldiers would go on." They then asked "what presents were given."

Black Horse told them "that they had all they wanted to eat, and the white chief wished all the Arrapahoes and Sioux, and all other Indians of that country, to go to Laramie and sign the treaty and get their presents." At this the Sioux unstrung their bows, and whipped Black Horse and the other Cheyennes over the back and face, crying "*Coo!*" which by the Indians is deemed a matter of prowess and a feat which secures them credit, as they count their "*Coos*" in a fight almost as proudly as they do the scalps of enemies.

After the Sioux left. Black Horse told French Pete that he must go to his village and from there to the mountains, for the Sioux meant war, but advised *him* to send a messenger to the white chief quick, or the Sioux would kill him. French Pete neglected the advice; but was on his return in the morning, when the Sioux, who had stolen Major Haymond's mules, and had come in contact with his men, came across the train and destroyed all the men who were with it.

On the same day Major Haymond's four companies were ordered to change their position and encamp just below the fort.

On the 19th a train with military escort, under Captain Burrows, was sent back to Fort Reno for provisions. The young men of the Cheyennes also returned from the Arkansas, and "Bob Tail" had an interview with the colonel, leaving his own robe as a pledge of his friendship.

About one o'clock a.m., July 24th, a courier from Clear Fork brought a dispatch from Captain Burrows that the Sioux were very numerous, and additional force was needed at once. Mr. Thomas Dillon also wrote that Mr. Kirkendall's train had been engaged all the afternoon, and he could not move without troops. A company of infantry, with a mountain howitzer, was soon started, and upon their approach in the morning, the Indians, numbering several hundred, fled, Torrence Callery, of Company G, had been killed; and one of the trains relieved, which had been taken back to Fort Reno temporarily, contained five officers of the regiment, with servants, baggage, Mrs. Lieutenant Wands and child, all of whom had been forwarded from Fort Laramie, under the prestige of the Laramie treaty, with only ten men as escort to headquarters. When this train had reached Crazy Woman's Fork it was attacked by fifty Indians, and Lieutenant Daniels, of Indiana, who was a little in advance selecting camping ground, was killed, scalped, and mutilated, while one of the Indians put on his clothes and danced within view of the party.

Chaplain David White, Lieutenants Templeton, Bradley, and Wands, with Mrs. Wands and child, survived, and the Henry rifle of Mr. Wands was specially efficacious in warding off and punishing the assailants.

Chaplain White, like the preachers of Cromwell, only prayed *internally*, while putting his time physically into the best exercise of self-defence. He thinks he did his duty; and the officers say that he thought it was just about the right thing to kill as many of the varmint as possible.

Lieutenant Kirtland's rescuing party from Reno was also very prompt, and Lieutenant Daniel's remains were escorted to that post and suitably buried.

The Cheyennes of Black Horse met Kirkendall's train and gave warning of the approach of the Sioux, just as they had at the council given indications of this same movement. The warning was disregarded, but the Sioux *did* come.

Thus commenced our first two weeks in our new home. A few more incidents will illustrate the experience that followed.

July 22nd. At Buffalo Springs, on the Dry Fork of Powder River, a citizen train was attacked, having one man killed and another wounded.

July 22nd. Indians appeared at Fort Reno, driving off one public mule.

July 22nd. Mr. Nye lost four animals near Fort Phil Kearney, and Mr. Axe and Mr. Dixon each had two mules stolen by Indians.

July 23rd. A citizen train was attacked at the Dry Fork of the Cheyenne, and two men were killed.

July 23rd. Louis Cheney's train was attacked; one man was killed, and horses, cattle, and private property were sacrificed.

July 28th. Indians attempted to drive off the public stock at Fort Reno, and failed; but took the cattle of citizen John B. Sloss. Pursuit; recovered them.

July 29th. A citizen train was attacked at Brown Springs, four miles east of the East Fork of the Cheyenne, and eight men were killed, two were wounded, and one of these died of his wounds. Their grave is still memorial of the confidence with which they left Laramie, assured that all was peace. These men, though too few in numbers, were well armed, but were deceived by a show of friendship; and one Indian shot a white man in the back just after shaking hands and receiving a present.

Meanwhile, the necessity of maintaining Fort Reno as an intermediate post on the route had been established. Another company was sent to reinforce its garrison. The Upper Yellowstone post was abandoned for want of troops, and early in August, Brevet Lieutenant-Colonel N. C. Kinney, with Captain Burrows and their two companies, were sent to the Big Horn River, distant ninety-one miles, to establish that post, subsequently known as Fort C. F. Smith.

The narrative of *all* hostile demonstrations need not be traced. Enough will be given to correct false ideas as to the feelings and operations of Indians during the year; and the reader will not be astonished that ladies, as well as gentlemen, perused the President's message of December 8th, 1866, which congratulated the country that the Indians were at peace, with something like inquisitiveness as to whether the colonel had reported the true condition to department headquarters, and whether department headquarters had read his report.

But to proceed. Grover, the artist, correspondent of Frank Leslie, was scalped one Sunday morning, while only a few minutes' walk from the post.

August 9th. In one of the frequent attacks upon the timber train, four mules were taken after the driver had cut them loose; but a party from the fort under Corporal Phillip recaptured the mules, killing one Indian and wounding a second.

August 12th. Indians drove off horses and cattle belonging to citizens encamped on the river bank near Reno. The cattle were recaptured.

August 14th. Joseph Postlewaite and Stockley Williams were killed within four miles of Fort Reno.

August 17th. Indians appeared in force near the same post, and drove off' seven public horses and seventeen mules. Other similar depredations occurred in August.

September 8th. At 6 o'clock a.m. Twenty mules were driven from a citizen herd, during a severe storm, within a mile of Fort Phil Kearney; and two other demonstrations were made the same day. The colonel with one party, and Lieutenant Adair with another, were out until after 9 o'clock at night in pursuit.

September 10th. Ten herders were attacked a mile south of the fort, losing thirty-three horses and seventy-eight mules. Pursuit was vigorous, but unsuccessful.

September 13th. At midnight a summons came from the hay contractors, Messrs. Crarv and Carter, at Goose Creek, for help, as one man had been killed, hay had been heaped upon five mowing-machines and set on fire, and two hundred and nine cattle had been stolen by the Indians, who had driven a herd of buffalo into the valley, and thus taken buffalo and cattle together out of reach.

Lieutenant Adair went at once with reinforcements, but found the Indians in too large force for continuance of the work.

The same day at 9 o'clock, Indians stampeded a public herd, wounding two of the herders. Captain Ten Eyck and Lieutenant Wands pursued until late at night. Private Donovan came in also with an arrow in his hip; but, just as he was always in an Indian fight, brave as a lion, started out again as soon as it was withdrawn.

September 14th. Private Gilchrist was killed.

September 16th. Peter Johnson, riding a few rods in advance of his party, which was returning from a hay field near Lake Smedt, was suddenly cut off by Indians. Search was made that night by a party under Quartermaster Brown, but his remains were not recovered.

September 17th. A large force demonstrated from the east, and took forty-eight head of cattle; but all were recaptured on pursuit.

September 20th. Indians attacked a citizen outfit lying in the angle of the two Pineys; but were repulsed by aid from the fort, losing one red man killed and another wounded.

September 23rd. Indians attacked and drove off twenty-four head of cattle. They were pursued by Quartermaster Brown, in company with twenty-three soldiers and citizens, and after a sharp fight at close quarters, the cattle were recaptured, and a loss was inflicted upon the Indians of thirteen killed and many wounded.

September 23rd. Lieutenant Matson, with an escort, bringing wagons from the hay field, was surrounded and corralled for some time by a superior force. He found upon the road the body of contractor Grull, who had been to Fort C. F. Smith with public stores, and was killed on his return with two of his drivers.

On the 17th, 21st, and 23rd, Indians had also been active near Fort Reno, driving off horses and cattle. Casper H. Walsh was killed; and at the Dry Fork of the Cheyenne, citizens W. R. Pettis and A. G. Overholt were wounded.

September 27th. Private Patrick Smith was scalped at the pinery, but crawled a half mile to the blockhouse, and survived twenty-four hours.

Two of the working party in the woods were also cut off from their comrades by nearly one hundred Indians, and were scalped before their eyes. A party of fifteen dashed at the nearest picket but did no harm.

Captain Bailey's mining party lost two of their best men.

On one occasion a messenger came in hot haste from the Pinery, reporting that they were besieged; that the Indians had fired through the loop-holes of the blockhouse; that the men were constantly under arms, unwilling as well as unable to work, and asking for a force to clear the Indians out of the bottom lands underneath, where the woods were very dense. The colonel went out with a small party and howitzer, shelled the woods, restored confidence, and the men resumed work. A person ignorant of the effect of a case shot, which scatters its eighty iron bullets quite dangerously, might think it very foolish to explode one where no enemy was *in sight*: but we saw those experiments repeated, where otherwise quite a skirmishing party would have been required, and as the Indians invariably ran away, and sometimes got hurt, the little howitzers were soon favourites and no objects of ridicule or contempt.

The foregoing are instances out of many Indian visits, but do not give all, even of the first two months of our residence in that country. Alarms were constant; attacks upon the trains were frequent, and this kind of visitation continued during the whole season. The ladies all came to the conclusion, no less than the officers affirmed it, that the Laramie treaty was "*Wau-nee-chee,*" no good!

Note.—A buffalo robe, similar to that engraved, was captured, showing the details of the fight of September 23rd, between Captain Brown and Red Cloud's band.

BATTLE DECORATIONS OF BUFFALO ROBE

CHAPTER 14

What Bridger and Beckwith Say

It was quite early after the establishment of Fort Philip Kearney that measures were taken to hold communication with the Crow Indians, to consult with the authorities of Montana, and determine the condition of the entire route to Virginia City. Major Bridger was selected for the mission, accompanied by Henry Williams, assistant guide, who proved himself valuable in almost every work he undertook. They made the through trip with comparative expedition, made complete notes of the journey, and besides their official reports, were very courteous in contributing their information to those who were desirous to keep a full record of all that transpired during our sojourn on the frontier.

They had first an interview with nearly six hundred warriors, not far from Clark's Fork. On that occasion "White Mouth," "Black Foot," and "Rotten Tail" declared their uniform and unanimous voice for peace; but said that in some instances the young men desired to join the Sioux, and thus come to some accommodation as to their title to the lands of which they had been robbed by both Sioux and Cheyennes.

Red Cloud had made them a visit and they had returned the visit, but would not join him against the whites. The "Man afraid of his Horses" told them that his young men were going on the war-path, and that the Sissetons, Bad Faces, Ogillallas from the Missouri, the Minneconjuns from the Black Hills, the Unkpapas, some Cheyennes and Arrapahoes, as well as the Gros Ventres of the Prairie, were united to drive away the whites, and would have big fights at the two new forts in the fall.

They also represented that "Iron Shell," with some of the young men of the Minneconjuns and Brulès, would go with Red Cloud, notwithstanding the Laramie treaty; that the Nes Perces and Flatheads were friendly, but the Pagans and Bloods were hostile, while the Blackfeet, Assiniboines, and Crees were friendly with both parties and would join no league against the whites.

Besides the visits of Bridger to other bands of Crows along the route from Big Horn to the Upper Yellowstone, James Beckwith, the famous *mulatto* of the plains, who had also lived among the Crows as an adopted chief, and had several Crow wives, was employed as an assistant guide, and was sent to their villages, where he subsequently sickened and died.

From these sources it was learned that in the fight of September 23rd the Sioux lost thirteen killed and had a great many wounded.

Other parties of Crows came to Fort C. F. Smith to hunt and trade in that vicinity, and not only showed uniform friendliness toward the whites and the new road, but offered two hundred and fifty young warriors to engage in operations against the Sioux. Major Bridger had great confidence in this proposition; but the officers had, it would seem, no authority to employ so many, as well as no means of arming and equipping them when employed.

All the statements of the Crows were substantially confirmed by Cheyennes at a subsequent visit. They represented "Red Cloud "and "The Man afraid of his Horses" to be in Tongue River valley, and "Buffalo Tongue," to be on Powder River; that the "Big Bellies," the "Bad Arrows," "Those that wear a Bone in the Nose," and "Those that put Meat in the Pot" were near the Big Horn River, and though friendly to the Crows were opposed to the road; that "Bob North," a white man with but one thumb, with twenty-five lodges and the "Big Medicine Man of the Arrapahoes," had also joined the aggressive party.

Still later in the season there was renewed and cumulative evidence that the Crows were truly friendly, but were unwilling to venture very far eastward for any purpose, until the Sioux were out of the way or the white soldiers were sufficiently numerous to guarantee their safety without sacrifice of life or property.

"White Mouth" and "Rotten Tail" told Mr. Bridger that they were half a day in riding through the hostile villages in Tongue River valley, and that fifteen hundred lodges of war parties were preparing to attack the white man at Fort Philip Kearney and Fort C. F. Smith.

All these statements were believed, and it is known that they had important influence in that vigorous prosecution of necessary work which followed, and rendered impossible any system of aggressive war on the part of the troops of the garrison.

Chapter 15

Reinforcements on the Way

The last days of August brought Brevet Brigadier-General Hazen on a tour of inspection, and his visit was greatly enjoyed by us all. He also brought the welcome news that two companies of regular cavalry had been ordered up immediately from Laramie, and that although he had waited a week for them at Fort Reno, they would certainly be but a few days behind him. The next day it was understood that official orders had been received to the same effect—that one regiment of infantry had left St. Louis by way of reinforcements westward, and that General Cooke had acquired the other two battalions of the 18th, with control of all operations on the Platte. This inspired everybody with good cheer, and the time was eagerly anticipated, by ladies no less than gentlemen, when adequate means would allow some opportunity to punish Indians more thoroughly and thus insure the integrity and security of the route.

On the last day of August General Hazen, accompanied by Lieutenant Bradley and twenty-six picked men of the mounted infantry, with Mr. Brannan as guide, started overland for Fort Ben- ton and other posts on the Upper Missouri. The loss of one-third of the mounted force seemed less annoying, as the two companies of cavalry were supposed to be not far behind, and yet, in fact, they *did not come that fall*. Half armed portions of one company straggled along in November, having old Enfield rifles or old-fashion carbines, and the first instalment of this company was but sixteen strong, under a sergeant, with orders to escort a train to Fort C. F. Smith.

All this no one could know in advance; and the constant looking for somebody to help watch, work, and fight was kept up until, as in respect of almost everything else relating to the post which was of importance to be known to the people at large, or at least the authorities at the head of affairs, it was left for the massacre of December 21st to arouse the impression that there were really some untamed red men roaming loose on the plains.

The mounted infantry were the sole dependence for carrying the mails, as these had been ordered to be carried weekly, at the rate of at least fifty miles per day; and the horses, which by the 10th of October had been reduced to less than forty, were poorly adapted for a swift express of over two hundred and thirty-five miles without a relay, and especially when they were almost daily required for active picket and outpost duty at the fort.

This mail was our sole reliance, as it made the trip both ways, and no cavalry or other mail parties came from Laramie to exchange with it, and so divide the labour between the two posts until subsequently, when mails were left at the ferry. Fort Philip Kearney therefore did not receive its mails from the east, but sent east when it wanted some news, and thus occupied a very prominent and independent position in Absaraka and the region adjacent thereto. Sometimes these trips were as long as three weeks, because night travel had to be relied upon through a portion of the route, and neither wagon-teams nor pack mules maintained their ambition as to speed and exactness, when they found that their natural inability to perform the feat was not regarded as excuse for failure.

The Indian habit of calling as early as daylight for loose stock, required also that the horses, when in garrison, should be early saddled, so that, at any moment, the girths could be tightened, the bridles be bitted, and a dash be made after such persistent trespassers. It was a source of congratulation, alike to men and to horses, that this habit never cost the garrison a life or a horse, while in many cases it defeated the plans of the Indians and secured the recapture of stolen stock. Mounted infantry, however, are a peculiar institution in that country. The long rifle, however well cared for, is forever in the way, and the soldier is spoiled for a footman and is almost useless in the saddle. It became a settled opinion, which the ladies shared with others, that the Sioux and Cheyenne light cavalry were much better adapted to the hills and valleys, the gorges and mountain passes, especially in a long race, or steeple-chase, than even the mounted men of the 18th.

Of course, it was difficult for men, unused to horseback-riding, to take to it *kindly*, at first; and the manual of arms was less convenient when yelping Indians were shaking buffalo robes and speeding the flight of arrows and bullets. We had, of course, to keep a mounted picket and prompt communication with working parties; and there was also some responsibility for helping Fort C F. Smith to some communication with the outer world.

Such men as Brannan, with his daring, who was scalped through his imprudence on his return from the trip with General Hazen; as Van Volzpah, with his experience and quiet coolness, who, after a life in Oregon and Washington Territories, and many successful trips to Laramie, was butchered at last, with his whole party; as miner Phillips, with his sound sense and solid honesty, who carried dispatches on the night of December 21st, and Captain Bailey, of the miners, who, after seventeen years in frontier explorations, retained the manners and habits of a pleasant gentleman, full of intrinsic worth and steady courage, could do anything with Indians or horses on a mail trip, that *anybody* could do; but in that bracing climate horses *would* need their forage when trips were frequent, and even the men were found to be limited to something like the ordinary finite range of physical ability and endurance.

And yet, nearly every ten days, and sometimes each week, brought us a mail, omitting such newspapers as were borrowed somewhere east, or were diverted to Salt Lake City, where there were more readers, as well as the leisure of security from the red men of the plains. New York papers were often ten weeks old, and nearly half the letters, for a portion of the time, bore the postal mark of Salt Lake City, additional to several others.

When horses diminished in numbers, and mounted escorts could not accompany the trains to the pinery, a new plan was adopted for the more prompt formation of the corral. Trains went out in two parallel lines with an intervening space of fifty or one hundred yards, so that, when an alarm was given, the front wagons turned in to meet each other; those on the flanks were trotted up with the mules inside, covered by the next wagon in advance; while the rear wagons of each line obliqued in to fill the fourth, or rear side of the square. It was a singular commentary on the recklessness of travellers, their ignorance of the feelings of Indians, their want of correct advice at Laramie, and the wisdom of the Indians themselves,—that, of all the outrages committed on trains in 1866, there was never a single persistent attack upon a good corral, neither was there loss of life when proper rules were regarded.

The apparent exception near Fort Philip Kearney, when Lieutenant Guinness was killed, in June, 1807, grew out of the great disparity of numbers, in part, and partly to the assurance of the Indians, derived from the massacre of December 21st, 1866. Brevet Major Powell, who resisted the attack of June, 1867, also resisted the tantalizing challenge of Indians, December 19th, 1866, and literally obeyed his orders, thereby saving himself and command from that utter destruction which befell others two days later.

For many months nearly all public references to attacks about that post, only made mention of attacks on *wood* trains; and the world at large seemed to regard it as if a detail had each time been sent for daily supply of fuel, instead of being employed on systematic labour in building a large post and fort.

The pinery, which is most accessible, is just seven miles from the fort, as indicated on the map of Fort Philip Kearney and surroundings. At the base of the upper mountain, as well as on the island below, blockhouses had been built, and the men for a long time remained over night for early morning work. A train of over ninety wagons was employed at one period, and the timber would be cut, loaded, and hauled the same day. All sizes were accessible, from timber that would work out thirty-inch clear boards and plank down to the slender pine of the thickets from two to three inches thick, which made a close framework or skeleton for support of a clay covering. Innumerable straight trees of from four to fifteen inches in diameter were found, which cut from thirty to forty feet in length, without a knot or branch; and these lay so closely in a wall as to need no chinking before the plaster was applied.

These timber parties always had their armed teamsters, their armed choppers, and armed guard. Chopping details varied from sixteen to thirty, with a special guard of about the same number, making, with teamsters, a resisting force of from seventy to one hundred men, and sometimes, early in the season, the force of teamsters and wagonmasters alone was nearly that number.

Timber was procured much nearer, but with more difficulty, in July and August; and the place last adopted proved ample for all purposes.

This work blended all kinds of labour appropriate for tools that chop, saw, hew, or finish *wood*. Shingles were rived from bolts sawed by the men, and many a "shingle bee" was held, at night, to expedite work and convince the sceptical that shingles, or anything else, could be made or *done*, when it *had* to be, and that civilization was still westward bound.

CHAPTER 16

Fort Philip Kearney and Surroundings

But for the presence of hostile Indians, the country about Fort Philip Kearney would be a charming field for hunting and picnic purposes. Soon after our arrival, the ladies ventured twice to the mountains, and the second time descended to Pine Island, where choice elk steaks, furnished by the timber choppers, and suitable accessories, supplied a delightful meal, and no Indian disturbed the pleasure. Judge J. T. Kinney, formerly Chief Justice of Utah, representing the business interests of Mr. Botsford, the sutler, was chief manager and steward, and under his skilful catering a dinner was provided that would not have dishonoured a city restaurant.

The bill of fare was not printed; but canned lobster, cove oysters, and salmon were a very fair first course; and, associated with the game, were jellies, pineapples, tomatoes, sweet corn, peas, pickles, and such creature comforts, while puddings, pies, and domestic cake, from doughnuts and gingerbread up to plum cake and jelly cake, with coffee, and Madame Cliquot for those who wished it, and pipes and cigars for the gentlemen, enabled everybody to satisfy desire.

A trip to Lake Smedt, which is but a little more than two miles distant, is another locality which could be made a pleasant summer resort, to say nothing of skates in winter. The western end of the lake is accessible by a gentle slope after crossing Starling Creek; and a few hours' work and the use of pine timber would make a convenient landing for sail boats and duck boats. The north shore is ragged and the hills are covered with fragments of coal, red lava, and melted boulders, which seem as if they had been thrown out of some great furnace. The south shore is hilly but less rocky. The water is deep and intensely alkaline, and there is neither inlet nor outlet as the little creek which is crossed before reaching the lake passes by the west end at a few hundred yards distance, and turns westward to the Piney Forks, emptying its stream below their junction.

A third ride, which requires the saddle, is to climb the mountains by an Indian trail just below the point where the Little Piney makes its exit, and visit Fort Ridge, more than seven hundred feet above the fort. This ridge received its name from an Indian fort near the summit. It is about thirty feet square, of loose stones of considerable size, and when visited, the inclosure was raised still higher by temporary abattis of pine logs. There were indications that a band had recently camped near it, having squaws with the party, and doubtless this place furnished one of the camp fires which had repeatedly been observed both by night and day. The view from the next higher range is fine beyond description.

Below the observer, the fort, the Pineys, Lake Smedt, and the branches of Peno Creek are drawn so near that it is difficult to realize that they are from seven to twelve miles distant. Beyond, and northward, the successive round-topped red buttes follow each other like an exaggerated style of the waves of some old cornfield which has been uncultivated for years; and thus they stretch on for nearly eighty miles before they are blended with the uneven horizon. In the northwest is the beautiful valley of Tongue River and its tributaries, with the Panther Mountains beyond. Westward the Big Horn Mountain range continues its cragged front, past Piney summit and Rocky Face Ridge, until lost to view. Eastward, the Black Hills, beyond Reno, and Pumpkin Buttes, loom up at a distance of a hundred miles, and Rock Creek and Clear Fork are traced until they disappear in the buttes of the north. Southward, Cloud Peak rises sublimely, with its hoary head piercing the clouds and furnishing an exhaustless reservoir for the hungry streams below.

The ascent is slow and requires frequent rests. Animals as well as men pant under the strain; the breath becomes short and laboured, giving no little pain with a sense of suffocation, and the perspiration drops from mules and horses as if they had just been lifted bodily from a complete emersion. But, when the topmost summit is attained, after threading the intricacies of a pine orchard half checked by young balsam and hemlock, the cup of coffee, with a sirloin of mountain sheep, cooked upon heated stones or spitted before the coals, acquire peculiar virtue and relish; and the mind never tires in study of the

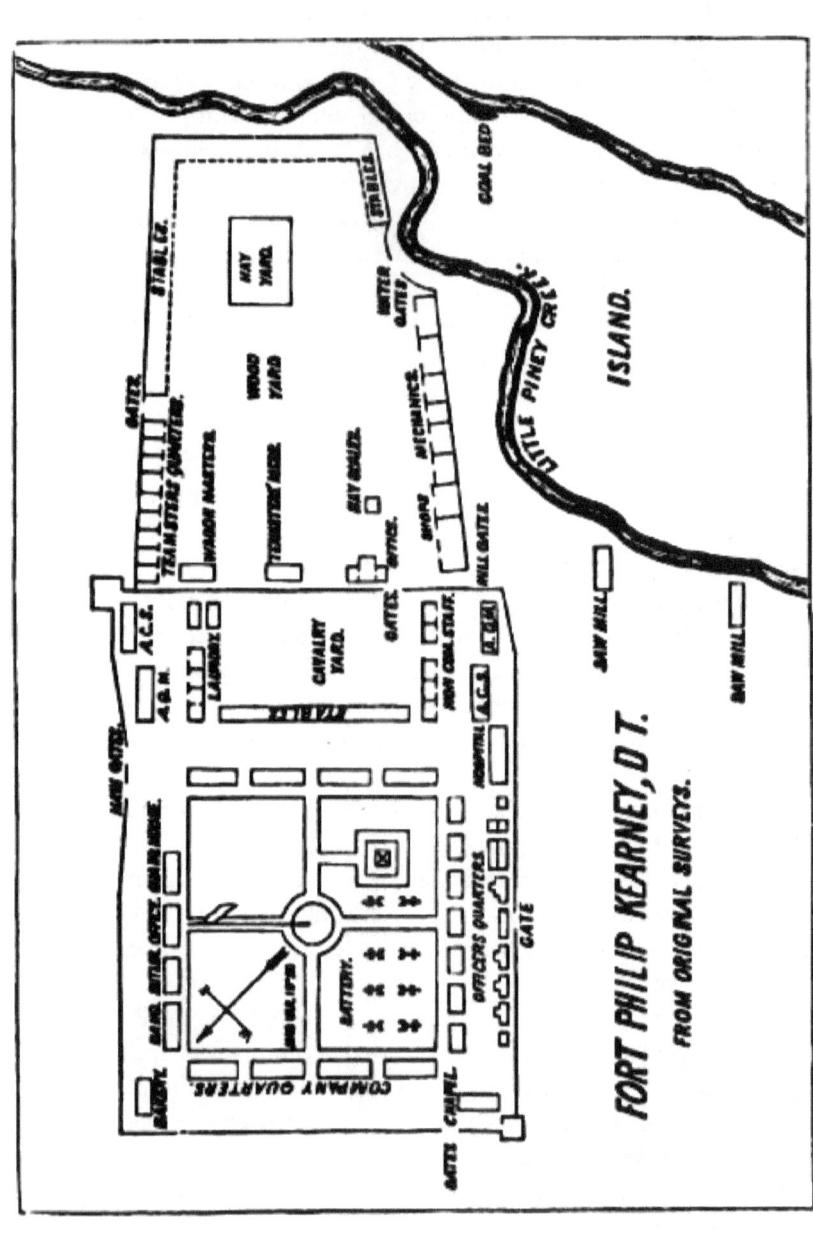

magnificent panorama disclosed.

The Big Piney itself is possessed of a variety of natural charms. The gorge through which the water rushes is nearly four hundred and fifty feet in height, and while the river soon buries itself in the pines below, so that the sighs of the winds through their branches are blended in solemn murmurs with the mad dash of cascades and the swift rush of the rapids, it often breaks out to the sunlight, and retains all its wildness and tumult of sounds, until it passes the fort, and, joined by its lesser sister, bears off for the Missouri through the intervening channels.

These are all rides for the saddle, although the ambulance can reach all but the mountain summit; and, until two narrow escapes, one on Big Piney and another beyond Pilot Hill, had taught the ladies the risk of exposure, it was no rare thing to see Mrs. Wands and others on a gallop for recreation and change.

The road from the fort to the pinery is itself over the gentle southern slope of Sullivant Hills, and at the highest point before entering the woods, there is a tine view of Tongue River, the red buttes, and the lake, only surpassed by that of Fort Ridge itself.

Pilot Hill, only a few hundred yards from the fort, has its own fine views, and the traveller from Powder River can see, at the distance of eleven miles, its picket on the summit, watching for his arrival or keeping close scrutiny of the enemies of his peace.

The old road was abandoned the same week the site of the fort was selected; and though Colonel Sawyer soon after came over the old road as in 1865, all trains subsequently took the short cut-off from the lake to the fort.

Opposite the fort, a gradual slope, slashed by occasional ravines, ends in a narrow table-land with another fine view of the fort, Peno valley, the mountains and the lake. In every direction are natural beauties which minister to the refined taste, and furnish, even at that distance from civilized life, such choice intercourse with nature, that separation from friends is softened and the hours of peace are like the moments of a pleasant dream.

The fort proper is six hundred feet by eight hundred, situated upon a natural plateau, so that there is a gradual slope from the front and rear, falling off nearly sixty feet in a few rods, thus affording a natural glacis, and giving to the position a positive strength, independent of other defences. A rectangle, two hundred by six hundred feet, is occupied by warehouses, cavalry stables, laundress quarters, and the non-commissioned staff.

About the parade-ground, already referred to, are officers' and men's quarters, offices, guardhouse, sutler's and band building.

The stockade is made of heavy pine trunks eleven feet long, hewn to a touching surface of four inches so as to join closely, being pointed and loop-holed, and firmly imbedded in the ground for three feet. Blockhouses are at two diagonal corners, and massive gates of plank with small wickets, all having substantial locks, are on three fronts, and on the fourth or southern front, back of the officers' quarters, is a small gate for sallies, or for officers' use.

Three framed warehouses, the hospital and four company quarters, built in 1866, are eighty-four feet long and twenty-four feet wide, with ceilings of ten feet. The windows to soldiers' quarters, as well as those designed for officers, have three sashes each, giving ample light and cheerfulness to the whole garrison. Regulation bunks, with arm racks, shelves for knapsacks, boots, etc., are conveniently arranged, so that a company can form for roll-call between the two lines.

A flag-staff, surrounded by an octagonal band platform, stand, and seats, occupies, the centre of the parade, and diverging walks, twelve feet wide, pass to each street, the magazine being in the centre of one of the squares.

East of, and opening from the fort, extending with nearly an equal area, to the little Piney is the corral, or quartermaster's yard. This is surrounded by a rough cottonwood stockade, and contains stabling for mules, hay and wood yards, hay scales, quarters for teamsters and mechanics, the blacksmith, wagonmakers, carpenters, saddlers, and armourers' shops, and the general apparatus and conveniences of such a place.

From this corral, one gate opens toward the sawmills, one toward the road from Powder River, and one to the clear waters of the Little Piney, which here makes a convenient bend perfectly protected by the re-entering angle of the stockade just at that point.

Two steam sawmills just above the mill gate, and but a few rods distant, furnish constant supplies of posts, plank, studding, rafters, lath and boards, and all lumber for every use.

The stockade of two thousand eight hundred feet circuit was completed in October, notwithstanding all other work and constant skirmishing went on, and, with the exception of most of the Sabbaths, there was no cessation of labour, whatever the weather, until the holidays of October 29th and 30th. On the first of November the same diligence was renewed, and each day's close was a new testimony to what a few men could accomplish under systematized labour and the will to work.

CHAPTER 17

Indian Response to a National Salute

The last day of October being the stated day of Muster-for-pay, it was declared a holiday, as the previous day had been one of preparation. The completed flag-staff was at last to receive its chief glory in flying the first garrison flag that ever rose over Absaraka.

The day was bright and lovely.

The whole command was in full dress, and after the inspection and review of the morning upon the plain before the fort, and the proper muster, the troops formed three sides of a square about the flag-staff, the fourth side having a platform for officers, ladies, and visitors, and the band taking station in the centre.

Probably the programme would not conform closely to all conventionalisms of army usage, or find precise antecedents in army regulations, but it appeared to be designed more particularly to bring hard-working day-labourers back to something like military dress forms of parade, and supply a little recreation to those whose only interval of rest was the occasional hours of sleep. Shut out from civilized life, the only drawback was the refusal of the colonel to let everybody give some old-fashioned cheering when the work was done. But all went off about as well as it would elsewhere, and as it suited those whom it was designed to gratify, it made no difference to mankind at large.

Judge Kinney read an appropriate poem of Miss Carmichael's chaste and spirited collection, Chaplain White offered the prayer, and principal musician Barnes, who, with William Daily, fashioned the flag-staff, presented to be read an original poem of his own, which at least did justice to his patriotic spirit.

The following was the address, and is such a brief *resumé* of the preceding work, and the results attained by the expedition of 1866 in a little more than three months of labour, that no apology is made for its repetition, although already known to many:

> Officers and Men,—Three and one-half months ago stakes were driven to define the now perfected outlines of Fort Philip Kearney. Aggressive Indians threatened to exterminate the command. Our advent cost us blood. Private Livensberger of Company F was the first victim, July 17th, 1866; Lieutenant Daniels, private Callery, of G Company; Gilchrist and Johnson, of E Company; Fitzpatrick and Hacket, of D Company; Patrick Smith, of H Company; and Oberly and Wasser have also, in the order named, given their lives to vindicate our pledge to never yield one foot of advance, but to guarantee a safe passage for all who seek a home in the lands beyond.
>
> Fifteen weeks have passed, varied by many skirmishes and both night and day alarms, but that pledge holds good. In every work done your arms have been at hand. In the pine tracts or hay fields, on picket or general guard duty, no one has failed to find a constant exposure to some hostile shaft, and to feel that a cunning adversary was watching every chance to harass and kill.
>
> And yet that pledge holds good. Stockade and blockhouse, embrasure and loop-hole, shell and bullet, have warned off danger, so that women and children now notice the savage as he appears, only to look for fresh occasion for you to punish him, and with righteous anger to avenge the dead.
>
> The Indian dead outnumbers your own four-fold, while your acquired experience and better cause afford you constant success in every encounter. This is not all. Substantial warehouses, containing a year's supply, spacious and enduring quarters, and a well-adapted magazine are other proofs of your diligence and spirit.
>
> The steam whistle and the rattle of the mower have followed your steps in this westward march of empire. You have built a central post that will bear comparison with any for security, completeness, and adaptation to the ends in view, wherever the other may be located, or however long in erection.[1]
>
> Surrounded by temptations to hunt the choicest game, and al-

---

1. Brevet Brigadier General W. B. Hazen, upon his tour of inspection, pronounced this stockade to be the best he had ever seen, excepting only one in British America, built by the Hudson Bay Company, with great labour and expense. The previous description of Fort Philip Kearney is in substance derived from the *Army and Navy Journal* and *New York Times*.

lured by tales of golden treasure just beyond you, you have spared your powder for your foes, and have given the labour of your hands to your proper work. Passing from guard-watching to fatigue-work, and, after one night in bed, often disturbed, returning to your post as sentry; attempting with success all trades and callings, and handling the broad-axe and hammer, the saw and the chisel, with the same success as that with which you have sped the bullet, your work has proven how well deserved was the confidence I reposed in all of you; and that same old pledge still holds good.

Coincident with your march to this point was the occupation of Fort Reno; first by Company B, afterward reinforced by Company F of this battalion, and the advance of Companies D and G to Fort C. F. Smith, nearly one hundred miles farther west. All these, like yourselves, having a share in the labour, the exposure, and the conflicts that throughout the whole length of the line attended its occupation, have sustained the past good record of the 18th Infantry, and thus also have vindicated your pledge.

And now, this day, laying aside the worn and tattered garments, which have done their part during weeks of toil and struggle, the veteran battalion of the 18th Infantry, from which perhaps I shall soon be parted in the changes of army life and organization, puts on its fresh full-dress attire for muster and review.

The crowning office, without which you would regard your work as scarcely begun, is now to be performed, and to its fulfilment I assign *soldiers*; neither discharging the duty myself, nor delegating it to some brother officer; but some veteran soldiers of good desert shall share with a sergeant from each of their companies, and the worthy man whose work rises high above us, the honour of raising our new and beautiful garrison flag to the top of the handsomest flag-staff in America.

It is the first full garrison flag that has floated between the Platte and Montana; and this beautiful pole, perfect in detail, as if wrought and finished in the navy yards of New York, Philadelphia, or Boston, will be to Sergeant Barnes, whose appropriate and well-intended verses will be read to you, a long remembered trophy of his patriotism and skill; a new impulse to your own future exertions; a new cause for pride as its stripes and stars are daily unfolded; a new source of courage to each traveller westward advancing; and a new terror to foes who dare to assail you.

With music and the roar of cannon we will greet its unfoldings.

This day shall be a holiday, and a fresh starting-point for future endeavour.

And yet, all is not said that I wish to say! While we exalt the national standard, and rejoice in its glory and its power, let us not forget the true source of that glory and power.

For our unexampled health and continued success; for that land of the free and home of the brave; for our institutions and their fruits, we owe all to the Great Ruler who made and has preserved us.

Let me, then, ask all, with uncovered heads and grateful hearts, to pause in our act of consecration while the chaplain shall invoke God's own blessing upon that act; so that while this banner rises heavenward, and so shall rise with each recurring sun, all hearts shall rise to the throne of the Infinite, and for this day, its duties and its pleasures, we shall become better men and better soldiers of the great Republic.

At the close of the prayer, the flag slowly rose to masthead, while national airs, the booming of cannon, and the sharp ring of *presented arms* paid it such tokens of respect as the occasion enjoined.

The afternoon was pleasant, and such recreation was indulged in as the men found agreeable. About three o'clock, Indians came out of the creek, and around the bend of Sullivant Hills, so quickly as to almost pass the west gate before they were discovered. They evidently hoped, by the suddenness of their movement, to cut off a few private horses that were grazing just south of the fort, but were disappointed. Others appeared upon the hills, and flashing mirrors were constantly passing signals for nearly an hour.

It would seem as if the salute had attracted their attention, and they had supposed that other Indians were near the fort, or the white men had some other exhibition for their gratification and surprise. They had at least the pleasure of seeing the stars and stripes, and thus getting new hints as to the proposed length of our visit. In the evening all the officers, in full dress, and the ladies of the garrison, attended the muster evening levee at the colonel's, where music, social dancing, and such an entertainment as was practicable, closed the day, and brought everybody up very closely to the grade of similar reunions in the States.

CHAPTER 18

Hostile Sioux and Friendly Cheyennes

One September morning was peculiarly bright and clear. A full moon had fairly invited the Indian deities to their best endeavour, but as a slight fall of snow half covered the earth all expectations of seeing red men gradually vanished from our minds. The timber train went as usual to the Pinery. A water party was at the larger creek before the fort. Details were at work on the ditch. Others were hewing, pointing, cutting loop-holes, or placing the completed trunks in the trenches. The sawmills were busy, and men who had just come off guard cheerfully lent their energies to work upon their company barracks. The touch of snow seemed to hurry everybody. The band were just marching from the guard parade when an alarm was given.

We could all see, and, after the children were looked up or "accounted for," did our share of watching.

A party of seven Indians dashed out of the thick Cottonwood at the confluence of the two Pineys and made boldly for the picket on Pilot Hill. It seemed that almost instantly the relief of the mounted picket, always saddled and ready, were out of the east gate upon a run, and yet it was plain that no riders or horses would be in time. The despised howitzers were brought into requisition, and a case shot was sent as a swifter messenger, with its relief of eighty bullets, and, as it hurtled through the air, the savages slackened speed a little to watch its advent. They found "the gun that shoots twice" too much for their dodging, and as its shell exploded over their heads, scattering its compliments and the earth in all directions, they turned their course and made for the brush as quickly as they had appeared. A second similar messenger dropped one Indian from the saddle, and all took to cover.

Directly opposite the fort, and only about seven hundred yards from the front gate, across the Piney, where Captain Bailey had encamped his party of miners, nearly fifty Indians made a dash for his horses; but the miners were quick as their foe, and were after them with revolvers and rifles; while again, "the gun that shoots twice" achieved a success. One Indian pony was shot by a miner, but, to our great disgust, his rider coolly leaped up behind another Indian and galloped off beyond the reach of harm.

A case shot and shell turned aside another party demonstrating from the west; but, simultaneously with the operations of these parties, a still larger force was spread out on the summit and slopes of Lodge Trail Ridge, just as if they had in view an attack upon the timber train while the other parties should skirmish and draw the attention of the garrison. A detachment was at once sent toward the woods, but the flashing looking-glasses all along the hills passed the quick signal that their plans had been foiled, and very soon all Indians had disappeared.

A messenger brought in word that Patrick Smith, belonging to the permanent blockhouse party in the woods, had dragged himself nearly a half mile to his camp, badly wounded with arrows, and scalped. He had managed to break off the shafts, so as not to be impeded in crawling through the thickets. Dr. Reid, acting assistant surgeon, at once went to his relief; but he died within twenty-four hours.

While the working party were felling trees, a party of Indians broke through the woods and killed two of the detail who were a little separated from their comrades.

About two o'clock in the afternoon the sudden, repeated shriek of the steam-whistle at the farther mill, and the equally hasty signal of the pickets, gave the alarm that Indians were again close by. We could all see fifteen Indians between the fort and the mountain, galloping from the west directly for Pilot Hill, with the plain purpose of capturing and scalping the picket under the very eyes of the garrison. Before they had half ascended the hill, Captain Brown and Lieutenant Adair, with a party, were in hot pursuit. Private Rover (who is of good Chicago family, and enlisted under the false name of Rover) was in charge of the picket. He had been signally brave in several tight places before.

On this occasion he dismounted his three men, turned the horses loose toward the fort with a good urging, and slowly fell off the northern slope, with arms at a "ready," to join the supporting party.

The horses came down the steep grade toward the fort on a run, passing through the Indians, who dare not stop them and could only give them a few arrows as they passed. The chief warrior reached the summit, and for an instant turned his pony, to imitate the usual signal of riding in a circle until flags were used; but the pressure of Captain Brown's party soon put the Indians and their ponies to their mettle. It was nearly night when the party returned, with wearied horses, to tell the tale of their adventures.

They brought with them a band of eight Cheyenne Indians and one squaw, whose broken-down ponies and miserable outfit showed that they were neither on the war-path nor very prosperous. It seems that Captain Brown, while pursuing the Sioux, saw them suddenly stop and have a short parley with a party coming from the east.

As the two separated, the latter came forward holding up a paper and showing themselves to be "Little Moon," "The Rabbit that Jumps," and "The Wolf that Lies Down," with a few others, on their way to the fort for provisions, and permission to go to Tongue River valley to hunt.

These chiefs were at the council in July, and said that Black Horse (who then was ill) was sick and in their camp at Rock Creek, and that old "White Head," the oldest living Cheyenne chief, was with them also: that they had been in the mountains as directed, and had crossed as far as Fort Caspar, where Brevet Major Morris had treated them well, and given them a letter to the colonel.

These Indians were permitted to camp on an island in Little Piney, under the notice of the sawmill guard, and by dusk were cooking their bacon and coffee, which had been presented by Colonel Carrington.

Men of the timber train came in, and told the soldiers that some of this very party were with those who had killed Oberly and Wasser. This rumour spread through the garrison. Added to the fact that many officers and citizens had doubts whether some of the band of "Black Horse" were not among our active enemies, this developed a spirit of vengeance that soon made itself demonstrative.

It seemed too bad, when no man could go out of the stockade unarmed, and any negligence insured the most horrible death and torture, that any red man should be sheltered and fed by the garrison, its commander, or Colonel Carrington, the district commander.

About 9 o'clock Chaplain White called and said that the men talked about killing the Cheyennes; and soon after a soldier opened the door and said that "the men were killing the Indians." The colonel started at once, with revolver in hand, and three reports, soon after heard, showed that some issue had been made. As a matter of fact, nearly ninety men had quietly armed, and in the darkness of the night formed themselves opposite the Indians, cocked their pieces, all ready to fire, when a guard arrived and they were ordered back to post. Anxious not to be recognized when the guard arrived and they were ordered back, they disobeyed Captain Ten Eyck and rushed for the east gate; but the colonel's shots, after hesitation to obey his order to halt, stopped the party.

So far as the light could determine, they were found to be some of the best men of the garrison. They quickly realized the disgrace that would have fallen upon the post and regiment had they perpetrated the massacre, and for many reasons were restored to their barracks with only admonition and caution as to future conduct.

In fact, the next day these same Indians had a conference, and in the judgment of everybody vindicated their good faith by such information of their own movements and those of the Sioux, as fully comported with advices from other sources.

Old "White Head" also came, with a few braves, and had a talk with some of the officers; but the band, after the risk of the night before, and having been instructed to keep off the road (as soldiers could no longer discriminate when they met Indians on the road, or about the working parties), left us and returned no more.

Other days were as full of changing adventures as this. Few were without their share of less painful incidents. A game of croquet was planned, and while the ladies could neither ride nor walk beyond the gates, some amusement was attempted between Indian alarms; the evening found its recreation in the authors' game, a quiet quadrille, good music, conversation, and other varieties, besides the needle and cookbook.

It may be added, before this last reference to the Cheyennes, that when they were passed by the Sioux whom Captain Brown chased from Pilot Hill, the Sioux contemptuously struck them and cried "Coo!" as they did in July, when unable to induce the same party to engage in war against the whites and the occupation of the road.

CHAPTER 19

Indians All in Their War-Paint

The nights in Absaraka were peculiarly beautiful when cloudless. The rarity of the atmosphere gave full play to the star-beams, and it seemed as if there were twice as many as in any firmament elsewhere.

Their first appearance was often mistaken for Indian signal fires, as they rose above the horizon, like the sun or moon, having orbs as marked and light as brilliant as when they attained the zenith. In the glory of the full moon the snow-clad mountains shone as silver; while the deep roar of the cascades of Big Piney Fork was hardly less grateful to the wakeful soul than its lullaby was soothing to the weary.

From sunset until morning, this melody increased in power, as if making most of its time when man was not too busy to notice or enjoy, or as if seeking to comfort and quiet him after his day of toil. Each midday's thaw upon the mountains in summer would reach the great gates of exit just at that grateful hour when the undisturbed slumber is sweetest and soundest, and all natural harmonies intensity the blessing of morning sleep.

Now and then the *aurora borealis* put forth its pyrotechnic energies in a profuse variety of merry dances, vaulting streamers, and gorgeous coronas; and then, again, the lunar rainbow, with its strangely unreal tints and novelties, would banish sleep and bring us all to a patient attention to its claims, and thorough admiration of its wonderful characteristics.

August and November contributed their aerolites and proper share of meteors, and the blazing sky-path of these eccentric visitors shone fresh and clear after the celestial traveller had exploded itself, or had been otherwise disposed of under the laws of its being or the programme of the meteorologist and astronomer. Other nights were such as Æneas knew when the gods were angry, or Odin permitted when the storm-king was riding in state or in vengeance. *Then*, every mountain gorge had its own blast, and every gulch, ravine, and valley had its fitful and unruly current. Tent-flies took the proportions and direction of inflated balloons, and the snapping and flapping was suggestive of sky for the roofing and all out-doors for the inclosure of the habitation we dwelt in.

Such winds do justice to the theory and mission of winds. They blow as winds can only blow when in real earnest: and it is inflexibly certain that the classical Æolus of early times who used to cave and lock up the winds he was familiar with, never gained jurisdiction over the winds of Absaraka; or the whole history of his career and successes is simply a myth, or poetic fiction of by-gone days. In early school hours, when Madame M——s thought Latin was a special accomplishment as a basis of good English, we received the history and adventures of Æolus with as much faith as anybody did, and if compelled, at last, to question any alleged circumstances connected with his career, it is a matter of reluctant conviction, and not of captious scepticism as to the history of the past.

Other night scenes than those portrayed by Nature were frequently contributed by the native inhabitants of the land.

While the garrison were in tents few ladies slept soundly; and officers and men alike threw themselves down for repose as if expecting each moment a summons to duty. Beyond the general guard lines, the pickets were thrown out in several directions to watch for the approach of Indians; and as each relief went out it changed its station, so that enemies who knew the former position of the detail could not know its place two hours afterward. Scarcely had the post been located, when these night visitations became frequent.

On one occasion brisk firing was heard on all sides, and the entire garrison was under arms, while Lieutenant Adair's whole company was sent out to support the pickets and ward off attack. Numerous fancies often blended with the real facts, and false alarms alternated with the genuine. Thus, wonderful reports would come in of the flight of arrows that innocently whizzed past the men on duty; and yet the closest scrutiny by lantern or morning light would fail to discover the projectiles themselves.

Sometimes a mule, straying from corral or parting his halter, became the victim of that constant vigilance which was the price of our lives and liberty; or sneaking wolves would be mistaken for sneaking Indians, whose habit of borrowing wolf-skins and wolf-cries to deceive us compelled instant attention to whatever had show of life. At other times crawling Indians would actually draw near enough to attempt a shot at the tents or sentries; and at all times, dawn of day was the only sure indication that an enemy was not close at hand. One sign, however, became a fair one. When wolves were loudest and nearest, the Indians seldom were near; and the old trappers claimed to distinguish between the genuine wolf-howl and the Indian imitation by the fact that the former produced no echo. Either the natural or the imitated was ugly enough, and sufficiently abundant for that style of music.

With completion of the stockade the guard was reduced, and some sense of security prevailed. Until then, it is certain that any considerable body of Indians, with a proper leader, could have dashed through the camp and performed substantial mischief. But while the stockade kept Indians out, it did not keep them away. Still they ventured their shots at the sentries, fired arrows into the beef cattle close outside, and tried all possible measures to decoy and capture any who were imprudent and careless.

About nine o'clock one evening, a volley near the front gate aroused the garrison. Close to the stockade, and just at the foot of the natural slope which surrounds it, a small corral of wagons belonging to the sutler inclosed a group of teamsters engaged at cards. The first indication of the presence of Indians was a volley fired under the wagon beds, which wounded three, and one of them fatally. A detail from the guard was soon on the spot, and the low ground was scouted as far as the creek; but the night being dark, no Indians were found.

Another evening, just after taps, an alarm was given by the sutler that his stock, which had been left on herd half a mile south of the fort, on the Little Piney, was attacked; and besides his own men. Captain Brown, with forty infantry, moved out as skirmishers from that face of the fort toward the creek.

Almost immediately a bright fire sprang up on the spur of Sullivant Hills, nearest the post on the west, around which the figures of Indians could be distinctly seen moving. The picket at the hay-ricks east of the fort, on Little Piney, fired two shots at horsemen on the creek, and there were other indications that several hostile parties were preying about us. The night was very dark, and objects could be seen but a short distance. The bright fire, made up of pine flambeaus or torches, alone furnished any show of a fair target, and received complimentary attention.

A careful range was given to the field howitzer, loaded with a twelve-pound spherical case shot, and three twelve-pound mountain howitzers were also loaded and trained in three other directions, where there was any probability of stirring up the skulkers. All were discharged at one word, and the first shell exploded directly over the fire, scattering its bullets and the Indians as well, while the fire was instantly extinguished and the night passed without further interruption. The stock were brought in safely, with the report that the Indians abandoned their game as soon as the party on the hills was scattered. It evidently was a novel surprise, that at night, and at the distance of several hundred yards, the white soldiers could reach them with such plentiful volleys as a case shot distributes.

The duties of the officer of the day at night were always exacting and full of incident; and indeed, while every day brought its probabilities of some Indian adventures near the fort or at the Pinery, every night had its special dangers, which unanticipated might involve great loss, if not the sacrifice of the post, its garrison, and stores.

Repeated attempts were made to approach the large hay-ricks for the purpose of setting them on fire; and while as a general rule large parties only appeared at the full of the moon, the forays of stealing and scalping bands were constantly harassing and probable.

Such demonstrations were seldom early in the evening. Just at daybreak, when sleep is soundest, and the faintest glimmer of light discloses unprotected stock or exposed positions, was the favourite hour with the sharp red man.

Two days after Captain Fetterman arrived, impressed with the opinion, to which he had often given language, that "a company of regulars could whip a thousand, and a regiment could whip the whole array of hostile tribes," he was permitted to make the experiment of lying in the Cottonwood thickets of Big Piney from two o'clock until ten o'clock in the morning, using hobbled mules for live bait to decoy the aborigines.

A beautiful Sunday morning dawned, and no Indians were seen; and so close was the covert that the glass did not reveal the secreted party. About nine o'clock Mrs. Wheatley rode in front of the fort with Mr. Reid, passing it nearly a half mile, where her husband's cattle were feeding, and at least a mile from the expected skirmish. The team soon came back upon the run, some Indians having dashed forth, driven off the cattle, and not capturing the wagon and passengers because of a presented rifle, or the assurance that the stock was theirs at all events, while a moment's delay would expose them to quick pursuit from the fort.

The Indians may or may not have known the plan for their surprise; but their sagacity and suspicion, their keen sight, and knowledge of woodcraft are seldom at loss; and while they were often foiled and disappointed, or repulsed with loss, they were always innocent of being surprised, and shrewdly made their own advances so covered that they were near the desired object before their presence was known.

So it was that nights in Absaraka, so cool and suggestive of sweetest sleep, were associated with wakefulness and danger; and at least one officer, whose responsibilities were as large as any, slept for weeks in succession without removal of garments, and nightly made his rounds to secure personal knowledge of the deportment of the guard and the condition of the post.

Habit, however, soon accustomed those who were not immediately on duty to trust the vigilance of the guard, and to sleep by snatches that grateful sleep which elsewhere never could be beat.

CHAPTER 20

Domestic, Social, and Religious Life, With the Episodes Therein Occurring

Woman had a choice field in Absaraka for the exercise of many industrial pursuits, and fortunate were those who in earlier days had been advised that other rooms than the parlour have their uses, and other fingering than that of the piano must be employed in roasting and boiling, in frying and broiling, in baking and stewing. It was found that yeast was to be made before the bread could be extra, that the hands were to be servants when no other servants could be had; and it was discovered by some that the dishcloth and washcloth, the broom and the duster were susceptible of as graceful manipulation as prinking irons, or the strings of lute and guitar.

In fact, every morning brought its round of ante-breakfast labour, with that restoring process by which dishes once used are brought back to proper condition for future uses. Female servants were scarce, independent, and disputant. The few taken with families had learned that their market value for washing was above everything reasonable in a household, and that a fortune was soon to be realized by selling villainous pies to soldiers at half a dollar or more for a pie.

Ladies found themselves obliged to turn milliners and dressmakers; and we know experimentally that our experience in fabricating boys' clothes alone was worth a good apprenticeship, if it should ever become necessary to rush to a trade for support.

Frank Leslie's and *Madame Demerest's* magazine became each a desideratum, and linsey-woolsey, delaines, and calico nowhere else underwent such endowment with fashionable shapes as in Absaraka.

Darning and stitching, hemming and hemstitching, cutting and basting were as inevitable as the need of clothes to wear. The triplet of "I never could, I never would, and I never will," became almost obsolete; and in their place was these other impulses, "I wouldn't, but I must and I will," or "I could, I can, and I *do!*" Unhappy were any who despised to begin, and, in the penalty of charcoal beefsteak, hot water soups, and dyspeptic biscuit, were driven to despair or disgust.

But any life on the plains is a good school, and its practical suggestions take all the starch and false pride as to work completely out of the unfortunate human creature who expects the spoon to be carried to the mouth by attendants, and a metropolitan table to be spread by the hands of a striker.

Primitive ways are to be learned; but the tent becomes neat and genteel, and the taste of its arrangement and adornment gives capital hints to the mind of the beauty of patience, and especially confirms the sacred maxim, that content with godliness is great gain.

The snapping of a tent-pole at midnight under three feet of snow; the blaze of the canvas, as the ambitious fire commissions the red-hot pipe to unroof your earthly tabernacle, at no small risk to bedding and trunks; the pretty little drifts that gracefully slip through the closely drawn entrance and sprinkle your bed, your furniture, and your wardrobe, all afford change and excitement, and not unseldom bring occasion to begin housekeeping anew. The frozen-up kettles, pots, and buckets demand recognition; while the milk, the cream, and the butter are incentives to new branches of industry and skill.

So when houses are used, one house will differ from another house in glory. The *adobe*, with its unplastered surface, and the dropping of dirt from the earth-covered roof, is one variety; and the log-cabin is another variety; either of which involves much ingenuity, not to say genius, as the mind struggles to give them neatness and comfort. Yet either of these soon becomes home; and its protection from summer's heat and winter's cold is often more grateful and complete than more pretending edifices of wood or brick. It is indeed not always easy to adapt a carpet to dirt floors, or the changing sizes of army habitations; nor is it pleasant to break up and begin housekeeping several times a year.

Always there is something you cannot carry with you, something which must be sold or given away. *Always* some favourite chair is broken and crockery mysteriously disappears, requiring new outlay at prices beyond reason, and trying the patience and temper by sound and certain tests. Custom familiarizes the different styles, shapes, and colours of plates and dishes, as they are replenished at different times and places; but while the tin-cup and plate are *splendid* on the march, they do not come up to the ideal of comeliness and elegance in preparation for a reception or dinner-party given to strangers.

When, after a successful trip of six hundred miles, our two cows were driven away one Sunday afternoon by some very mean Indians, there ensued another of those episodes which distract the mind and mar all plans as to butter and cream for cake and for coffee. The wolves took our nice turkey hen just as she was ready to give us a brood of little turkeys; while half of our young chickens in that bracing climate gaped themselves to death. Yet, with all these sacrifices and losses from repeated change, there were real cosy times in tents, houses, or in cabins.

The good nature and good sense of Uncle Samuel had furnished canned provisions, greatly to our personal comfort and pecuniary convenience; but fresh vegetables were most precious and rare. A few potatoes from Bozeman City, sent with the regards of Brevet Lieutenant-Colonel Kinney, were a great treat; and Major Almstedt, paymaster, was good enough to spare a half cabbage and eleven onions, through one of his trips, to astonish the palate, and minister to a craving for something novel from the United States. Ingenuity was tasked to invent new cookery for cove oysters and other savoury preserved edibles; and wild plums, gooseberries, currants, grapes, and cherries furnished a preserve basis quite palatable and natural.

Wild meats would have been abundant; but the stringent Indian game laws of that country treated all hunting by the white man as poaching, and the preserves were skilfully guarded, to cut off' so far as possible every impulse to trespass.

Evenings had their readings, their games, and quiet quadrilles. Music was a never-failing relief for body and mind; and the interchange of patterns, books, and receipts kept up material for new industry and new themes for deliberation or chit-chat. Sickness, though rare, brought its sympathies, and its little interchange of good things and delicacies; and with the occasional pressure of unsatisfied longings there was developed a peculiarly apt illustration of the idea that people really don't want much of anything, and the Scripture was confirmed that "*a man's life consisteth not in the abundance of what a man possesseth.*"

Change and frequent parting brought those peculiar separations that nowhere else are so tender as in army life on the frontier. Captain

Haymond, Lieutenants Phisterer and D'Isay left us for recruiting service only two weeks after we reached our destination; and subsequently, Lieutenant Adair and Lieutenant Bisbee, wife and child. Others came, and quite a coterie shared in the round of evening sociables, which relieved the tension of continual excitement, and brought into being some features similar in kind to those of by-gone times at home.

Nor was the Sabbath neglected. Each new building, that was available in turn, became our sanctuary, as there was not time to build exclusively for chapel purposes. The sutler's store, the commissary building, company headquarters, and the band pavilion of evergreens successively shared the honour. The string band accompanied the voices, and, far away from the church-going bell and the heaven-directing spires, the praise of God was sung and Divine help implored. Few are the sanctuaries in civilized states where the *Magnificat, Gloria in Excelsis, There is a light in the window, Old Hundred,* and *Coronation* were supported by a better orchestra or sung with more spirit.

The garrison itself had its own occasional social gatherings; and such was the general sobriety, the patient obedience and thorough absorption of the men in the plans of their commander, that drunkenness was rare and profanity less than usual. The stringent orders against verbal or personal abuse, the public reprimand administered on one occasion, and the governing principle that while obedience must be cheerful and immediate, the rights of the soldier as a man must be regarded, inspired the men with confidence and new ambition to fulfil their full measure of duty.

Chapter 21

Indian Warfare

When even a woman shares the contingencies of entering a new country with troops, she must learn something besides the lessons of housewifery, endurance, and patience.

When days, weeks, and months pass with constantly recurring opportunities of seeing Indians in small and in large parties dashing at pickets, driving in wood parties, harassing water details, and, with dancing and yelling, challenging the garrison to pursuit; when, now and then, one, two, or more casualties mark the issues of a day, and these culminate, until at last live wagon-loads of bodies give evidence of the cunning barbarity and numbers of the foe; when night alarms are common, and three men are shot within thirty yards of the gates; when the stockade becomes a prison-wall, and over its trunks are seen only the signs of precaution or active warfare; when the men are never idle, but all are daily engrossed in essential labour, with no signs of reinforcement or aid; when the usual thankless task of opening a new country with its uncertainties and enmities, with resources absurdly deficient, meets only obloquy and abuse for the principal actors, she acquires *somehow*, whether by instinct or observation, it matters not which, an idea that Indians *will fight*, and sometimes do become quite wicked and dangerous. Surely, their ways are not as our ways, and their ponies are not like our horses. Their commissariat and their forage are not in trains or on pack mules; their campaigns are not extensively advertised in advance, nor do they move by regular stages or established routes.

Yes, even a woman, after several hundred miles of journey alternately in the ambulance or side saddle, sometimes in corral expecting its aid for safety, and again in the winding defile, where the very place excites the keenest scrutiny and is suggestive of noble red men with the nobility ignored, will see some peculiarities of Indian warfare when Indians are really venomous, and will draw conclusions for friends to consider, even if they only elicit a smile at her timidity, simplicity, or weakness.

James, the novelist, never compelled his solitary horseman to fight a Sioux, and, had the Knight of the Leopard, at the Diamond of the Desert, met more than one quiver of the darts of the Saracen, his adventures might have ended while his career was scarcely begun. Not unlike the Arab is the Indian of the Northwest. Isolated, yet in communication through the little mirrors which flash the sunlight and pass his signals for miles; separated, yet by the lance, pennon, and flags combined, when opportunity is inviting; dashing directly forward at a run, with the person crouched on the pony's neck, and wheeling only to throw himself out of sight and pass his arrows and bullets under the animal's neck before he returns for a fresh venture; fleeing everywhere, apparently at random, so that his pursuer must take choice of object of quest only to find his hot pursuit fruitless, with gathered numbers in his line of retreat; shooting up and down red buttes, where the horse of the white man breaks down at once; running on foot, with the trotting pony just behind him seeking a rest from the burden of his master; imitating the cry of the wolf and the hoot of the owl, when it will hide his night visit,—these Indians are everywhere, where you suppose they are not; and are certain to be nowhere, where you suppose them to be, sure.

In ambush and decoy, *splendid*; in horsemanship, *perfect*; in strategy, *cunning*; in battle, *wary* and careful of life; in victory, jubilant; and in vengeance, fiendish and terrible.

Too few to waste life fruitlessly; too superstitious to leave their dead to the enemy; too cunning or niggardly of resources to offer fair fight; too fond of their choice hunting-grounds to yield willing possession to the stranger,—they wait and watch, and watch and wait, to gather the scalps of the unwary and ignorant, and bear off their trophies to new feasts, new orgies, and new endeavour.

So reluctant are they to attack a foe under cover, that during the year 1866—once before stated—not a train was lost or seriously embarrassed when in corral; nor was any considerable party assailed when it sought judicious and substantial defence. Yet, daring and watchful, none better estimate the foe they contend with. When white men have delivered their fire, and the gleam of the ramrod has shown that the single-shooting arm was in use, then follows the wild dash, with revolvers and arrows, so quick and so spirited that their loss is as nothing, and swift ponies take them safely away for renewal of attack. Circling and intermingling to confuse all aim, affecting retreat seemingly to break up their array, and by some ravine, gulch, *cañon*, or thicket to appear on fresh and better vantage-ground, they approximate ubiquity, and till the terse description of the veteran Bridger, "Where there ain't no Injuns, you'll find 'em thickest."

Good judges of numbers, and quick to estimate the strength and designs of an enemy; keen to maintain their scouts and secure due notice of reinforcements; rarely, though sometimes, fighting in masses, but then with such involved and concerted disorder as to insure their purpose, when the plan is to overwhelm alive and capture for the torture,—this same Indian must find in his final master a better-armed and well-disciplined foe, who has studied his country and his nature, and this before his peace-offerings will be abiding and honest, or his hunting-grounds shall become the peaceful path of the traveller.

With all this, these same Indians have read the book of fate, and in the establishment of mutually supporting and well-garrisoned strongholds they will be foiled as to protracted interruption of emigration and travel. When this end is reached, and the great route through Absaraka is occupied and guarded, the game will flee the range of the white man's rifle, and the desperate Indian must abandon his home, fight himself to death, or yield to the white man's mercy.

Fired by the progress of the settler and the soldier; seeing as never before the last retreat of the buffalo, the elk, and the deer invaded by a permanent intruder; looking at his rights as violated, and the promises of many agents as unfulfilled; taught by nature, if not by the white man, that he is the lawful tenant of the waste he roams over until he has bartered his right away,—he has some reason to exclaim, as Red Cloud assured Black Horse, when the latter, in July, 1866, said, "Let us take the white man's hand and what he gives us, rather than fight him longer and lose all,"—the answer was: "White man lies and steals. My lodges were many, but now they are few. The white man wants *all*. The white man must fight, and the Indian will die where his fathers died."

Growing conscious of the white man's power, knowing how vain is an open field struggle, they avoid such determining issues, and waylay in detail, gradually enlarging their sphere of action, and thereby gathering in the young men and disaffected of other bands, until common cause may be had of all whose wrongs or temper inspire them to keep the war-path longer.

The frequent change of dwelling-place in a great area of hunting-ground gives them peculiar aptitude for this warfare and peculiar immunity from punishment. A single pony will bear and drag the lodge poles of a *tepah*, and the squaws will not only relieve the warriors of all menial details, but with the old men and boys are no despicable protectors of a village when the fighting men are in pursuit of game or scalps.

Thus Indian fighting is no parade of ceremony specifically described in regulations, nor an issue between fair and generous opponents. It is at all times destruction for the white man to fail, and his exposures, his perils, and even his successes, so much less heralded and estimated than in more artificial war with those of his own race, only bring him the personal consciousness of duty done to balance wasting years, loss of social life, and a bare support. With all this, and the sometimes recurring feeling of bitterness prompting the desire to exterminate his foe and thereby visit upon him some of the horrid scenes he has passed through, there comes the inevitable sentiment of pity, and even of sympathy with the bold warrior in his great struggle; and in a dash over the plains, or breathing the pure air of the mountains, the sense of freedom and independence brings such contrast with the machinery and formalities of much that is called civilized life, that it seems but natural that the red man in his pride and strength should bear aloft the spear-point, and with new resolve fight the way through to his final home in the Spirit land.

CHAPTER 22

The Arrow Beats the Revolver

Popular opinion has regarded the Indian bow and arrow as something primitive and well enough for the pursuit of game, but quite useless in a contest with the white man. This idea would be excellent if the Indian warriors would calmly march up in line of battle and risk their masses so armed against others armed with the rifle. But the Indian comes as the hornet comes, in clouds or singly, yet never trying to sting until his ascendency is assured and his own exposure is slight.

At fifty yards a well-shapen, iron-pointed arrow is dangerous and very sure. A handful drawn from the quiver and discharged successively will make a more rapid fire than that of the revolver, and at very short range will farther penetrate a piece of plank or timber than the ball of an ordinary Colt's navy pistol.

The arrow-head varies in length and shape, and the shaft itself slightly changes, according to the tastes of different bands or tribes; and yet so constantly are arrows exchanged in gambling or barter that the character of the arrow used does not invariably determine the tribe engaged. Such were many of the arrows taken from the bodies of Captains Fetterman, Brown, Lieutenant Grummond, and others, after the massacre of December, 1866. All the peculiarities there found have been seen in the quivers of the Kittekehas, Chowees, Petropowetaws, and other Pawnees, all of whom are friendly, and some of whom are now, as in the winter of 1865-6, in the employ of the United States.

The head is often barbed, but not generally, and is from two to three and a half inches in length, made of iron, and ground to a double edge. The shaft, which is about twenty-five inches in length, is winged by three feathers of the eagle, sage-hen, or wild-goose, and from the sinew wrapping of the head to that which binds the feathers is deeply marked by three grooves or blood-seams, so that when the flesh of man or beast closes about the shaft, these seams act as conduits and gradually bleed the victim to death. These grooves are with some Indians straight, and with others are zigzag or winding from midway down to the feathers.

The bows of Ogillalla and Brulè Sioux, Arrapahoes, Cheyennes, and most of the Indians east of the Rocky Mountains, are from thirty-two to forty inches long, of great elasticity and tension, so that they easily drive an arrow through a two-inch plank, and even through a man or buffalo.

The hatchet is generally that which is furnished by Indian agents or traders, often having the head and handle hollow and connected for use as a pipe; and, when possible, the handle itself is profusely studded with brass nails such as once distinguished parlour sofas and chairs.

Rifles, both English and American, abound. The "Hawkins" is a favourite, carrying what is called the "trade ball," and requiring a patch; but many of the old guides, trappers, and half-breeds still cling to their use as in the days of Pathfinder and other heroes of Cooper.

The quiver and bow-case are made of deerskin, bearskin, otter and other hides, or furs; and the armament of Hawkeye, which now hangs before the writer, is elaborate with tassels and pendants from well-dressed beaver.

The shield is worn by many of the leading braves, and is formed of several thicknesses of hide fastened through and through about the edge with sinew, and studded with brass nails, or ornamented with silver and other bright metal.

The spear varies from five and a half to seven feet in length, having a head nearly eighteen inches long, with a small pennon; and the heel of the shaft is balanced with eagle feathers, while others are caught along the shaft, giving steadiness to the flight, and suiting the diversified tastes of the owner.

The right and left hair of the warrior or brave is brought before the ear, braided or twisted, and wrapped with strings or ribbons, and falling upon the breast; while a third braid, falling behind and below the scalp-lock or tuft, often is covered with a succession of silver medallions hammered from coin, gradually diminishing in size from four inches to one inch as the series approaches the ground.

Earrings, necklaces, bracelets, and armlets are of brass, beads, bears' claws, or silver, but more generally of beautiful combinations of shells from the Pacific, seventy-five of which have been the price of a pony, and show the close relations of trade maintained between the tribes of the opposite slopes of the Rocky Mountains.

Moccasins, leggings, breech-cloth, and a buffalo robe belted about the waist, leaving the breast bare, is the sole dress of the majority. Others have jackets more or less fancifully decorated with small bullet buttons, and every article of dress that an American soldier uses is at once assumed when its possession is acquired. Trowsers are, however, cut off at the hip, as their own style of protection is habitually preferred. Gifts of clothing are quickly put on; and a present of gentlemen's underclothes once given to a Pawnee was so quickly substituted for his original garments as barely to allow escape from the room during the process.

The women vary little in costume except in a wrapping something like a petticoat or skirt, but wear less paint. The hair-parting is, however, invariably painted vermilion when visiting or in full dress, and cheeks, chin, and arms have their share of brilliant tints. Warriors, squaws, and children alike use the bow and arrow, but the women are peculiarly apt with knife and hatchet. The youngsters have a javelin exercise which is admirably fitted to prepare them for their future life. A small hoop is held by the thumb and forefinger of the right hand, while within the hand is the spear. The hoop is thrown forward on the ground, and the javelin is sent after and through the ring with great dexterity and success. This, with the cast of the hatchet and play of the knife, takes the place of the white boy's baseball or marbles; and the blunt-headed arrow brings down birds and small game that would be spoiled by the keener shaft.

The revolver is becoming quite common, and is used with more dexterity and skill than is the rifle. The following instance will illustrate a remarkable failure in rifle firing. Soon after Captain Fetterman arrived, he rode to the Pinery with Lieutenant Bisbee, Captain Ten Eyck, and one or two other officers who had just arrived, to see the locality. They descended to Pine Island just after the last timber-wagon had come out on the road, and in advance of their escort. They were received by a volley of from fifteen to twenty rifle shots, which were fired from a rest upon a fallen tree, at a distance of only fifty paces, as actually measured, without injury to anybody. A second volley equally failed to touch a man.

A little bugle-boy brought word to the garrison that all were killed, for he saw the Indians as they fired and the officers as they disappeared. They were compelled to skirmish down the island before they could extricate themselves from the dilemma. A supporting party went out,

Tepee, or tepah—Indian lodge

but met them returning, and thus relieved the anxiety of the garrison.

The Indians not only use mirrors and flags for signal purposes, but many carry with them good field and spy-glasses, some of English styles, procured from Canada, and others are supplied by traders on the frontier.

The domestic life of the Indian, with the barbarity of the sun-dance and the filth of his home, have been often described; but the plenitude of furs in the land of Absaraka have furnished peculiar facilities for adornment and somewhat better wardrobes than are usual nearer the Lower Missouri and Mississippi waters. Their *tepah* (*tepee*, or lodge) is the model from which the Sibley tent was derived, and will accommodate several families; but nothing else on the face of the earth, will furnish a more curious medley of contents than does a *tepah* where two or three families, of all ages and sizes, with all their worldly goods and hopes are huddled, piled, and crammed about its fire, and where the fitful wind and lazy squaws are combined in the effort to smoke buffalo tongues, strips of meat, and *Injun* all together.

The picture is complete, by way of contrast, if a kettle of boiling water over the fire has received a fat dog just after his throat felt the knife, and a white officer, on a pile of furs, is doing his best to show how gracefully he can endure the honours and dinner specially designed for his presence. All this, too, while other officers and ladies are cheerfully waiting outside in the glad consciousness of escape from the hospitality of a chief.

Bells, triangles, and common horns have found their way among these Indians, and they eagerly adopt from the white man whatever makes noise or show.

CHAPTER 23

Extracts From Journal

Fort Philip Kearney, December 6th, 1866. I hardly know how to take up my sadly interrupted journal. This day, with its bright morning, brought its sweet promise of rest from Indian alarms, and throughout the garrison all work was pushed with vigour; but the evening adds another sad chapter to the history of our frontier life.

The garrison waited anxiously until nearly nine o'clock before the distant bugle-note indicated the return of parties which, since nine in the morning, have been in pursuit of Indians. It seems hardly possible that poor Bingham, the gentle, manly, and soldierly young officer, who has already won the esteem of everybody, has already, so soon after his arrival, fallen a victim to his ardour and the craft of our foes. It seems that such a disaster has been necessary, to check the natural impulse of everyone who comes here to chase Indians regardless of number or rules. Mr. Grummond and Mr. Wands have given me the whole history, and it is of God's mercy that any one escaped. Captain Fetterman has been in, and says "he has learned a lesson, and that this Indian war has become a hand-to hand fight, requiring the utmost caution," and he wants no more such risks.

When the Indians attacked the wood train in the morning. Captain Fetterman was sent with mounted infantry and a part of Lieutenant Bingham's cavalry to drive the Indians over Lodge Trail Ridge, while the colonel, with Lieutenant Grummond and about twenty-five or thirty mounted men, crossed Big Piney to intercept the party chased by Captain Fetterman. Nearly two hundred Indians were in front of Captain Fetterman, hotly engaging his party, when fifteen of the cavalry, with Lieutenant Bingham, left him, for some reason unknown to everybody. The colonel's party pushed for the scene of action, and met the cavalry dismounted on one of the forks of Peno, but without

Mr. Bingham. It seems that he had dashed westward after he saw the colonel's party galloping down the hills, and Mr. Grummond, by some sudden impulse, was led to leave his own party and join Mr. Bingham, both disappearing suddenly and nearly alone.

The colonel's party followed down the valley, according to original plan, until the opening below showed a large force of Indians beyond, and fast gathering on the flanks. Only seven men and a bugle-boy turned the point with him, and Indians were constantly circling around to draw their fire. Private McGuire's horse went down with him, as he gratefully tells his story, and an Indian was crawling along to scalp him, when the party stopped for him and he was lifted up. The recall was sounded, and Corporal Baker hearing it rode over a hill from the north, reporting that Lieutenant Bingham had certainly gone beyond the second hill, though just then there were at least eighty Indians in sight before that hill.

Soon after Captain Fetterman came up, having crossed over to the other party after the defection of the cavalry, and a movement was made at once for the rescue of Lieutenant Bingham. Lieutenant Wands, who had superseded Captain Brown as regimental quartermaster, was to have started with the colonel, but being delayed to exchange his horse, by mistake joined the other party. He had been grazed by a ball, and probably his coolness and his Henry rifle saved that detachment after Lieutenant Bingham left it, as the others fired revolvers, even at several hundred yards, and Lieutenant Bingham threw his away.

The party rode but a few rods on the hill when suddenly a shout was heard: "For God's sake, come down quick," and through a gulch where the road was visible seven Indians were seen with their spear-heads close upon the backs of four of our men, one of whom was Lieutenant Grummond.

Mr. Wands thinks, from the formation of the ground, that had they passed that ravine a moment sooner or later, they would have seen nothing of Mr. Grummond's party until they should have found their bodies on return.

A few moments later the body of Lieutenant Bingham was found, and that of Sergeant Bowers, who was still living, though his skull was cleft through with a hatchet. He had killed three Indians with his revolver before he was overpowered. Private Donovan, always so brave, was with the party. They had been surrounded by thirty Indians while Lieutenants Grummond and Bingham were pursuing a dismounted Indian and cutting at him with sabres.

An ambulance was sent for, and Captain Arnold went out with forty men to reinforce the party. The remains of Lieutenant Bingham are in hospital, to be cared for and prepared for burial.

******

December 9th, 1866. Lieutenant Bingham and Sergeant Bowers were buried today. Lieutenant Grummond conducted the Masonic services, assisted by Mr. Weston, Mr. Saunders, Mr. Beckwith and others, while Chaplain White conducted the religious portion.

Thus our cemetery fills up with only the victims of violence! Everything in nature is so beautiful, and the climate is so restoring and healthful, that one could look upon such frontier life with something like complacency were it not for these savages, or even if the long and anxiously expected reinforcements could be seen or heard from. Sometimes it seems as if nobody cared if we had help or not.

Sergeant Bowers was such a favourite with Captain Brown that he placed his own corps-badge upon the breast of the remains; and the men feel especially vindictive and anxious for revenge, as Bowers had so often led the hay parties and successfully skirmished in defence of their work.

The officers feel more than ever the necessity of completing all necessary work and preparing for winter, and many believe that we may shortly expect, as the Crows indicated, the return of Indians in still larger force, to try and cut off work and supplies, if they do not dare to come near the fort and attempt its capture by surprise.

After the funeral. Lieutenant Grummond came in to speak of the services at the grave, which were very impressive, and again expressed his gratitude for his preservation. The lesson will not be lost, and shows what madness it is to follow these Indians very far with insufficient force, and what great peril may come to the post and whole line of road by rash impulses and disregard of the special work that presses so hard.

We think now that we shall not soon hear from Fort C. F. Smith, as Lieutenant Bingham had just returned from that post, having an escort of twenty-five men; and Brevet Lieutenant-Colonel Kinney, who has just made us a week's visit, thinks it unsafe to undertake the trip with less than an escort of fifty good men.

Our mail is overdue, and no doubt the courier and mail party are detained as guides to troops. The sentries understand they are not to fire at messengers coming from the east, and we shall soon have letters and papers after a long intermission. Perhaps the news of our difficulties has by this time been received, and nearly six months of trial may be succeeded by six months of triumph. We learn, as did Crusoe, how much can be done during comparative isolation from a civilized world.

Note.—Red Cloud had command in person on the 6th of December, and white signal-flags were displayed, covering a line of seven miles.

Chapter 24

Fetterman's Massacre

December, 21st, 1866, was to us the saddest day of the year. Though snow covered the mountains, and there was every indication of the return of severe weather, the morning was quite pleasant. Men only wore blouses at their work, and the train, although much later than usual, went to the Pinery with a strong guard, so that the teamsters, choppers, and escort, all armed, numbered not far from ninety men.

The children ran in about 11 o'clock, shouting "Indians!" and the pickets on Pilot Hill could be distinctly seen giving the signal of "many Indians," on the line of the wood road; and news was also furnished that the train was in corral only a short distance from the garrison.

The officers and all the ladies were soon watching for other usual demonstrations, while a detail was being organized to relieve the train.

Brevet Lieutenant-Colonel Fetterman, then walking back and forth before his quarters, near where the colonel was giving his instructions, asked and obtained permission to go with the detachment.

Lieutenant Grummond, also at his own request, took a part of Company C, 2nd United States Cavalry,—making the whole force just seventy-eight officers and men. Captain Brown, unknown to the officers of the garrison, as well as citizens Wheatley and Fisher, both experienced frontiersmen and good shots, also joined the party.

It was just at the time when a few more trains of saw-logs would furnish ample lumber material to complete the office building and a fifth company quarters, already well under progress.

The orders were given in front of Lieutenant Grummond's house, next the colonel's, and those who were present heard them repeated with distinctness and special urgency. Lieutenant Wands was also instructed to repeat them. As if peculiarly impressed with some anticipations of rashness in the movement, the colonel, just after the command left, went across the parade-ground to a sentry platform, halted the mounted party, and gave additional orders, understood in the garrison, and by those who heard them, to be the substantial repetition of the former.

The health of Mrs. Grummond was such that Lieutenant Wands and other friends urged him, for his family's sake, to be prudent, and avoid all rash movements and any pursuit that would draw them over Lodge Trail Ridge, and to report to Brevet Lieutenant-Colonel Fetterman the orders he had received. These orders were, in so many words, "to relieve the train, and under no circumstances to cross the ridge." Everybody knew why special emphasis was given to these orders.

Only two days before. Brevet Major Powell had been sent out to relieve a train, and obeyed his orders literally, although, as he afterward said, he was sorely tempted to pursue, but became afterward convinced that certain destruction would have been the result. Major Powell was in fact assigned to command the relieving party on the 21st; but when Brevet Lieutenant-Colonel Fetterman stepped forward and claimed it by seniority of rank, he was permitted to go and received his instructions.

The day before, and succeeding that on which Major Powell had reported several hundred Indians present, the colonel himself took charge of trains to the pinery, spending the day in building a bridge over the creek and superintending the chopping parties and guard detail. All the indications were that the numerous Indian villages on Tongue River would lose no chance to do mischief, and the garrison was insufficiently supplied with arms, even of old styles, for the men actually at the post. Before Captain Fetterman left, a few Indian pickets were seen on Lodge Trail Ridge, and a few were below the fort at the road crossing. Two or three case shot, dropped near them, dismounted one and brought nearly thirty out of the brush. These at once disappeared.

After the detachment had been gone a short time, finding that Captain Fetterman had left without a surgeon, the colonel sent Dr. Hines, with one of his own orderlies, to join the train and report to Captain Fetterman; Doctor Hines started, but soon returned with the news that the train had safely pursued its route to the woods; that Captain Fetterman was on the ridge to the north, out of view, and that there was so many Indians in sight that he could not join the party. It was about noon, and a man rushed in to say that firing was renewed.

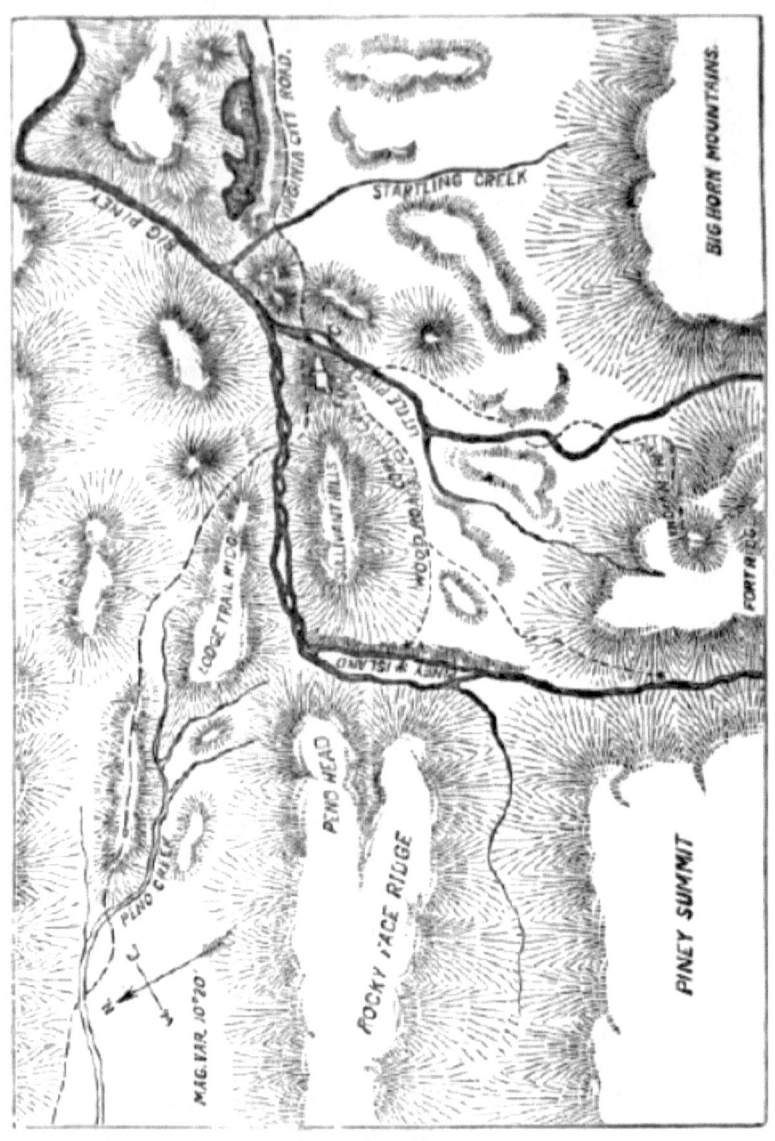

* Indicates block-houses in woods for working parties.
..... Dotted line, roads to Pino Island and Mountain.
— — Broken line, road to Virginia City, crossing narrow divide where bodies of Fetterman's command were found.
C, cemetery at foot of Pilot Hill.
☐ Corral, on road to woods, where train was attacked December 21st, 1866.

FORT PHILIP KEARNEY AND SURROUNDINGS, FROM ORIGINAL SURVEYS.

Every shot could be heard, and there was little doubt that a desperate fight was going on in the valley of Peno Creek beyond the ridge. The presence of Lieutenant Grummond with the party gave us new anxiety, and many heartfelt prayers were offered that he might return in safety. The colonel was on the "lookout," on headquarters building, and gave his orders before coming down.

It seemed long, but was hardly twelve minutes before Captain Ten Eyck, Lieutenant Matson, Dr. Hines, and Dr. Ould, with a relieving party, were moving, on the run, for the scene of action. We had all watched Captain Fetterman until the curve of Sullivant Hills shut him off, and then he was on the southern slope of the ridge, apparently intending to cut off the retreat of the Indians from the train. Wagons and ambulances were hurried up; the whole garrison was on the alert; extra ammunition for both parties was started, and even the prisoners were put on duty to give the guard and all available men their perfect freedom for whatever might transpire. Couriers were sent to the woods to bring back the train and its guard, to secure its support, as well as from the fear that the diversion of Captain Fetterman from his orders might still involve its destruction; and shortly Captain Arnold came to report that the whole force of armed men left at the post, including guard and everything, was but one hundred and nineteen men.

Until the wagons galloped out of the gate, we could see a solitary Indian on the highest part of Lodge Trail Ridge; but he soon disappeared. All this time firing was increasing in intensity, and in little more than thirty minutes,—after one or two quick volleys, the rattle of file-firing, and a few scattering shots,—a perfect silence ensued. There were then many anxious hearts, and *waiting* was perfectly terrible! The movements of Captain Ten Eyck were watched with intensest interest. The pickets could give no information, and a messenger sent upon Sullivant Hills could see neither Indians nor troops. It was just before Captain Ten Eyck's party reached the top of the hill across the Piney, north of the Virginia City road, that all firing ceased.

Soon Orderly Sample was seen to break away from the command and make for the fort, with his horse, on the run. He brought the message that the valleys were full of Indians, and that several hundred were on the road below, yelling and challenging them to come down; but nothing could be seen of Fetterman. As was afterward learned, this party was on the very field of carnage, and doubtless they were completing their robbery and butchery. It was after dark when Captain Ten Eyck returned, with forty-nine of the bodies, and made the terrible announcement that all were killed.

To a woman whose house and heart received the widow as a sister, and whose office it was to advise her of the facts, the recital of the scenes of that day, even at this late period, is full of pain; but at the time, the Christian fortitude and holy calmness with which Mrs. Grummond looked upward to her Heavenly Father for wisdom and strength, inspired all with something of her same patience to know the worst and meet its issues.

The body of Lieutenant Grummond had not been rescued, and there was some faint hope that stragglers might yet come in and break the absolute gloom of the tragedy by some explanatory and redeeming feature.

At last the wood train came in, having seen nothing of Fetterman, not even having heard the firing, or suspected any additional danger after repulsing their own immediate assailants. Imagination only can suggest how wide-sweeping would have been the massacre had any considerable portion of the hostile bands renewed the attack upon the train after the successful decoy of the others to inevitable destruction.

With the next morning came a meeting of officers, with universal disinclination, generally expressed, to venture a search for the remaining dead. The safety of any small party seemed doubtful, and the post itself might be imperilled by a large draft upon the garrison. But the colonel had made up his mind, and freely expressed his purpose "not to let the Indians have the conviction that the dead could not be rescued;" and besides this, the very men who had passed through the war without blanching began to form ideas of the numbers and barbarity of the Indians, which threatened to take away one-half their real strength.

So the colonel informed Mrs. Grummond that he should go in person, and would bring home her husband. Captain Ten Eyck, Lieutenant Matson, and Dr. Ould went with the party. Long after they left, and they left with the cheerful Godspeed of every woman and soldier of the garrison, on a holy mission, the pickets, which were distributed on the line of march, indicated their progress, and showed that neither the fort nor the detachment could be threatened without such connection of signals as would advise both and secure co-operation whatever might ensue.

Long after dark, the wagons and command returned with the remaining dead, slowly passing to the hospital and other buildings made ready for their reception.

Lieutenant Grummond's body was found, and eventually accompanied us on our midwinter's march back over the plains.

A careful roll-call of the garrison was had, and the body of every missing man was found. Wheatley and Fisher were discovered near a pile of rocks, surrounded by expended cartridges, proving that their Henry rifles had done good service. All the bodies lay along or near a narrow divide over which the road ran, and to which no doubt the assailed party had retreated when overwhelming numbers bore down upon them. Captains Fetterman and Brown were at the point nearest the fort, each with a revolver shot in the left temple, and so scorched with powder as to leave no doubt that they shot each other when hope had fled. So ended lives that were full of pride and confidence in the morning.

Captain Brown's repeated dashes, and especially his success on the 23rd of September, had inspired him with perfectly reckless daring in pursuit of Indians; and only the night before the massacre he made a call, with spurs fastened in the buttonholes of his coat, leggings wrapped, and two revolvers accessible, declaring, by way of explanation, that he was ready by day and night, and must have *one scalp* before leaving for Laramie, to which place he had been ordered. He had inspired Captain Fetterman, who had been but a short time in the country, and already had great contempt for our adversaries, with the same mad determination to chase whenever they could, regardless of numbers; and together they planned an expedition of a week's trip to Tongue River valley, with a mixed party of ninety citizens and soldiers, to destroy the Indian villages and clear out all enemies. Disapproval of the plan did not change their belief in its feasibility and wisdom; but here were eighty-one officers and men, and among them the veterans of a long war, utterly destroyed in their hands, only six or seven miles on the route to that same Tongue River valley.

This massacre proved the value and integrity of Major Bridger and his statements, and no less showed the wisdom of a settled policy not to precipitate or undertake a general war while there was but a handful of men at the post; and the army had not yet received such increase as could promise any considerable support.

A kind Providence spared many, and the line of road opened in the summer of 1866 was maintained. Other regiments have strengthened the garrisons, and a year of changes finds the Indians still numerous and unpunished, but with the line still maintained; while the fruits of the labour of 1866 are yet to be valued when that country shall be occupied and sufficiently understood. If the line be abandoned by its garrisons, as is probable, to give better security for the Union Pacific Railroad, and if its choice hunting-grounds be given to the Indians, who seem to have a right to them at present, it cannot be doubted that the work done will have its value, and Eastern Montana will ultimately perfect its communications with the Missouri through the field of so much struggle and duty.

CHAPTER 25

The Funeral, and Burial of Fourscore and One Victims of the Massacre

The bodies of the dead were first deposited in the spare ward of the hospital, two hospital-tents, and a double cabin. Details from each company assisted in their care and recognition. Many gave their best uniforms, decently to clothe their comrades,—and the noblest traits of the soldier were touchingly developed as they carefully handled the mutilated fragments, drew out or cut off the arrows, and decently composed all for the burial.

A long line of pine cases, duly numbered, was arranged by companies along the officers' street, near the hospital, and as each body was placed in its plain receptacle, the number and name was taken, for the future reference of friends.

The detail to dig a grave for this great entombment was well armed, and accompanied by a guard; but so intense was the cold that constant relays were required, and the interment was not achieved until Wednesday after the fight.

Over the great pit, fifty feet long and seven feet deep, a mound was raised, and the dead were buried with a sad and solemn stillness that will long leave its memory with those who had souls to estimate the circumstances and lessons of that dire calamity.

As if Nature herself were shocked by the enormity of the Indian torture there inflicted, and would still the passions of all, or forbid their immediate indulgence, it so happened that from the very night of December 21st the winter became unmitigated in its severity, requiring guards to be changed at least half hourly, preventing out-of-door inspections of the guard, and driving officers, ladies, and men to beaver, buffalo, or wolf skins for protection from the cold.

The relief, as they hastened to their regular distribution, presented no bad idea of Lapland or Siberian life. The tastes, workmanship, and capital of the wearers were variously illustrated in their personal wardrobes. A uniform cap being useless and hardly endurable, even with coat-cape fastened, hood-like, over the head, the soldiers had permission to suit themselves in respect of substantial comfort. Mittens that ended at the shoulder; buffalo boots and leggings nearly to the thigh; hats as tall as a Polander's, with bushy wolf tails *pendant*; and tippets, comforts, coats, and vests of skins made an odd style of uniform under the existing Regulations for the better government of the Army of the United States.

There were, indeed, times when the smallest possible number of men were allowed to be exposed, and *these* only while the corporal could return to the guard-house and fresh relief might promptly follow up the same routine of constant change. Some were frosted in crossing the parade, some on their sentry platforms; and guard duty with keeping warm were the principal work of all who had no part in hauling water, cutting wood, the care of stock, or the issue of supplies.

The holidays were sad as they were cold. Lights were burned in all quarters, and one non-commissioned officer was always on duty in each building, so that in case of alarm there could not be an instant's delay in the use of the whole command. Each company knew its place and the distribution of the loop-holes; the gunners slept in tents near their guns, and all things were ripe for the destruction of assailants should any venture to attack.

The constant and drifting snowstorms soon so lifted their crests by the west flank of the stockade that officers walked over its trunks, and when a trench ten feet wide was cleared, the next snow or wind would fill it, as only snow can snow and winds can blow in that suburb of Cloud Peak, the home of perpetual snow.

The men themselves, who, at the October muster, looked forward to the holidays and December muster with glad anticipations, forbore all demonstrations usual to such a period, and sensibly felt the weight of the great loss incurred.

Of the sergeants who had distinguished themselves in the previous war, or had actively operated in the labours of 1866, nearly all of the most prominent had fallen: Lang, a martinet, trim, upright, and soldierly; Bissell, calm, mature, and carrying into his profession the sturdy habits of business which had marked his life in Chicago before a hasty indiscretion impelled him to the army; Smith, the pride of the mounted infantry; Morgan, and many others, deserve an enduring monument over their last resting-place no less than heroes of more exalted stations from more memorable battlefields.

The whole garrison shared the gloom. Charades, tableaus, Shakespearian readings, the usual muster evening levee at the colonel's, and all the social reunions which had been anticipated as bringing something pleasant, and in the similitude of civilized life, were dropped as unseasonable and almost unholy. Present and exacting duty admitted no dalliance with pleasures that were at other times rational and refreshing; and a calm, sedate, but genial sympathy brought most to a closer fraternity, almost confirming the sacred proverb, "*That it is better to go to the house of mourning than to the house of feasting.*"

But no calm review, no wealth of language can bring before the minds of strangers to those scenes any conception of the realities experienced; neither would a literal catalogue of mutilations and outrages upon the persons of the fallen bring within the range of any imagination the capacity to present them as they were to the understanding of others. The aggregate of wrongs to single individuals would sum up the shocking features of many battlefields; and the sum of all inflicted upon the entire party can have no precedent by which to estimate their horrors.

Nor was the abandonment of the proper recreation of the holidays the sole result.

Plans had been made looking to a short winter expedition, under the advice of General Cooke, that "three hundred infantry, with much suffering, could perhaps do more in winter than three thousand cavalry in summer." The exact method of doing this had not been settled upon, it is believed, though much talked of in social circles, where the ladies had the privilege of listening; and it was known that the colonel was determined, as soon as reinforced, to make such reconnoissances and outside movements as would test its practicability without risk to the post; but the destruction of Fetterman's command within a few miles of the post engendered doubts, which were freely expressed by the officers, whether the force that could be made available, even after a successful march and surprise, could entirely or signally destroy the villages of Red Cloud, with his warriors, his knifing squaws, and shooting *papooses*.

Underlying these facts was the general congratulation that a successful maintenance of the post until spring should reopen the road to travel, would be a practical assurance to the Indian of the ultimate extinction of his hunting-grounds and the end of his supremacy in Absaraka. Others suggested that perhaps Red Cloud had concluded to keep himself vigorously awake, and try the surprise part himself, or so occupy himself as to consolidate all hostile bands into some comprehensive system of hostility to the post and the white man generally.

Besides this, it was a matter of notoriety and fact that, while the officers were anxious for repeating arms or breech-loaders, only old styles of rifles were on the way, and also that ammunition, not more than four or five months previously started from Leavenworth, was resting itself at some place not disclosed to the white warriors of Absaraka. Then the reinforcements had not come; and as the affair of the 21st, with the details of the same, had actually engrossed the time and energies of the whole garrison, the entire plan of destroying the Indians of the Northwest, while the mercury was motionless and the snow was all in motion, was temporarily dropped.

True it was that the spirit which drove Fetterman to hasty disobedience and certain destruction, *viz.*, a desire to settle accounts for some of the outrages perpetrated during our six months' sojourn, had somewhat decidedly inspired all the ladies, as well as the officers and men, with a longing to do something explosive and brilliant; but the ladies had so often been told not to discuss military matters, and the tide of events having unfavourably settled the prospect of our husbands' gaining glory by miraculous adventures with Red Cloud, there was a quiet acquiescence in the condition of self-defence.

A stranger might have almost thought we were besieged. The commanders of Forts C. F. Smith and Reno so construed their condition; and the constant watchfulness, strict discipline, and ever-present preparation for all contingencies savoured not a little of the same essence, as we passed the holidays of 1866-7 at Fort Philip Kearney, Absaraka.

Chapter 26

Comedy of Errors

Has any military event in history, whether sacred or profane, immediately after its occurrence called forth more elaborate and general explanation, and involved more contradictory and absurd criticism, all "founded upon fact," yet ignorant of that valuable article, than the massacre near Fort Phil Kearney, December 21st, 1866?

Of course the public could not be expected to know, nor the press to announce, that the only means of communication between that post and Fort Laramie, the nearest mail and telegraph station, was through two hundred and thirty-five miles of hostile country and through couriers sent by the post commander himself.

Neither could the great American people *wait* for information; but they must know exactly and fully all the particulars for perusal while coffee was cooling at the next morning's breakfast-table.

It was, of course, to be expected that the Illustrated Papers should act promptly and perspicuously, with all the embellishment and accuracy which wood engraving affords, and do this so truly to life that it would be at once recognized by all actors in its scenes; and it was equally certain and necessary that a "special artist," some "actual observer," or a "special correspondent," should furnish the editor's *sanctum* with the right material for his use in advance of the mails. There was certainly no difficulty as to historical precedents or illustrations of Indian warfare from which to combine a proper sketch, and accordingly the work was begun, even before the couriers had reached Laramie with details of the transaction itself.

As there was no one to contradict, and no one who knew the truth, a large margin was left for the play of the fancy, and the imagination was drawn upon with great freedom and success. The people were of course greatly shocked by the tragedy, and were certain that somebody was terribly to blame. The Indians were supposed to be so quiet and peaceful that nobody asked whether the massacre was one of a series; but statesmen as well as editors, those who claimed to know all about Indian affairs, and those who never saw a live Indian out of a city show, devised theory upon theory, to the great delight of their own complacent souls and with all the wonderful wisdom of absolute ignorance.

It could not be expected, in the urgent demand for particulars, that truth and justice would be the essential features of the whole; and the sensation had to be used just at the time, or somebody's paper or somebody's friend would suppose that somebody else, who was regularly compensated to cater to the popular passion for the startling and novel, was ignorant of that of which he knew nothing. So it happened that numberless journals *obtained, at last, the true version of that sad affair.*

Not to name those papers and thus arouse invidious distinctions where so many showed brilliant powers of imagination, a few choice selections will do honour to them all and injustice to none.

Albany, a city set on a hill, Argus-eyed and sagacious, had a corresponding pre-eminence in the way of invention and preciseness of detail. It portrayed, as *"from reliable information,"* the fearful climax, "when the last band of survivors were driven to the gates of the fort, knocking and screaming in vain for admission; when the last cartridge from revolver, carbine, and rifle was expended; when the sabres and butts of muskets were broken; and when, leaning against the gates, weary and bleeding and all resistance fruitless, all fell in one heap of mangled humanity, unsupported and uncared for." This sketch closed its recital with the startling announcement that the commanding officer, whom it doomed to future obloquy, with two full companies, was looking on, afraid either to fire or open the gates lest the garrison within should be massacred by the infuriated savages and the post should be sacked!

Blockhouses, of course, reserved their fire! Loop-holes shone with the glaring eyes of frightened soldiery, but not with the gleaming rifle! Four howitzers, which could have swept the slope and bottom land, were silent and innocent of harm to anybody!

And yet, as a matter of fact, the fight was not within sight of the fort; and its capacity for defence or the support of any party nearby was superior to the whole force of Indians in Tongue River valley.

One "Illustrated Paper" had a report "from the only eyewitness of the massacre." This person was said "to have been cut off" from his party by Indians, and from a thicket only two hundred and fifty yards distant from the fight he saw the repeated charges of the cavalry, the dashing adventures of officers and men, and the last shot discharged by the last survivor through his own brain."

And yet, as a matter of fact, the very person accredited with this narrow escape and these providential aids to a close observation, did not see a shot fired by the party, or any part of the conflict; but went out with Captain Ten Eyck's relieving party, after failing to find Fetterman's party when firing was heard, and saw what Captain Ten Eyck saw of the fight, and that was—nothing.

A second "Illustrated Paper" had an engraving of the fight, and indicated in advance what should be done with the post commander. Others were hardly outdone by this. All had a convenient scapegoat for the whole affair. The gallantry and prowess of some were praised, while dereliction and cowardice were branded upon others.

Even the metropolitan papers of New York and Washington could not possibly wait, but discharged their shafts, regardless of character or truth. Thus pamphlets, letters, editorials, and pictures expressed their theories or positive statements; so that beyond the opinion of Lieutenant-General Sherman accompanying a soldier's letter, published at Washington in a pamphlet, with other documents sent to Congress upon the massacre, and a critique of the *Cincinnati Gazette* upon the pamphlet itself (author unknown to us), no correct account of the tragedy has ever gained access to the people at large.

To those who were present under the shadow of such a calamity, it seemed harsh and brutal that, more than two thousand miles away, there should be such quick and morbid ambition to criticise and abuse; and the ladies were not a whit behind the officers and men in thoroughly wishing that delegations from the eastern cities could spend some days in that country to try a few dashes after Indians, and take a turn at guard or picket duty, and live a time where newspapers are sometimes two months in coming, where bacon takes the place of sea-food, and desiccated materials put on the name and function of vegetables.

We had become perfectly accustomed and hardened to correspondents from the plains, whose warped or false representations discredited every good thing. Thus, for instance, three papers among those of the largest circulation in the country declared that the commanding officer was constantly giving powder to his enemies, and that ladies threw packages of sugar and coffee over the stockade to the squaws. A tender-hearted, sympathetic, but temporary *attaché* of the Indian Bureau knew just how the massacre occurred—*viz.*, that the poor, hungry, starving women of the Sioux had come to beg, and their husbands had come to ask a little powder for hunting and to have an order revoked as to gifts of arms to Indians, and, being fired upon, they became desperate and took immediate vengeance.

This critic, whose narration had its place on the tables of members of Congress, said a wood train could not have more than six men with it, and could not possibly have been attacked by three hundred Indians. He did not know how slowly six men would have built a post; nor that the timber trains sometimes numbered ninety or more wagons, each drawn by six mules; that each team required a driver; that the work required choppers and loaders and a guard to protect them; and that six men could not do this.

Some supposed that the whole was caused by ignorance of the Indian tricks and habits, and of the surrounding country, notwithstanding the fact that some of the officers not involved in the skirmish had spent the summer and fall in just such warfare and in reconnoissance of the country for miles in all directions.

Every conceivable hypothesis but the correct one was adopted, and everybody *guessed*, without seeming to think that possibly the authorities of the fort itself knew something of the affair, and were old enough to make some official report of the matter.

One said that the soldiers abused the squaws and the women of the country, although, except at the July meeting with the Cheyennes and the short stay of French Pete's rescued wife, there was never a squaw at the fort.

At least three disappointed aspirants for civil berths became newspaper correspondents and traducers; but the sting of their falsehoods was innocuous, as their inducement was understood.

One and all gloried in abuse; and no wonder is it that the hard labour of 1866, its skirmishes and exposures, its chases and its losses, were never told, lest credit should inure to the pioneer expedition to Absaraka.

The information supplied, and that manufactured, alike furnished some amusement to the garrison; but, for the sake of many friends who were anxious to learn the truth, it would have been grateful to the feelings had the truth been made known, to accompany the false as its antidote. At last the United States Senate called for the report of the commanding officer, at the April session, 1867, and again at the July session; and when it appears, some additional light may be furnished by which to confirm or disprove this comedy of errors.

Note.—Although Brigadier-General P. St. George Cooke removed Colonel Carrington from Fort Phil Kearney, without waiting for that officer's report, no sooner was that report received by Lieutenant-General Sherman, than General Cooke was himself relieved, and General Augur was assigned to fill his place.

Note.—(Edition of 1878.) The general history of operations, the text of 24, and the Official Report of Appendix 1., are deemed sufficient explanation of Fetterman's massacre, without the Report of Col. Carrington, although its use has been authorized by the War Department.

CHAPTER 27

March to Fort Reno

New Year's Day, 1867, was without its anticipated festivities. All honour to the 27th Infantry,—until then the 2nd Battalion of the 18th Infantry, and which on the last day of December severed its relations with the old regiment,—that during the holiday week they accepted their sad lesson, and with manly self-denial refrained from those indulgences which are so common at Christmas and the advent of a New Year.

On New Year's Day the Military Reservation was finally announced, in orders, giving to the burial-place of the victims of that great disaster a memorial character, honourable to the courage of the fallen.

A few days after, Brevet Brigadier-General H. W. Wessels, Lieutenant-Colonel of the 18th, a soldier with laurels and a gentleman without blemish, arrived with two companies of cavalry and four companies of infantry, of which one company was to be left at Fort Reno, his former post.

Orders came to remove headquarters to Fort Caspar, and all preparation was duly made. General Dandy, chief quartermaster, with discernment and courtesy, fitted up army wagons for the women and children, and deserves due thanks for our earthly salvation, as that preparation alone secured us a safe deliverance during the trip that ensued.

"*After night cometh the morning,*" and at Crazy Woman's Fork, January 25th, 1867, the order of nature was regularly preserved. We left Fort Philip Kearney at half-past one p.m. of the 23rd, just at the hour fixed. Packing had been done, wagons were loaded, houses had been evacuated for newcomers, and although the snow again began its fantastic drifting and plentiful resupply, the march had to be made, and the extinct road could hardly become more distinct, but possibly even worse.

By ten o'clock at night, by dint of shovelling and picking at proper intervals, nearly six miles had been attained, and the train corralled on a commanding summit to wait for the coming moon.

Lieutenant Bowman had been detailed to command the escort of twenty cavalry and forty infantry as far as Fort Reno, and discharged his trust with unwavering diligence and acceptance.

At one o'clock a.m. the bugle sounded, and just at three o'clock our invaluable guide and scout. Captain Bailey, reported "that himself and moon were ready." The sky had cleared, the stars were brilliant, and the *aurora borealis* faintly endeavoured to show itself and cheer our onward way.

It is picturesque so to travel. Napoleon, it is reported, travelled over snow, but left his family; and the novelty of the movement of officers, their wives and children, and the usual families of band musicians, with their liberal allowance of future trumpeters, flutists, and drummers, gave this march a distinguishing feature not usually credited to that masterly winter trip of Napoleon to Italy by the way of the Alps. The wheels creaked, the mules made their usual vocal sounds at the early disturbance of their feed, and everybody shrunk into clothing as closely as possible to evade the increasing cold.

The thermometer hanging in our wagon allowed the mercury to do its share of shrinkage, and lingered about thirteen degrees below zero, with great apparent hesitation, if not positive reluctance, at being kept out of the bulb. Stalking in front, leading his pony, stamping through drifts and feeling his way, guide Bailey led off with inordinate self-possession, not to say coolness, and soon after daylight we were once more in camp at Clear Fork. Breakfast was soon over, the mules were fed, and the march proceeded. It was the remark of Captain Arnold that it was "*stunning cold*," and before twenty-four hours more were passed it became clearly evident that he had the right idea, and that expression will hereafter be to us not a provincialism of doubtful origin, but a *Simon pure* exponent of that style of cold.

Of course for awhile there was a keen watch for Indians, since as they see everything and know everything, it was just possible that they might envy us our horses, mules, and scalps; but the country was covered with buffalo, who did not even pay us the compliment of being scared, and in fact for twenty-five miles they were never out of view. Their quiet labour in the snow, wallowing and trampling for grass, was also a positive assurance, so said Bailey, that they had no red men in company.

So we ploughed, dug, and plodded on. Before night we were at Crazy Woman's Fork. That any one of the party left it alive, and made the next march, now seems a wonder. The corral was formed in the grove at the bend of the stream, and wood was abundant after digging it out of the snow, but there a wood fire actually lost one-half its virtue. As fast as snow melted and rolled from the billets, which were heaped on as high as a man could reach, the same melted snow turned to ice, and each fire was soon girt about by constantly thickening ice. To stand fronted to the flame, then reversed, and to do this constantly that fearfully long night, was the resort of almost everybody.

Cooking was out of the question. Hatchets broke our bread, and water was sufficiently warmed to thaw the chunks. Slices were not attempted. Thanks to our little stoves, the ladies essayed the luxury of *steeped*, not to say hot coffee, and with partial success. None of the special artists who portrayed the massacre accompanied us, but the picture of an entertainment given to Lieutenant Bowman, escort commander, and Captain Arnold, is still before us.

The general train formed a complete circle, with headquarters wagons in the centre. By every fire were groups bending forward with outstretched hands to gather a little vital warmth. Hopeless of supper, most of the women and children closed themselves up in their wagons, and from each little stove-pipe the white smoke told all night how hopefully they were struggling to worry it through. Children were crying of cold, and men were multiplying expletives. Drivers left their teams, and began to avow that they "never would drive another rod until it was warmer." All at once the colonel and a party of officers approached our wagon and knocked. The door partly opened, and we know how it must have looked as a tin cup suddenly gleaming by the camp-fire was quickly delivered, and its recipient hastened to a blaze to imbibe its contents while yet unfrozen. Then another and another went out in the same careful way, and the door slammed again.

Next, with the same caution, were passed forth bread, with pieces of the last turkey of Fort Phil Kearney, which, having been chopped with the hatchet, had also been softened over the fire, after the coffee had been concocted. As the door opened, we suppose the view must have been about as follows: In the foreground, a lady sitting upon a pile of wood, with feet to the stove, though these were covered with high buffalo boots, her head enveloped in a beaver hood, her form wrapped in linsey-woolsey and buffalo skins, and her hands stirring something like turkey knobs and bread chunks over the stove. In the background, in a perfect nest of wolf skins and beaver, two boys with caps, boots, and coats trimmed with the same material, and pushing themselves as close to that little sheet-iron arrangement as safety and culinary duties would permit; on the right and left a sabre, shotgun, rifle, and revolver, with pendant pails and cooking utensils; at the extreme end, a thermometer, worn out and desolate.

The iron itself seemed jealous of doing any radiation whatever, and some dry pine wood which had been brought with us burned out so quickly, and lost so much courage and efficiency by constant replenishing, that it really was not the fault of the stove, for it could not possibly be heated through between times. It *never was red hot*, and its very top would neither thaw nor toast bread, unless when a kettle let down within had contact with the flame that struggled to do its best.

Lieutenant Wands, with indomitable tact and energy, was everywhere, between the necessary warnings, encouraging drivers, cheering up soldiers, keeping himself alive, and doing good generally. Everybody had some adventure. Mules got mad and broke loose, dashing just where they pleased, as if bound to keep up circulation by constant exercise.

Sometimes a party would be seen coming with a great log, struggling through snow nearly waist deep, and now and then some desperate character would throw himself down, determined to have a sleep if he froze to death. This was of course stopped, and with chattering teeth and aching limbs and benumbed feet, general stamping was resorted to, to keep circulation busy after the manner of the mules.

Mrs. Wands and Mrs. Grummond had the same school of practice in keeping up fires, and little Bobby Wands had the same ambition to burn his buffalo boots as other little boys we know of.

The convenient window in the wagon door, when the frost was scraped off, was a capital place for study of human nature under adverse circumstances; and it is morally certain that any one of those wagons, in the exact condition as then seen, would have been worth to P. T. Barnum the restorative equivalent of his loss in the great fire.

At last the sentry called "one o'clock," and all through camp was repeated, "Good! it's one o'clock!" Some were for having reveille sounded at once; but guide Bailey, who had tried the ascent out of the bottom to the summit, eastward, found that no exit could be had until daylight. It was no doubt a lovely place for Indians, if they had been on that bluff, but they were not; and but for the shelter of the hill no living creature could have withstood the exposure.

From one o'clock to three, each hour was called, and at three the thermometer gave out entirely. The mercury settled in the bulb, froze itself stiff, and treated that sheet-iron stove with outrageous contempt.

Forty below zero! and the night dragged its hours so slowly! By four o'clock patience gave out also. Do or die was the impulse of all, and the slow work of getting frozen hands to put on frozen harness began, or rather such a thing was ordered to be done. Whether the teamsters thought the bugle summons was the thawing out of an old call, as once happened in the experience of the celebrated traveller Baron Munchausen, or they were too nearly frozen to appreciate their import, is not certain; but call after call failed to get them from their fires, until a verbal order, concise and to the point, promised all to be left behind, without wagon or rations, that were not ready to start punctually at six.

With the dawn came the report of the sad work of the night. Assistant Surgeon Hines had the fingers of both hands frozen, and they were already quite black; while many teamsters and nearly half of the escort were more or less frozen, some of them requiring amputations as soon as we reached Fort Reno.

With great difficulty, by the assistance of those comparatively uninjured, and the exercise of the positive authority of the officers, the train was at last ready. From the bottom land there was a sharp rise of nearly sixty feet to the bluff, and the first teams that tried it, even after the drifts had been shovelled away, repeatedly fell for want of foothold, and back came loaded wagons, dragging the kicking, tangled mules with them. Details of men took charge of the wheels, whips on either side, and ropes ahead, gave additional impulse; and in three hours the entire train had successfully passed the first sixteenth of a mile out of twenty-six to be made to Reno.

Just as the last wagons were buried in a deep cut, half a mile from the river, the alarm of "Indians" was given. A messenger came and reported that the rear was attacked. Teams were put to the gallop, the train was closed up, half frozen men in the wagons took their arms, and Lieutenant Wands, with a mounted party, dashed back to bring up the rear, and ascertain the facts. All proved a false alarm; but an hour was lost.

Fortunately the day was still and clear. The glare of the sun was at times blinding; but the goggles, which on the plains are used both against snow-blindness and dust, enabled all to get along tolerably well. Buffalo kept us company until within a few miles of Reno. Messengers were sent on in advance, and at dusk we safely passed its gates, and received at the hands of Captain Proctor, Adjutant Kirtland, and other officers, not only quarters, but all creature comforts for the whole party. Such was the first sixty-five miles march returning from Absaraka. Such were three days of our second winter on the plains. If we claim no special credit for endurance, and have never questioned the necessity of such a march at such a season, certainly, like good wives, we followed wherever led, and we do not envy any officer's wife, of however long experience, her claim to have had a harder trip after such a summer. Perhaps some have. Ours was ample for us.

It is now like a dream, when it comes to mind, that nearly one-half of more than fifty demonstrations of hostile Indians in the Mountain District were under the very eyes of the ladies of the garrison and their children. The lesson is not forgotten, as we no less recall the Mercy that spared us. Nor does a single sentiment of complaint or reflection upon the Indians, the *weather*, or anybody else, have its place in our recollections of the past. It was our impulse and duty to go, and we went. No regrets are entertained; but sometimes it seems that we should have had more enjoyment and quiet had there been more men along, and that the Indians would have treated larger numbers with greater respect; and sometimes it seems very strange that that trip to Fort Caspar, just then, was such a matter of life or death to the nation, as to make it a question of life or death to us.

CHAPTER 28

Fort Reno to Fort Caspar—Thence to the United States

Nearly three days were spent at Reno changing the infantry escort and providing for those who suffered. Lieutenant Jacobs, son of Dr. Jacobs, an old friend, at our birthplace, Danville, Kentucky, was its commander.

Our days' marches were *forced*, as far as snow would permit, and were—1st, Dry Fork of the Cheyenne; 2nd, "Wind River; 3rd, Brown Springs, four miles east of the South Fork of the Cheyenne; 4th, the North Platte, near mouth of Sage Creek; 5th, Deer Creek Station, burned by Indians in 1865; and 6th, to Caspar. Indians had kept out of sight, and the headquarters of the 18th were again approaching a home. Lieutenant Wands, guide Bailey, and others rode forward, to give notice of our speedy arrival; when, all at once, we found our ambulance closed in by others, and upon looking out discovered the whole train on a trot, in column of six wagons front, and thus moving all in mass. The quick passing of an orderly was all that had been noticed, and without the sound of a bugle or other warning we found ourselves preparing for Indians, only six miles from Caspar. A party of red men had passed between the train and those who with Lieutenant Wands had gone in advance, and galloping close up to the telegraph office, had run off the stock of the horses just after the officers had dismounted at the fort.

The colonel, who was riding along a ridge somewhat in advance, recognized a mounted party crossing the Platte to be Indians, closed up the train and moved on; but pursuit was hopeless, as the Indians had seen the escort turn the hill in full view, and were nearly across the Platte three miles distant when discovered.

Soon we were met by Brevet Major Norris, a friend of old times, with his company of the 2nd Cavalry, and returned with him to post, where he had already anticipated our wants. Here also Brevet Major Morris, Captain Freeman and wife, and Lieutenant Carpenter, all old officers of the 18th, competed in their welcomes, with other officers previously unknown, to us all. Here also, to our great delight, we met Mrs. Potter and her husband, the new adjutant of the regiment, who, after long service as acting assistant adjutant-general during the war, and as commandant of the District of Utah, while colonel of the 6th U. S. Volunteers, had been appointed to the 18th Infantry and at once placed on the staff. Mrs. Potter and little Carroll had just arrived from Laramie upon advices of change of headquarters.

The first thing done was to disencumber ourselves of blankets and furs. The next, was to open our eyes as Lieutenant Wands inquired where most would we prefer to go rather than remain at Caspar, the most barren and insignificant post on the plains. The apparent joke as to *preference* was earnest of a welcome fact; for sure enough. General Augur, upon assuming command at Omaha, had changed the headquarters station to McPherson, and thus we at once began to prepare ourselves to double our track to Sage Creek and extend our winter's march over the path of 1866, and within ninety-seven miles of old Kearney. Orders had miscarried, or the trip to Caspar would have been spared us.

The next day Captain Kellogg of the 18th, with his most estimable and lovely wife, arrived, and the associations of olden times were agreeably renewed.

Goodbyes quickly followed, and with Brevet Major Morris of the 18th in charge of the new escort we were again on the way. The second day we reached the North Platte again, where Lieutenant Jacobs, who had now to return to Reno, bade his farewell, leaving pleasant memories of his courtesies as a gentleman and efficiency in charge of the escort.

Before stopping, on the sixth day of February, the colonel had the misfortune to be accidentally shot while riding rapidly to close up the train, by the discharge of his revolver, which had been badly repaired at Caspar, the ball entering the scarpal space, grazing both femoral artery and sciatic nerve, following the bone around to the outside of the limb, where it lodged. Instead of returning to Caspar, he ordered the train crowded forward to Laramie, and at noon of Saturday, the ninth of February, the corral was formed in the Laramie River bottom near the post.

The whole-hearted Mr. Bullock threw open his house, and, with Surgeon Shell, heaped upon the party that remained for twelve days with the colonel every comfort and attention that home itself could have furnished. The second day heavy snow fell, and the last of headquarters did not reach Fort McPherson until March 2nd) although Adjutant Potter and Quartermaster Wands, with their families and part of the baggage, were sent a few days in advance. The trip from Laramie was without escort, none being attainable, although there had been an outrage perpetrated but a few days before between the post and Fort Mitchell; still, no danger was apprehended. The ride of fifty-three miles to the latter post was made in one day; and two or three days of rest passed delightfully, as Captain Hughes of the 18th, and Assistant Surgeon Cunningham, nephew of Lieutenant-General Cunningham of the British Army, were our excellent and willing entertainers. They had given the same cordial greeting to the advance train, and thus Reno, Caspar, and Mitchell had alike kept up that old army hospitality which was once its pride and is the essential and redeeming feature of its isolated social life.

Scott's Bluffs, Fortification Rocks, Chimney Rock, and Courthouse Rock, had a different language as they rose before us, cold and snow-clad; but even winter could impart no more gloom to their barren features; and the same cedars peeped through the snow that had dotted the sterile sides and *cañons* in the heat of summer.

Captain Neil, Dr. Latham, Mr. Adams and wife, and young Janney, of Columbus, Ohio, were still at Sedgwick, but otherwise few *old* friends were met. Brevet Lieutenant- Colonel Dodge of the 30th Infantry, which was in camp across the river, and Lieutenant Bennett also called. The sight of a full regiment reminded us how constantly General Wessels and the upper garrisons were watching daily for their arrival, and how long we had lived in the same expectancy.

The Platte was crossed on the ice; but it would hardly have been the fair thing to have passed it without recognition, so our ambulance broke through a few times, and three or four little scares were undergone for old acquaintance sake.

From Fort Sedgwick to Fort McPherson the drifting sands of summer had been overshadowed by the deep and drifting snows of winter; but with Valentine and Baker and Morrow to yield their best for our physical necessities, the journey soon came to an end.

We had been to Absaraka and back again! All phases of life, all eccentricities of climate and temperature, all grades of exposure and danger, and intercourse with all styles of human nature had been experienced or encountered.

Fort McPherson became home for a time. Here were some reminders of old times, as the spring of 1867 brought Indian depredations to the very vicinity. Here, too, were Indian councils, Indian visits, and Indian promises. Here, too, the Special Indian Commission spent a month in seeking interviews with the Ogillallas and Brulè Sioux of the Republican, and taking the testimony of Colonel Carrington as to the facts concerning Fetterman's massacre.

Here, too, a court of inquiry met to take testimony, and we had the pleasure of again meeting Captains Haymond and Phisterer, who left Fort Phil Kearney, August 1st, 1866, and had been summoned from Pittsburg and New York as witnesses respecting the affair of December 21st following their departure.

Here, also, were visits from Generals Sherman, Augur, and Custer; and here, also. Spotted Tail, Standing Elk, Swift Bear, Two Strike, Pawnee Killer, The Whistler, Long Bull, The Man that walks under the Ground, Joe Smith, Sharp Nose, and The White Antelope had talks, and gave pledges of friendship.

Here, also, the courtesy of Brevet Lieutenant-Colonel Mizner, of the 2nd Cavalry, and his wife, and the officers of his command, and the sisterly welcome of Mrs. Potter made our arrival pleasant and our stay delightful, crowning with something like the amenities of old-fashion times in the States, our return from Absaraka, Home of the Crows.

But changes still occurred! Mr. Wands had been transferred to the 36th Infantry, and with his family soon returned westward again. Lieutenant Brent succeeded him as regimental quartermaster. Colonel Mizner took his turn to visit the Indian country farther west, and his accomplished wife anticipated our own trip eastward a few weeks. As at the outset so at the close of our trip across the plains and back again, the same kind Providence guided and guarded our footsteps, and more than ever brought home to the soul the sweet assurance of his presence

Wherever we wander,
Wherever we roam.

CHAPTER 29

In Memoriam

The dead of 1866, in the occupation of Absaraka, were those who were worthy. Officers and men alike had done duty well, and the majority had an honourable record before they engaged a new enemy in a new country.

Brevet Lieutenant-Colonel William J. Fetterman, son of Captain George Fetterman, deceased, an old army officer, was born in garrison, and was instinct with the ambition of a soldier.

He was appointed a lieutenant in the 18th United States Infantry in May, 1861, and joined the regimental headquarters almost immediately. In the School of Instruction for officers, organized by the colonel of the regiment in July, 1861, he was ambitious and proficient, and in his duties as recruiting officer in Ohio realized substantial success, while, no less, commanding esteem by his refinement, gentlemanly manners, and adaptation to social life.

After he accompanied the regiment to the field, and when the changes incident to the war had placed the field officers of the regiment on detached duty, as generals of volunteers, Captain Fetterman commanded the detachment, and earned the reputation of being a brave soldier.

His return to the regiment in November, 1866, had been sought, and no less looked for with glad anticipation, as officers were so few, and his social and professional character alike made him a favourite.

As the senior officer serving with the 2nd Battalion, just taking the new style of the 27th Infantry, it was naturally expected that he would take command of it whenever the colonel should join the 1st Battalion, which was to retain the old number, but had its companies on the lower route.

That he was impatient because Indians were not summarily punished, and permitted this feeling and contempt of the enemy to drive him to hopeless ruin, where a simple deference to the orders and known policy of his commander, and still higher authority would have brought no loss of life whatever, is matter of history; yet, such was the esteem entertained for him by his colonel and many friends, that as the grave received his remains, and the battlefield evinced the vigour of his desperate defence, no bitter reflections mingle with the necessity of rendering equal justice to the living.

In the prime of manhood and the pride of a noble spirit, he reached forth for laurels that were beyond his reach; and with all the support that human energy and quick haste could furnish, the error could not be retrieved, and his brief Indian campaign and life closed together, when he had just reached his new field of labour, inexperienced in its methods and contingencies, and incurring the saddest penalty for neglect of the experience of others.

In life he was a gentleman. In death he was mourned and honoured.

Captain Frederick H. Brown, enlisted in the 18th Infantry at Columbus, Ohio, was at once appointed a sergeant at regimental headquarters, and then quartermaster sergeant. Among the first appointments from the ranks, under the then existing law requiring the colonel to fill the vacancies of second lieutenant, Mr. Brown was second. He was almost immediately appointed regimental quartermaster and commissary, as his antecedent experience in the commission business at Toledo had peculiarly fitted him for such duty. This office, in the field and out of it, he filled until promoted captain, late in 1866, when he received orders to join his company at Fort Laramie.

He had become so attached to the country about Fort Philip Kearney, and so enthused by his purpose to take the scalp of "Red Cloud," that Indian skirmishing fastened itself upon his nature with the hold of some constitutional disease.

With it all he felt a deep sense of neglect that the flood of brevets which rolled over the regiment omitted his name; and when one officer was breveted for services in the Atlanta campaign, although, during the whole period, that officer was at the North, and others had honours for similar erroneously designated services, he became impatient, eager, and reckless.

His intimacy in the family of the writer brought forth frequent sketches of his history and disappointments; and while he could cheerfully accept and reason upon the circumstances of the command, and intellectually recognize the impossibility of doing more than was being done to punish the savages, his restless spirit would hardly let him fill up the measure of his necessary duty, so set was his purpose to do some service that would command the recognition of his six years' of connection with the 18th Infantry.

On the night before his death, already adverted to, when he called, equipped for immediate duty, and at a time of the evening when there was no show for service, he was peculiarly earnest in his regret that he must leave without "Red Cloud's" scalp. He asked for the colonel, and said "he wished they would hurry up reinforcements. He was going to have one more fight if he had to work night and day to finish his papers." He adverted to the colonel's refusal to permit himself and Captain Fetterman to go to Tongue River valley on a trip with the mounted men, and said "he knew it was impossible, but he just felt that he could kill a dozen himself."

Those who knew Captain Brown, or, as all the officers styled him, "Fred," know how he overflowed with genial humour, and interested himself in whatever imparted social life to the march, or garrison life. His relation of an Indian skirmish on the 23rd of September was frequent; and just before his death he made up its history, which he said "showed one good fight he had with the rascals."

That *his* impulses led Brevet Lieutenant-Colonel Fetterman to disobey orders on the 21st of December, at the sacrifice of the whole detachment, is not questioned; and yet we have no heart for blame when the strength of his friendship, his pride in his regiment, his disappointment as to honourable mention, and his brave but false estimate of the spirit of the Indian, challenge so much of our regard as memory brings him back to us, as when we parted but a few hours before he left earth's scenes forever. He said "he would always keep a shot for himself;" and doubtless thereby saved himself from torture.

Lieutenant George W. Grummond, who fell in the same memorable slaughter, had achieved success in the war with the rebellion as captain and field officer of Michigan volunteers, and was understood to have been breveted brigadier-general of volunteers before he ceased his connection with the Army of the Cumberland. Our narrative has shown how narrow was his escape on the 6th of December; and the sketch of Fetterman's massacre shows how closely he obeyed his orders to remain with Captain Fetterman. His ambition prompted him to volunteer to accompany that party, and the fact that his remains were found with those of Sergeant Lang and a few others, more than a quarter of a mile in advance of the other dead, indicates that he either was covering the retreat or was disabled and killed in a gallant defence. He had a soldier's spirit, and in social relations was genial and already esteemed by all. He alone, of the fallen, left a widow to mourn his loss, and his remains returned with her to Tennessee, where they received their final burial.

CHAPTER 30

Omaha to Virginia City, Montana

The foregoing narrative has given the distances for the best *day-by-day* marches, and such facts as to wood, grass, and water as are of practical value along the route from the Union Pacific Railroad to Fort Philip Kearney.

The westward-bound traveller will find at Omaha such extensive supplies of merchandise and outfit, at the establishments of W. R. King & Co., Jewett & Ely, John M. McCormick & Co., Hurfords, Lehmen & Co., Stephens and Wilcox, C. F. Catlin, S. & A. B. Saunders, and fifty other grocery, hardware, dry goods, and stationery houses, that he will find himself not a whit at loss if he has reached that city without much antecedent outlay; while the Union Pacific Railroad regularly transports its burdens beyond the first spur of the Rocky Mountains, passing *en route* the wagon departure at Horse Shoe Creek, and again at Cheyenne, affording a comparatively easy route to Laramie and points beyond.

To those who travel with their own wagons and substance, this narrative gives many hints; but the whole line from Leavenworth, or Nebraska City, on the south side of the Platte, has been temporarily impaired by the Indian encroachments, the westward tide of travel, and the natural laws of that advance. With no affectation of scientific research more than to collect such botanical, floral, and geological specimens as the circumstances of the march would permit and a natural taste for such study would prompt, our information from competent sources, in company, sets forth Southern and Middle Nebraska as full of promise. The beautiful farming lands back of Omaha will find their contesting claimants; while salt, building material, and indications of coal show that the State is capable of expansion and self-support with little extrinsic aid.

Beyond Nebraska, and apart from the accommodations of the Union Pacific Railroad, the ox and mule teams still hold supremacy, and for their benefit some further information is given.

The trip of Major James Bridger and guide Henry Williams in 1866, who were sent forward by Colonel Carrington to visit the authorities of Montana and survey the route, or shorten it and open a new route, furnishes many facts additional to those contained in the report of Colonel Sawyer, and their notes, somewhat abridged, are by permission freely used for our present purpose, with the confidence that this will always be an avenue for travel, though interrupted in the settlement of Indian questions for a time.

The following statement closely approximates the odometer measurement of General Hazen in 1866, and while this is twenty miles less than Colonel Sawyer's route, the course of travel adopted by Major Bridger confirms his opinion that nearly thirty miles more can be saved as soon as the government or emigration can safely operate and improve the road:

Fort Philip Kearney to Fort C. F. Smith	91 miles.
Fort C. F. Smith to Clarke's Fork	63 "
Clarke's Fork to Yellowstone Ferry	90 "
Yellowstone Ferry to Bozeman City	51 "
Bozeman City to Virginia City	70 "
Total	365 miles.

The first distance is divisible as follows:

Fort Philip Kearney to Peno Creek Branch	5 miles.
To N. Bank of Peno Creek, with timber, grass, and water	7 "
To Second Crossing of Peno Creek, with same supplies	6 "
To Crossing of Goose Creek, with same supplies	4 "
To Brown's Fork of Tongue River, with same supplies	13 "
To East Fork of Little Horn River, with same supplies	17 "
To Grass Lodge Creek, with same supplies	15 "
To Rotten Grass Creek, with same supplies	16 "
To Fort C. F. Smith, Bridger's Cut-off.	8 "
Total	91 miles

Between Tongue River and Little Horn River eight forks are crossed, the largest of which, "Colonel Kinney's Fork," is quite a stream of clear water, with nearly two feet of depth in the autumn.

Between Little Horn and Big Horn Rivers are nine small streams of constant water.

The Big Horn River is nearly three hundred and thirty yards wide, with from three to six feet of water, and is crossed by a substantial ferry. In 1866 Kirkendall's train lost a wagonmaster by attempting to ford it; but it can be forded, with some little risk to stock and merchandise, at a low stage of water. It is unsafe for strangers, and the ferry is indispensable to general travel.

Fort C. F. Smith, on the Big Horn River, was built by Brevet Lieutenant-Colonel N. C. Kinney, Captain of the 18th Infantry in 1866, and suffered less from Indian adventures on account of the vicinity of the friendly Crow Indians, and because it was west of the main hunting-ground of the Arrapahoes, Cheyennes, and Sioux. It is the last residence of white men until the traveller reaches Bozeman City.

Associated with Captain Kinney in the building of Fort C. F. Smith, and with wonderful vigour and patience resisting the effect of wounds and apprehended heart disease, should be mentioned Brevet Major Thomas B. Burrows. His father is well known as the veteran friend of education in Pennsylvania.

The second distance, before referred to, is divisible as follows:

From Fort C. F. Smith to Dubois Creek, a fork of Beauvàis Fork of Big Horn River, N.W. by N. 10 miles.
This stream is about fifteen feet wide. Road good except the crossings of two small creeks, and distant from the mountains about seven miles. The timber is ash and box elder.

To North Fork of Dubois Creek, N.W. by N 10 miles.
Road crosses small creeks and ravines, and is quite bad. The stream is narrow, and eight miles from the mountains. Grass good, and timber for fuel.

To South Fork of Prior's River, N.W 8 miles.
Road passes one long canon, cutting the divide between Big Horn and Rocky Ranges, crossing several creeks, and in places quite rough. Grass good.

To Ice Water Spring, N.W. by N 15 miles.
At four miles is water in a small branch. At five miles farther is Millard's Spring, with good grass and water. This spring rises and flows from a high, level prairie, four miles from the base

of the mountains, forming a branch of Prior's River, three feet wide and twelve inches deep. At six miles farther comes Ice Water Spring, with good grass, but no timber, although at Prior's River, two miles beyond, the timber is abundant. Road is in many places quite rocky. Ice Water Springs rise from a mound in the prairie, supplying four small streams which unite in a channel six feet wide and three feet deep, flowing with great rapidity.

To Spring Creek, W.N.W   8 miles.
Road crosses Prior River and its four miles of beautiful valley, thence up the valley of Spring Creek, or North Fork of Prior's River. Here are many steep bluffs until the road attains the summit of the divide between Prior's River and Clark's Fork, Grass excellent. Only sufficient timber for fuel.

To Clark's Fork, nearly W   12 miles.
The road is good, and all prairie except two dry creek-crossings, which are not decidedly bad. Clark's Fork is here nearly one hundred yards wide, with a rich valley and abundance of grass and timber.

                               Total   63 miles.

The third distance is divisible as follows:

To Rocky Fork   7 miles.
This stream is forty-five yards wide, about three feet deep, with good ford. Luxuriant timber and grass. Ten miles from the mountains.

To Berdan's Creek—Branch of Rocky Fork   12 miles.
Rocky Fork is crossed twice. Good camping-grounds are found every three miles. Grass and timber abundant.

To South Fork of Rosebud   10 miles.
Three miles up Berdan's Creek. Road rough until the main divide is reached, between this creek and the South Fork of Rosebud. Stream about fifteen feet wide and two feet deep, abounding in beaver dams. Grass good; but only sufficient timber for fuel. Road runs six miles from mountains.

To Rosebud River Camp   8 miles.
Down South Fork of Rosebud one mile; thence crossing a di-

vide of three miles. Rosebud is nearly twenty-five yards wide and two and one-half feet deep. Cottonwood and willow timber is plentiful, and grass good. Thence down Rosebud four miles to best camp. About ten miles from the mountains.

To Stillwater, W.S.W　　　　　　　　　　　　　　6 miles.
Road crosses the main Rosebud and follows up Stillwater Fork of Rosebud. Road good, timber heavy, and grass good. Stream is about sixty-five yards wide, three feet deep, and quite a rocky ford. About six miles from the mountains.

To Emmil's Fork　　　　　　　　　　　　　　　　18 miles.
The road runs W.S.W., to North Fork of the Stillwater. Grass and timber very heavy, and camping-grounds every three miles. One divide is crossed before reaching Emmil's Fork, which here empties into the Yellowstone River. Emmil's Fork, named from the massacre of Emmil's party, in 1822, is about twenty feet wide and eighteen inches deep. The Yellowstone is here about one hundred and twenty yards wide and from three to five feet deep. The valley is from six to fifteen miles wide, and timber is very heavy.

To Big Boulder Creek　　　　　　　　　　　　　17 miles.
Eight miles up Yellowstone valley, crossing "Lower Cross Creek" at five miles, and "Upper or Big Cross Creek" three miles beyond. Road, grass, and timber good; thence the road is over level prairie nine miles, with abundance of grass and timber.

To Yellowstone Ferry　　　　　　　　　　　　　12 miles.
Road good. Timber is mostly on the north bank. The ferry is diagonally across the river, of nearly two hundred and seventy-five yards.

　　　　　　　　　　　Total　　　　　　　　90 miles.

The fourth distance is divisible as follows:

Yellowstone Ferry to Warm Spring, S.W　　　　4½ miles.
Up the Yellowstone River, after crossing, four and a half miles. Road here bears west toward the hills, becoming very heavy, and crossing a succession of small creeks and ravines.

To Twenty-five Yard River　　　　　　　　　　10½ miles.
Southwest five miles across the ridge to the Yellowstone. Road

difficult, crossing sidling hills. Up the valley two miles to foot of "Big Hill." Across the ridge, with better road, 3½ miles. This river derives its name from its width. Plenty of young timber, and grass good.

To Beaver or Pass Creek   17 miles.
Road runs S.W. by S. Road for ten miles very good, until leaving the river and entering the pass called Flat Head or Clarke's Pass. The last eight miles crosses a number of spring creeks, which flow from the snow range. No timber in this pass, except small pine and aspen.

To Cold Spring Creek   10 miles.
Up Beaver or Pass Creek. Road very rough. Grass good. Timber in abundance, of small varieties of pine and aspen.

To Head-waters, Cold Spring Creek   5 miles.
Road crosses the divide to the east Branch of Gallatin River. Timber largely destroyed by fire several years ago.

To Bozeman City   4 miles.
Down the East Gallatin River. Here is a successful flour-mill, and a small but thrifty village.

                          Total   51 miles.

The fifth distance is divisible as follows. Road adopted in 1866:

To Madison River   33 miles.
Southwest to West Gallatin River thirteen miles. Road runs across the valley, which is twelve miles, and nearly all occupied by farms, with abundance of grass, and well watered by small streams from the mountains. This river is about one hundred and fifty yards wide, and from two to two and one-half feet deep, very swift, with a heavy growth of cottonwood timber. Thence, southwest by south, nearly twenty miles across the dividing ridge to the Madison River. Road good; grass abundant; but little timber near the road.

To Meadow Creek   21 miles.
Road crosses Madison River. This river is nearly two hundred yards wide and three feet deep. Thence up the stream five miles, westward up a *cañon* four miles, to main divide of Hot Spring valley. This spring boils up vigorously, and with temperature

unpleasant to the hand. Near are the first quartz leads. The road is good, but rough. Thence south, across the divide, to Meadow Creek, twelve miles.

To Virginia City—by cut-off	16 miles.
The usual road is twenty-two miles.	
Total	70 miles.

Aggregate distances 365 miles.

CHAPTER 31

Indian Affairs on the Plains— Incidents of 1865-7

The entire history of the relations between the United States and the Indian tribes of the Northwest, during the last twelve years, (as at time of first publication), has been affected by the mistakes of 1866. The massacre of that year was the direct fruit of scant treaties and violated law, and succeeding bloodshed has been the natural result of efforts made to settle the habitation and status of the Indians who at that time were recognized as rightful occupants of Dacotah.

The reports and documents as to this period are voluminous and exhaustive. During the winter of 1865-6 the Indians were comparatively quiet. During October, Generals Harney and Sanborn made a treaty, at the mouth of the Little Arkansas, assigning to the Cheyennes and Arrapahoes a new reservation, partly in southern Kansas and partly in the Indian Territory. This was designed to remove them from the vicinity of Colorado; but the treaty "permitted them to reside upon, and range at pleasure through, the unsettled portions of that part of the country which lay between the Arkansas and Platte Rivers," and which they claimed as their own. This treaty accomplished nearly as much for peace as had the presence of the large force of volunteers then scattered over the plains.

The Minnesota war also ended, and the chief question for consideration was that of protecting overland travel, and securing a route for the proposed Union Pacific Railroad.

General Curtis wrote from Fort Sully, May 30th, 1866, that the proposed "Cheyenne and Black Hills" expedition had been abandoned, adding, "There may be some bitter complaints of this interference with the desire of our frontier men to spread over all parts of the Indian country, but justice and humanity will be advanced by this change of orders."

General Pope, whose Department included Minnesota, Iowa, Missouri, Kansas, Dacotah, Montana, Nebraska, Colorado, Utah, and New Mexico, wrote in February: "At present there is almost a general pacification in the Indian country within this department." Of the Omaha, Atcheson, and Leavenworth routes, converging at Fort Kearney, he says, "All these are safe to travel, even in small parties." In treating generally of western emigration, he uses the following terms:

> What right under our treaties with Indians have we to be roaming over the whole mining territory, as well as the plains to the east of them, molesting the Indians, in violation of treaties and right, which we solemnly pledged ourselves to prevent? How can we expect the Indian to observe a treaty which he sees us violate every day, to his injury? How can the Indian keep peace under such circumstances? We promised to protect him from our people, and do not fulfil our promise. He is forced to protect himself, and tempted every day by the careless and irregular manner in which parties of whites travel through the territory, to do as the whites do,—seize, whenever he can, anything he covets. The Indian cannot keep peace, even if he would.

The marching of Indian Commissioners with long wagon-trains of presents, the widely heralded assurance that thousands of red men would assemble at Laramie to establish definite terms of permanent peace alike induced quiet on the border and faith in good results. The treaty movement was right, and the Indians assembled in good faith, for a conference on equal terms; but that treaty did not cover the real issue at stake.

Fetterman's massacre, near Fort Phil Kearney, at once aroused the entire Indian population from the Arkansas line to the upper Missouri, and precipitated into hostility toward the whites, many bands or tribes which, at most, would only have robbed in small parties but for the stimulus of that carnage. All military reports of that period recognize this fact. It does not seem to have been understood that the Laramie treaty of 1866 affected and sought to reach Indians who were accustomed to roam south, as well as north, and that every tribe, there represented, had some members who did not assent to its terms, and who, in fact, sympathized with Red Cloud when he withdrew the young men from the conference to go upon the war-path. It is equally important to realize that *chiefs* are simply "braves," who control by virtue of their superior merit and will; that the union of bands in single tribes is very loose, unless against a common foe, and that they are to be caught, or approached and tamed, separately.

Because one band is either hostile or friendly is not the assurance of the temper of the next band in order. Hence war, except against Indians armed for war, or committed to war, only develops *more* war, distrust, and failure. There was more of truth than passion in the words of Sitting Bull in 1877: "*When you find a white man who will not lie, you may come back to me.*" And there was truth in the statement of General Sherman, "that every locality wanted a force at its command equal to resist the Indians of the whole Northwest," It is equally true that ranchmen, squatters, half-breeds, and trappers were reckless in robbing red men, but howled for protection if the Indian took his own property back.

The period covered by the narrative, in this volume, will be still better understood by a fuller statement of the facts which immediately preceded and followed the expedition of May, 1866. The writer took command of old Fort Kearney, Nebraska, late in 1865, and of the East Sub-District of Nebraska, in February, 1866. The 18th U. S. Infantry was the only Regular Army regiment which could be placed on the frontier. One battalion was sent on the Fort Riley route, and the third was on recruiting service. The 7th Iowa, 10th Ohio, 12th Missouri, 1st Nebraska, and 2nd West Virginia Regiments were clamorous "to return to their homes before corn-planting."

The 6th and 7th U. S. Volunteers were still on the plains; but as they had been paroled during the civil war, for temporary service on the frontier, they demanded their discharge when the civil war ended. The Union Pacific Railroad was still a future enterprise, and the border States, having in mind the *Report of Colonel Sawyer's Trip in 1864-5*, were urgent that a wagon-road should be immediately laid out around the Big Horn Range to Virginia City. By reference to chapter 5 of the narrative, it will be seen that the Niobrara route was also to be kept open and a fort built at foot of the Cheyenne Black Hills. Along the Platte River there was comparative quiet.

The Plum Creek and Julesburg raids, and Chivington's more frightful slaughter of defenceless Indians were still fresh in mind, but hostile operations were confined to the movements of small bands, who ran off stock, imposed upon a ranch, or robbed a defenceless train. During the winter of 1865-6 and the ensuing spring, the small force, then disposable, was sufficient to prevent incursions and guard the emigrant trains which almost daily passed westward.

Under direction of the government a careful survey of the Platte River was made in March, 1866, with view to a proposed bridge-crossing for the Union Pacific Railroad at Fort Kearney. Scouting-parties visited the Republican and its forks, and brought back an actual detailed account of the timber which could be used for bridge-piles, without encountering an Indian or crossing a fresh trail.

A large body of Pawnees, of various bands, headed by Pe-ta-la-sha-ra (Chowee) visited the post, left their squaws upon the islands of the Platte, to tan beaver-skins in peace, and made a protracted buffalo-hunt on the Republican, without contact with hostile Sioux or Cheyennes. In view of past raids, and the proposed discharge of so many volunteers, it was deemed necessary to supplement the small force on the overland stage-routes, by calling Pawnees, fast foes of the Sioux, into the United States service. A battalion of four companies, under Major North, was mustered in, and notwithstanding the ludicrous tableau presented, when four hundred Indians sat erect in McClelland saddles, clothed in full uniform, cap and ostrich feather included, and armed with carbine, revolver, hatchet, knife, etc., it did look warlike, because the men could easily strip, for real work, and they would fight Sioux as a matter of luxury.

The winter passed quietly. The proposed Montana expedition was organized, and fulfilled its destiny, as detailed in Mrs. Carrington's narrative; and the careful reader of its quiet paragraphs will find many suggestions which, in the light of subsequent history, reflect much light upon the merits of that enterprise.

It is a matter of history that neither General Pope, who ordered the expedition, nor General Sherman, who believed that it would ensure a safe emigrant route to Montana, had been furnished with, or knew of, the old treaties as to that particular country which it would violate; neither had it been clearly announced that the success of the proposed Laramie conference would hinge upon a cheerful modification, or the faithful execution of those treaties. In urging the retention of the belt between the Arkansas and Platte Rivers for public transit. General Sherman expressly made the condition, "that it did not violate some one of the solemn treaties made with those Indians, who are very captions, and claim to the very letter the execution on our part of those treaties, the obligations of which they know so perfectly."

It must also be borne in mind that the Conner expedition of 1865,

La-Hic-Ta-Pa-La-Sha.
Pipe Chief—Pawnee.

and the first establishment of the Powder River post, Fort Reno, was a committal of the government to the occupation of territory which had yet to be acquired by the United States; and that this involved the necessity of increasing the military force upon the Plains beyond the demands of ordinary times.

It was true that small bodies of emigrants occasionally suffered, but no less true that judiciously organized trains passed safely, and that no widespread combination of tribes was realized until the forced occupation of the Big Horn country introduced a costly and protracted war. The Indian was assailed in his last covert, on the only soil where game remained, and it was understood by him to be, as it was in fact, his final struggle for independence and self-support, after the manner of his fathers.

With this glance at the circumstances under which the military occupation of that country was initiated, there is to be associated the state of affairs which existed along the Platte, and thence southward, across the Republican, during the spring and summer of 1867, shortly after the massacre.

The Union Pacific Railroad was in progress of construction at the rate of from two to three miles a day, and its protection became the chief employment of troops. Regimental headquarters of the 18th Infantry were at Fort McPherson, with a garrison of Battery C, 3rd U. S. Artillery, and Company D, 2nd U. S. Cavalry. Small parties of Indians would steal stock or annoy working-parties, but the chief active hostility was along the posts of the lower line, and in the valley of the Republican. This valley was hunted over indiscriminately by Cheyennes and Sioux, and equally by Indians who were friendly and those who were hostile to the whites. The policy of the post commander, as enjoined by Generals Sherman and Augur, was to persuade all who had in good faith signed the treaty at Laramie to go north of the Platte, so that hostile Indians could be dealt with by themselves.

In chapter 28 of the narrative of this volume, the visits of Generals Sherman, Augur, and Custer, and of many noted Indian chiefs, are briefly noticed. General Custer, in *Life on the Plains*,[1] and in *The Galaxy* magazine for May and June, 1872, also mentions his halt near Fort McPherson. Much light is cast upon subsequent military movements by reference to the details of conferences held with Indians at that post, during May and June, 1867, including one at which General

---

1. *My Life on the Plains or Personal Experiences With Indians* by George A. Custer also published by Leonaur.

PE-TA-LA-SHA-RA.
PAWNEE CHIEF—CHOWEE BAND.

Custer was present.

"Spotted Tail," "Standing Elk," and other Brulè and Ogallalla chiefs, came with a large number of braves and their families to give assurance of the good faith with which they kept the pledges made at Laramie, and to accept a home and support. These were assigned to Brady's Island, near the post, as a rendezvous, and General Augur promptly sent a month's rations from Omaha, in addition to those furnished from the fort. The name of Spotted Tail has become so celebrated for his loyalty to obligation and his exceptional respect for his Indian wife, that their portraits are given, as well as some incidents connected with their visit. He was taken upon an engine at North Platte station, then just established, and was whisked by his camp of wondering people at a speed of nearly thirty miles an hour, as if some iron monster was running away with their chief. He looked at a watch, held in the hand of the accompanying officer, then at the driving-wheels, then made the motion of shooting an arrow, and then relaxed into his commonplace acceptance of the facts.

At one interview, when pipes had done all possible soothing, and all were ready to talk, powder was asked for. When told that the Great Chief at St. Louis must first consent, he counted the estimated days of delay with grunts of unqualified disfavour. The quick use of the telegraph in his presence, and a quick answer, restored his kind demeanour, and taught him a little of the white man's craft. On one occasion a thousand rations were issued, and in an hour the *sugar* had disappeared. Around the pile of bacon, flour, beans and hominy, a circle of nearly fifty old women danced, and their song of thanksgiving, as with shrill screams and distorted faces they whirled and leaped and swung their bodies, was more as one might imagine the rejoicings of fiends over some fresh soul lost, than as the expression of grateful hearts; and the horrid shrieks could only have been more thrilling if they had been a formal prelude to the scalping of their honoured host.

Spotted Tail manifested profound respect for his wife. When, with others of the band, they were suffering extremely for certain medical applications, which was attended to by Post Surgeon Davis, they delicately declined to enter the house of the post commander, but, as he passed the *piazza* and recognized the mistress of the house, whom he met near Laramie, he turned to his squaw, who walked behind him, and *both* joined in a bow of that recognition.

The settlement of "Spotted Tail" at Brady's Island left open the adjustment of troubles with the Cheyennes and Sioux, who still lingered

Cin-Te-Gi-Le-Ska.
Spotted Tail and his Squaw.—Brulè Sioux

in the valley of the Republican and points still farther south.

Nine commissioners had been sent west to investigate the Indian matter, particularly the Fetterman Massacre (see *Appendix*), and they were daily expected to take Colonel Carrington's testimony. General Augur, department commander, directed that officer, then commanding post, to send messengers to "Pawnee-Killer," "The Whistler," and other chiefs, and tell them that honourable terms of friendship would be conceded if they would come to a conference. These Indians came at different times and made short visits. Each visit, however, brought representative men, and in spite of the monotony of Indian interviews, three are put on record, so that those who read the history of succeeding operations may recognize the chiefs and judge of their conduct.

Chapter 32

Indian Affairs on the Plains— Incidents of 1867

On the 19th of April the Cheyenne village, on Pawnee Fork, in Western Kansas, had been destroyed by General Hancock's command, the Indian women and old men having abandoned it on the near approach of the troops. Pawnee Killer was among the chiefs who visited General Hancock's camp, April 14th, when an effort was made to induce them to send for their families. "Most of them," says General Custer, "exhibiting unmistakable signs of gratification at this apparently peaceful termination of our encounter." A fruitless pursuit of these Indians, both Sioux and Cheyennes, followed this failure to bring back their families and the destruction of their town. A long succession of raids upon stage stations had aroused that entire region to demand the punishment of the offenders. These events were not understood at Fort McPherson at the time of the visits now referred to, neither were the antecedents of "Pawnee Killer" specially alluded to in the conference with him, at which General Custer was present. (These conferences are transcribed literally, from the notes of the interviews.)

MAY 21ST, 1867. "THE WHISTLER," OGALLALLA SIOUX, CAME IN
WITH A PARTY.

Question by Colonel Carrington: "Did you get my letter? Where were you?"

Answer. "I was at the Arkansas. I think good, and no wrong. I come to shake hands and say what is good. I and White Antelope made treaty at Laramie, and swore to do nothing against the whites. We have a paper, and travel by it."

Colonel C. "Will you show me the paper?"

(The paper endorses "The Whistler," "Bull Fly," and "Yellow Jacket.")

Colonel C. "Where is your home now?"

Answer. "This side of the Arkansas. That is where I have been since the whites said they would not go through my country with soldiers."

Colonel C. "How long were you on the Arkansas?"

Answer. "Twenty-seven sleeps, and we came to White-Man's Fork."

Colonel C. "How many lodges?"

Answer. "One hundred."

Colonel C. "Who has fought you? The white chief believes that you were good at Laramie, and is glad you did not hurt the whites. Who has hurt you since the treaty, whites or Indians?"

Interpreter. "He says there is no one who gave him anything back; he went to shake hands with whites near Fort Lyon, other side of Island Wood Creek. When they went there, they did not throw away their lodges; were satisfied; women got scared; threw away (left) their lodges. If they wanted to fight, would get it. Came here for protection. Interpreter told them, there, the country did not belong to them."

"Sharp Nose" and "Brave Heart" (Brulè Sioux).

Interpreter. "He says, no big chief. You are chief; ho thinks you head chief."

Colonel C. "I am big chief here; have been twelve moons up to Big Horn."

Interpreter. "He says he has nothing bad for you. He is a small man, but has something to say."

Colonel C. "Tell him to speak."

Answer. "Was at Laramie. The chiefs there gave him that paper. Whenever he sees an officer he wishes to shake hands."

Colonel C. "Ask him where they want to stop. Did the Cheyennes drive them away?"

Answer. "He is afraid of Cheyennes."

Colonel C. "Does he want to live near white man or hunt?"

Answer. "The other side of Turkey Creek; plenty of buffalo; Solomon Fork."

Colonel C. "Tell him if they want to stay, chief and braves will see them tomorrow, and give them things to eat."

Answer. "That paper I have, I will use."

Colonel C. "Tell him it's good."

Answer. "He has that paper" (and shakes hands).

Colonel C. "We tell all white men to shake hands with Indians with such papers."

Answer. "On this side of Arkansas white men thick as grass—shook hands. They told him to come near and put lodges near." (This reference seems to be to Gen. Hancock's march.) "Women and young men got scared,—threw away all their things. Come for protection,—three hundred lodges. He and a few come and ask for something, lodges, etc. All the rest are coming. Give him some kettles and pans."

Colonel C. "When will the rest be here?"

Answer. "All the horses are poor,—*sometime*,—wish to hear what you think. He comes from this side the Arkansas; nothing to eat for twenty days,—they rest at White-Man's Fork."

Colonel C. "Any Brulès?"

Answer. "No."

Colonel C. "How many?"

Answer. "Three hundred and sixty lodges. He has been on this road. Never thought wrong of whites. Some Indians fight. He wants to take care of his band,—wants peace,—wants you to give them some white men to go with them, in case of trouble to tell them where to go."

Colonel C. "Tell him I will give him some kettles, pans, etc., and things to eat, and any lodges I can spare, and send word to Great Father for what I have not, to send them what he thinks best."

Answer. "He says he don't want to fight. Government promised to help them. Wants wagons and goods and men to go with them,—means nothing bad. *How!*" (Shakes hands.) "You have made his heart glad,—*he* is satisfied."

Colonel C. "Have they been to Beauvais's?" (A ranch up the road.)

Answer. "No, sir."

Long Bull (Oh-than-ca-pas-ka). (Credentials presented, signed by Gen. Curtis, Fort Sully, October 28th, 1865.) "He loves his people."

Colonel C. "Tell him it is very good. The white chief will hear him."

Answer. "They" (others) "have talked,—thinks the same as others. Big head chief, at Moran's." (A ranch up the road.)

Colonel C. "Who are the chiefs left behind?"

Answer. "Slow Dog is back at village, and Man that has been wounded with a small wound in the body (*Small Wound*). He says they are the main men there. He is an old man; goes by the men that are there,—some are fighting men. He comes for something good. He has been on Solomon's Fork. Never received any goods from the government,—wants them *now*,—needs them. He heard there was a big man of the government here. He came to see as quick as he could. He has made robes and traded them,—now is poor."

Colonel C. "Tell him that the white men from the Great Father are gone to Laramie; will be kind to him till they come back. Where are their ponies?"

Answer. "At Mr. Bonjier's."

Colonel C. "Tell them when our talk is over, I will give them some hay and something to eat. Ask them if they want to talk tomorrow."

(No answer; but shake hands.)

The "White Antelope" (Brulè). "He is no head man, he is a soldier; he has come with his lodge. His heart is good. He has been to war with other Indians; tries to keep them from war with the whites. *He heard from all Indians there were no soldiers to go between Plum Creek and Solomon's Fork. These Indians are poor.*" (Very likely that White Antelope had some idea as to the treaty of 1865.)

Colonel C. "Do they want to live in one place, or to go and hunt?"

Answer. "They want thirty days' rations, for all; want to go and tell the news to their people."

Colonel C. "When?"

Answer. "Today."

Colonel C. "What they want now is food for the present party?"

Answer. "Yes, sir."

Colonel C. "I am willing to give them two white men."

Answer. "He wants white men with Indian women, to teach them the ways of the whites; wants to go back."

Colonel C. "Do all wish to go this evening?" (No answer.)

Colonel C. "How many have come ?"

Answer. "One hundred and one in all; nine lodges have come in, the rest are back. About three hundred and fifty are at mouth of Black Wood; it empties in Republican, near White-Man's Fork."

Colonel C. "Tell them, since they came, I sent to Laramie over the wire, to General Sully, Big Man of the Commission. He is coming here; has left Laramie; there are six of them."

Colonel C. "How many miles is their village off the main road?"

Answer. "Sixty-five miles."

The following letter was given to "The Whistler," and, as appears hereafter, he made its contents known to other chiefs:

> Fort McPherson, Nebraska, May 21st, 1867
> To The Whistler, who came to see me, and to all the Ogallalla Sioux south of the Platte River.
> Come and see me if you want peace. I will feed you, and give you protection and provisions for your people; and while you are at peace the whites will protect and take care of you. Come to Moran's House.
>
> Henry B. Carrington,
> Colonel 18th U. S. Infantry,
> Brevet Brigadier-General U. S. A.

Tougon is here. (A half-breed interpreter.)

(Moran's Ranch was particularly named, so that collisions might be avoided and none come at random to the road.)

It is to be noticed that the statement of these Indians as to their contact with General Hancock's column, so far as it goes, is in harmony with the actual facts.

On the 2nd of June, a messenger reported that another party of Indians had arrived at Jack Morrow's ranch, nine miles west of the post, and wished an interview. They were directed to come to the fort. This they declined to do, and the orderly reported that some of Morrow's best horses, which had been grazing on the prairie, had disappeared. A part of Battery C, 3rd Artillery, under Brevet Lieutenant-Colonel Ransom, was at once sent with wagons, and with orders to escort or bring them to the fort, forthwith, and that they must send runners for the missing horses. This they did, and then came to the fort.

The Man that Walks Alone on the Ground (Ogallalla Sioux) first spoke.

Question by Col. Carrington.—"Did you come from the Republican?"

Answer. "No; we came from Beaver Creek."

Colonel C. "Where is The Whistler?"

Answer. "He is at Beaver Creek."

Colonel C. "Did he get the rations that I sent him?"

Answer. "He did."

Colonel C. "Did he say he was coming here again soon ?"

Answer. "He did; and said that he and his band would go north of the Platte River, where the Brulès went."

Colonel C. "I wish to tell you that the white soldiers in large numbers are coming here, and driving the hostile Cheyennes this way. I want friendly Indians to keep on the north side of the Platte River."

Answer, "I and my men want to cross the river."

(Orders had been received to furnish Lieutenant-Colonel Custer's detachment of the 7th Cavalry with rations if they touched Fort McPherson during a proposed scout.)

Colonel C. (to interpreter). "Ask him who stole the stock this morning. The white chief is very angry about it, and I want the horses brought back."

Answer. "He says that he got in with Whistler at Beaver Creek, and they were talking of coming on the road, and some of them did come, and the Cheyennes run off the horses, and that *he*, The Man that Walks Alone on the Ground, induced the Cheyennes to return the stock, which was done, except two horses, and Joe Smith (present at the conference) promised to return them or give two mules in their place."

Colonel C. "Did The Man that Walks Alone on the Ground or Joe Smith suppose that we were going to fight them?"

Answer. "They did."

Colonel C. "When I first sent out word to have them come in why did they not come?"

Answer by interpreter. "He says that Whistler told them that the white chief had a good heart, and told all the band to come in to the post, and when they got ready to come, they were told that the white soldiers would fight them and were then afraid to come."

Colonel C. "Ask him if they would like to go north of the *North Platte*, to the Sand Hills, and be taken care of and fed by the government?"

Question, in reply. "Are you an officer?"

Colonel C. "Yes; I am a big chief, and command all the country around here."

Interpreter. "He says he has a family, and wishes to go with them and his band *north of the North Platte,* provided the government will feed them and take care of them. He, and his father's fathers before him, had lived and hunted on this river, and he thinks that he has the best right to it."

Colonel C. "Tell him that I control this country here, and I will furnish means to take care of them if they go across the river and be at peace with the whites, and not steal their stock."

Answer. "We want it to be as it used to be,—at peace with the whites."

Colonel C. "Ask him if the Cheyennes (southern) have not a bad heart."

Answer. "Some of them have a very bad heart, and say they won't kill the whites, but will steal their stock, and that there are a great many now about Plum Creek and about Julesburg, stealing stock. The Cheyenne Chief, Black Kettle, don't want to fight. He is now on the other side of Fort Lyons."

Colonel C. "Is The Whistler a good Indian?"

Answer. "Yes."

Colonel C. "How many days would it take to come here, if I send them across the river?"

Answer. "He says that their horses are very poor. He will go back and see his people, and move as soon as he can." (These pledges were afterwards redeemed by some of the band.)

Colonel C. "Tell him that I got a dispatch from the Great Chief. General Sherman is coming here next Tuesday. Would he like to remain and have a talk with him?"

Answer. "Joe Smith will remain, but he and the others will go back to their village."

Colonel C. "Tell them if they want to be friends to the whites they must let me know where they are, so that I can keep the soldiers away, and not disturb them."

Answer. "He says he has sent some of his men back to the village this day to bring (take) good news back."

Colonel C. "Where is their village?"

Answer. "It is thirty-five miles southwest of White-Man's Fork, on Black Wood."

Colonel C. "Tell them, if they want to be at peace with the white man, they must keep away from the roads, and not interfere with trains. The white chief has a good heart and straight tongue, and will take care of his friends; but his enemies he will punish."

Interpreter. "Joseph Smith says, he came here last summer; he didn't want to fight the whites,—that he is a soldier at the head of the Ogallallas. The Man that Walks Alone on the Ground says, that he would like to have two white men to go along to the village and help him to move."

Colonel C. "Tell him he can have them, and ask him who he would like to have."

Answer. "He would like to have these two." (Pointing to the interpreters.)

Colonel C. "Do they want to go back to Morrow's tonight?"

Answer. "They do; and, they say, will remain until tomorrow, and Joe Smith will remain until Tuesday, when he will come here and see General Sherman. They say they are now ready to leave, and bid you goodnight."

A week later, General Custer's column,—six companies of the 7th United States Cavalry,—arrived, fresh from the pursuit of the Cheyennes, whose village was burned in April. Meanwhile a state of alarm prevailed at the ranches on the south side of the Platte, and constant demands were made for guard-details, far beyond the capacity of the garrison to furnish. Ranchmen would not keep their stock in corral, but left them on herd, still insisting upon protection for the stock. Details were refused.

On the 10th of June, after the burial of Major Cooper, of the 7th Cavalry, General Custer moved his camp up the Platte, near Morrow's, where hay was procurable, and Pawnee Killer, who had come in on invitation, was taken to the camp for a conference. The following is the official record of that conference as taken down at the time:

INTERVIEW BETWEEN GENERALS CARRINGTON, CUSTER, AND INDIAN CHIEFS PAWNEE KILLER AND FIVE (5) OF HIS TRIBE (OGALLALA SIOUX), AT GENERAL CUSTER'S CAMP, NEAR MORROW'S RANCH, JUNE 13TH, 1867.

Question by General Carrington: "Ask them what they came in for."

Answer by Pawnee Killer: "Two parties of Indians had been to the road, and went back to the village and told them lies, and now they came to see for themselves."

General Carrington. "Ask him if the Indian has a good heart; if he has seen Whistler since he (Whistler) saw the white chief." (General Carrington.)

Answer. "Yes."

Question. "Did he (Whistler) tell him that the white chief had a good heart?"

Answer. "He says that Whistler told them in the village to come to the road in a month and a half, and said that he would get tents, when they come,—from the white chief." (This is a correct report of the promise made to Whistler in the interview already quoted.)

General C. "Oh, yes. I did tell Whistler that I would give them provisions and tents if they would go north of the Platte. Where is The Man that Stands Alone on the Ground?"

Answer. "He says that he is at the village."

General C. "Did he say the whites treated him kindly?"

Answer. "He says they all talk alike; the same as Whistler."

General C. "The white chief would be at peace with all Indians if they would come in."

Answer. "He says they all talk alike, that come from you."

General C. "Did you know that Spotted Tail, Swift Bear, Two Strike, and Standing Elk were here with the white chief, and that I gave them, for one moon, to eat?" (Rations for a month.)

Answer. "He says he knows it."

General C. "Ask him if the Ogallallas would like to go to the north of the Platte, to be away from the hostile Indians."

Answer. "He thinks that all the big men should talk the same way."

Question. "How long since he left the village?"

Answer. "Two days and nights. He says you talk well and good."

Question. "Is it good (honest) to him?"

Answer. "He says he thinks good, if he can,—the same as you think. Some of the Indians tell him stories, and he came in to see for himself."

Question. "Ask him if The Whistler is coming here again."

Answer. "He says he is now after something to make lodges, as they have no buffalo now."

Question. "Ask him if all of the Indians south of the Platte want to come here and be taken care of by the whites."

Answer. "He says he thinks they all want to come inside of thirty or forty days; his horses are very poor."

Question. "Ask him if they will keep from the road until they come here. All those who come directly to me I will give tents and feed them; but they must keep away from the road, as the Great Father at Washington directs me to provide for them if they come here, and keep away from the roads."

Answer. "He says he is afraid to go with other people; there is (are) no Cheyennes with his people. They split eight or ten days ago; he says he is a fool, or has been a fool, but now will do better. He says Spotted Tail shook hands with the Great Father (at Laramie), but he Pawnee

Killer, did not, and is sorry for it now. The whites hunt for gold, and I am the same. I hunt for food and shelter, and if he moves over the river will you let him move back when the fighting is over?"

General C. "Tell him that the Big Men from Washington said, Give the Ogallallas all the country from the Platte to the Republican; and since the Cheyennes are hostile there, and the whites can't tell the hostile from the friendly Indians, they want all friendly Indians to stay north of the Platte."

Answer. "He says that is good."

General C. "I know they can't kill buffalo while fighting is going on, but I will feed them, north of the Platte; and when all Indians are peaceable, then we will let them hunt south of the Platte, so they don't go on the road."

Answer. "He says that he heard about being sent over the river, and that is the reason why he came in to know for himself, whether he can come back again after the fighting is over."

General' C. "Will he go north of the Platte River and stay there until we give him permission to go south again?"

Answer. "He says he will."

Question. "Don't he think he can come in sooner than forty days? I want him to come as soon as he can."

Answer. "He thinks he may come sooner, but wants time enough, fearing he may be delayed."

Question. "Ask him are there any Indians on White-Man's Fork."

Answer. "He says there are no Indians now on White-Man's Fork. They are on the South Fork of the Beaver Creek."

Question. "How many lodges, and how many fighting men?"

Answer. "He says they have sixty fighting men."

(Question. "Ask him who are the soldiers and chiefs who don't want to come; as Joe Smith and Whistler told me that some did not want to come."

Answer. "He says they all want to come and shake hands with the white officers and he friendly. He says his heart is good, and what his grandfather told him he still remembers,—to have an honest heart; and he says you don't think wrong, and want to shake hands with him, and as he has now parted with the Cheyennes he wants to be friendly, and all his tribe, with the whites, as the Great Father told him to be good."

General C. "Tell him he talks good; he has a good heart, like we have toward them. Ask him if they have much meat or food."

Answer. "He says they have been surrounded with meat, they moved where the buffalo are."

General C. "Tell him that all these soldiers are this white chief's men (General Custer's), and he has three times as many on the Smoky Hill" (route).

Question by General Custer. "Tell him if he hadn't come in yesterday, I would have gone on this morning. I heard that some friendly Indians were coming in, and I told my men that if I met Indians the first day from here I would be friendly with them, because they had General Carrington's papers; and all Indians we met after one day's march from here, we would make war with them, because war is my business, and your coming in may be the means of establishing peace between them and the whites. I am going to stay here one day more, so as I can send word to another big chief, who is at Sedgwick (General Sherman), He told me to come here and kill all Indians I met, and you came here yesterday and said you want peace, and I believe you. I sent that word to the big chief at Sedgwick. I have told the big chief that I believe that the Indian's heart is good, and that we will let the Sioux alone if they be friendly with us, but will make war with the Cheyennes. I would like to have you stay here till tomorrow evening; I expect to hear from the big chief that is at Sedgwick. This chief (General Carrington) will give you provisions for your party, enough to take you back. That is all I want to say now."

Answer. "I am in a hurry; I want to go back and tell my people the good news. I am the man to do it; I will tell my soldiers all to cross the river."

General Carrington. "I will cross them all over the river as soon as they come, and it shall cost them nothing."

Answer. "That's all I want to know."

(The expense of crossing by Morrow's boat was proverbially terrifying to white men and Indians alike.)

General C. "They must come in near Morrow's ranch, and not beyond."

Answer. "I want to go back immediately to my people, in order to hurry them to move, and would like to have some rations to take back; and as the whites are going to fight the Cheyennes, I want to tell my people to go north of the Platte. I want to go back to tell them to move, and tell them all I know, as you have told me, about going to war with the Cheyennes."

Question. "How will you carry rations we shall give you? We have no fresh meat, but will give you coffee, sugar, and hard bread."

Answer. "We want some tobacco."

General Custer. "'We have none of that. If they wait till tomorrow we could give them some."

Interpreter. "They want a white man to meet them at Red Willow, when they are coming back. They will come down the Republican, and then to Morrow's ranch."

General Custer, for self and General Carrington. "Tell them that we both have a good heart and true; that Indians come on the road and kill people and steal stock. We will kill all we catch hereafter on this road. The wire was not working, and that was the reason I did not move today. I was waiting to hear from the big chief at Sedgwick. There is a great deal of white soldiers coming, but we want our friends to move before they come."

Answer. "He says he wants you to keep them off till he can cross the river."

General Carrington. "Tell him that all Indians who *come on the road* are by us considered hostile, and all who wish to be friendly must not come on the road."

Answer. "He says he quit the Cheyennes, and is now going to fight them."

General C. "Tell him that we don't want them to fight the Cheyennes. We have men enough to do that ourselves. All we want of them is to go north of the river, out of the way of the Cheyennes. Ask him if he is pleased with the interview."

Answer. "He says yes; he shook hands with you to signify it."

These three independent interviews showed that the messages sent out had been correctly reported.

Pawnee Killer sat upon a camp-lounge cushion, underneath which General Custer had left one of his revolvers. The chief showed evident impatience toward the close of the interview, and after loading the ponies with bacon, etc., all they could carry, the party rode briskly away. The revolver was missed when too late for pursuit.

The following line from General Custer, that evening, gives his impression of the interview:

> June 12th (13th), 6 p.m.
>
> My Dear General,—I have telegraphed General Sherman the result of the talk with Pawnee Killer and the other Sioux, who

came in today in response to your invitation. I believe the Sioux are sincere in their desire for peace, and that if we exercise good judgment, we can separate the Sioux from the Cheyennes, and make friends of the former. I hope you will succeed in keeping the band together. (Then followed a friendly invitation for the ladies of the post to visit the camp that evening.)

    (Signed)   Truly your friend,
              Geo. a. Custer,
            Brevet Major-General.

Responsive to telegram as to the unreasonable demands of the settlers, came the following practical message from General Sherman:

          Sedgwick, July 13th, 1867.
General Carrington, Commanding.—Despatch of today received. I don't understand about the thirty friendly mounted Sioux reported by General Custer camped on Medicine Lodge Creek. Have word sent to them, if it is south of the Platte. Tell them they must join Spotted Tail immediately, else they will be confounded with the hostile Sioux. Your letter, asking me to come to McPherson with Senatorial party, only just reached me today. If the people along the south side of the Platte are stampeded, I can't help it. General Custer reported no trail from Fort Hays to McPherson. I hope his present movement will denounce the party that have been making so much noise along the Platte. We are not going to guard every ranch on the south side, and the people may start for the north side if they won't fight for their possession.

              W. T. Sherman,
           Lieutenant-General U. S. A.

General Sherman stopped at the camp of General Custer, and at the Post, and the cavalry column moved south. Within ten days Pawnee Killer had a collision with General Custer's column, and protracted hostilities followed. In a subsequent engagement with the same force, Black Kettle, an unquestionably bad Indian, was killed, and the 7th Cavalry, under their gallant lieutenant-colonel, became as distinguished for brisk work in the saddle, as the 2nd Cavalry had been, for its almost ubiquitous service wherever required in the Department of the Platte.

The operations on the lower line at once suspended the anticipated removal, northward, of some of the Indians; but still quite a number eventually joined Spotted Tail, and thus kept clear of a collision with the opposing forces. In view of large supplies and the small force on the line of the Platte, it is not improbable that the Indians left the Smoky Hill route, where troops were in force, to strike where there was less power to resist. In that case the sweep of General Custer, making McPherson a supply station, where he could also confer with General Sherman, defeated the plan.

Of their final action, General Augur, commanding Department of the Platte, under date of Oct. 23rd, 1869, thus writes:

> More than a year ago, when 'Spotted Tail' went to the reservation set apart for all these bands, certain of them, under the leadership of 'Pawnee Killer,' 'The Whistler,' 'Tall Bull,' 'Little Wound,' and others, refused to go. When the Cheyennes were driven south, last winter (1867-8), 'Tall Bull,' and a few other prominent head soldiers, joined their bands on the Republican, and it is their straggling bands that have committed all the depredations in northern Kansas and southern Nebraska during the past year. The Indians north of the Platte gave comparatively little trouble.

In July, Lieutenant-Colonel Wessells took command of the 18th Infantry during the colonel's invalid absence. In 1868-9, headquarters were at Fort Sedgwick, but the Indian operations were confined to a few attempts to annoy details guarding work on the line of the Union Pacific Railroad, and substantial order prevailed along the Platte.

During this period William Blackmore, Esq., of London, to whom the government has formally extended its acknowledgments for his invaluable photograph negatives of Indian chiefs, visited Fort Sedgwick in company with Major Bridges, of the 1st Regiment of (British) Foot Guards. Mr. Blackmore's contributions to American archaeological inquiry have been supplemented by the endowment and equipment of a museum at Salisbury, England, where is stowed a collection of Indian relics of war and the chase elsewhere unsurpassed. It is not out of place for an American officer to honour his labours, and testify of the generosity with which that gentleman, during 1875, both at London and Salisbury, repaid his host of Fort Sedgwick the attentions there accorded.

Red Cloud and Mr. Blackmore, of London.

CHAPTER 33

Indian Affairs on the Plains— Incidents, 1867-1873

The principal events which transpired immediately after Fetterman's massacre require notice, in order that the long line of consequences which followed operations in 1866 may be traced up to the present time.

The closing winter and spring, 1866-7, were periods of light warfare in the Big Horn and Tongue River valleys. In January, 1867, the snow had drifted to the height of the stockade, eight feet, and the difficulty of marching is illustrated in Chapter 27. of the narrative. Reports from officers who remained longer at the fort show, that continued storms, wind, and intense cold so crowded spring into summer, that active movements, even to haul fuel, were almost impracticable.

Every effort to induce Red Cloud to accept terms of peace was answered by his demand for the evacuation of the country and the demolition of the forts. The hostility of his band could not be repressed by vague assurances that the matter was under advisement, nor by the simple omission to reinforce the garrison and thoroughly occupy the line with troops. Failure to pursue and punish was regarded as acceptance of his victory; and the Indian could not comprehend how the nation had sufficient power in reserve to avenge the massacre, and yet could not hurry a force forward to do it.

On the 20th of July, 1867, Congress authorized a mixed commission of army officers and civilians to communicate with all hostile tribes and negotiate terms of permanent peace.

In 1868 the following treaty was announced:

The Sioux retained the right to hunt in Nebraska, on any lands north of the North Platte, and on the Republican Fork of the Smoky River.

Subsequently, in 1874, Congress appropriated twenty-five thousand dollars to redeem the right to hunt in Nebraska, but it was not until May, 1875, that the modified terms of the contract were formally settled between the parties in interest. The treaty of 1868 also stipulated that:

> The country north of the North Platte, in Nebraska, and east of the summits of the Big Horn Mountains should be held and considered unceded Indian territory, and that no white person or persons should be permitted to settle upon or occupy any portion of the same; nor, without the consent of the Indians first had and obtained, should pass through the same.

This was yielding more than the Sioux claimed at Laramie, in 1864, when the negotiations were cut short by the forcible possession of that territory. This clause thus recognized a large tract of neutral territory, bounded on the south by Nebraska; but this north line was still undefined, and involved much difficulty, when, on its final establishment, it was found to cut far north of the previous understanding of the Indian parties to the treaty.

Owing to the fact that the Union Pacific Railroad was fast making Montana accessible, the scarcity of troops, and other immediately prudential reasons, the President, on the 2nd day of March, 1868, ordered the Big Horn country to be given up. For want of ready transportation,—as wagons had first to be sent out for removal of the stores,—the movement could not be executed until August. Meanwhile, the ceaseless irritating annoyances of 1866 had to be inflicted upon the new garrisons and new post commanders, and they realized, personally, what it was to be without the means of responsive punishment of savage enemies, to be tenants at their will, and to esteem it a great triumph to receive occasional mails and recapture portions of stolen herds. Some of the official reports read very like Chapter 13 of this narrative, and illustrate the condition of the frontier.

October 1st, 1867.—A dash at the mules with the hay party; fourteen mules and seven horses run off.

October 12th.—Indians attempted to capture mules belonging to the pinery, four and a half miles from the post. (It was when sent simply to succour a similar train, that Fetterman took an independent departure, and sacrificed himself and his command.)

October 13th.—Forty-one mules run off by Indians at Fort Reno.

October 17th.—One man killed and scalped by Indians at the pinery.

October 20th.—Detachment of 2nd Cavalry attacked at Crazy Woman's Fork.

October 25th.—Indians twice attempted to run off the stock of three trains *en route* from Fort Reno.

March 12th, 1868.—Mail party from Fort Reno attacked on Dry Fork of the Cheyenne.

March 13th.—Indians captured a train between Fetterman and Laramie Peak sawmill.

March 14th.—Indians captured a mule train near post sawmill.

March 18th.—Indians captured twenty-nine mules of sawmill train, and killed one man.

March 18th.—Indians attacked Bruce's camp, near Box Elder, and ran off sixty head of cattle.

March 24th.—Ranches burned, and ranchmen killed, between Forts Laramie and Fetterman.

Of the Indian operations in the Department of the Platte, General Augur says: "It is more in the nature of disconnected raids for stealing animals, and getting other plunder, than of a systematic and permanent war. The raiding parties have been small, and scattered along the various lines of communication in this department." Still, on the 30th of September, 1867, he thus emphasizes the nature of the warfare in the Big Horn country, and the value of the line:

> The Montana route alone, between Laramie and C. F. Smith, near the Yellowstone, has occupied two regiments of infantry—the 18th and 27th—and half a regiment of cavalry, and they have barely maintained themselves upon it, and kept it open for their own supplies. The troops at the forts upon it have to fight almost daily to secure their supplies of wood and hay. K, therefore, these posts are now given up, it will be at a loss of all that has been expended upon them, and with almost a certainty that their re-establishment will be demanded in a few years. This

route, substantially, must become the great highway between Colorado, Nebraska, and Montana. Its proximity, in its whole extent, to what will undoubtedly be Indian country, will render necessary the very posts now existing upon it.

This was the condition of things, notwithstanding twenty-six companies were upon the line which eight companies had to open and defend in 1866; and it will hereafter appear that the extensive operations of after-years had to be conducted through this very region, without the advantage of those posts for rendezvous, rest, and supplies, and that new forts had to be established to command the same country.

The people at large know nothing of the trials, hardships, and exasperating endurances of frontier service, at such periods as this narrative and General Augur's report embody. They look for battles and victories, little knowing through what ordeals an officer must run the gauntlet, to save property, life, or honour, while conscious that if he do not perish, his reward must be in the sense of duty done. No consideration of personal comfort is possible. In referring to the return of Colonel J. J. Reynolds to Fort Fetterman in March, 1876, after destruction of the camp of Crazy Horse on Powder River, General Sherman, in his annual report for that year, writes:

The nights following the attack on Crazy Horse's village were so cold that the men were not allowed to sleep for fear of consequences.

The record of such a night, with the mercury 40° below zero, and when the use of black-snake whips alone roused men from overpowering lethargy, is set forth, in chapter 28, as part of the experience of an officer's wife on the Plains. But while the people do not realize the cost of such exposure, on the march or in the field, neither do they realize how delay or failure in the confirmation of favourable treaties, or in the appropriation of money to give them effect, exasperated the Indians, until the whole frontier became dotted with war spots, and all that had been done through the efforts of General Sherman and others, acting legitimately and purely as Peace Commissioners, was stripped of half its value. It is right that these facts should be placed outside of Executive Documents, and be recognized, so that neither the army, Indians, frontiersmen, the Interior Department, or Congress, should carry the whole burden of so much bloodshed and waste.

The commission which organized under the Act of July 20th, 1867, consisted of N. G. Taylor, President; J. B. Henderson; W. T. Sherman, Lieutenant-General; Wm. S. Harney, Brevet Major-General; John B. Sanborn; Alfred H. Terry, Brevet Major-General; S. F. Tappan; and C. C. Augur, Brevet Major-General. Their report of January 7th, 1868, is a faithful exposition of the condition of affairs, and an expressive commentary upon the delay for funds, and the difficulties attending the employment of so many and so changing systems of policy in dealing with the Indian tribes. It also confirms the assurance that the out-flow from the Laramie Treaty of 1866, and the enforced temporary abandonment of the Big Horn region, after actual possession and such terrible retribution, embodied two principles equally dangerous in dealing with savages, *viz.*: 1st, Disregard of treaties, and 2nd, Failure to punish wholesale slaughter.

In his official report of September 26th, 1868, General Sheridan, then commanding the department of the Missouri, thus writes in respect to his own command:

> The motives of the peace commissioners were humane, but there was an error of judgment in making peace with the Indians last fall. They should have been punished and made to give up the plunder captured, and which they now hold; and after properly submitting to the military and disgorging their plunder, they could have been turned over to the civil agents. This error has given more victims to savage ferocity. The present system of dealing with Indians, I think, is an error. There are too many fingers in the pie, too many ends to be subserved, and too much money to be made; and it is the interest of the nation, and of humanity, to put an end to this inhuman farce. The Peace Commission, the Indian Department, the military, and the Indian, make a baulky team. The Public Treasury is depleted and innocent people plundered in this quadrangular arrangement, in which the treasury and the unarmed settlers are the greatest sufferers.

Of the *animus* of the army, he makes a statement which is true, and deserving of universal recognition. It is this:

> I desire to say with all emphasis, what every army officer on the frontier will corroborate, that there is no class of men in this country who are so disinclined to war with the Indians as the army stationed among them. The army has nothing to gain by war with the Indians; on the contrary, it has everything to lose. In such a war it suffers all the hardship and privation, exposed

as it is to the charge of assassination if Indians are killed, to the charge of inefficiency if they are not; to misrepresentation by the agents who fatten on the plunder of Indians, and misunderstood by worthy people at a distance who are deceived by these very agents.

The year 1868 blazed with the war-fires which kindled in 1867. Hon. Schuyler Colfax telegraphed from Denver, September 7th, 1868:

> Hostile Indians have been striking simultaneously at isolated settlements of Colorado for a circuit of over two hundred miles. Men, women, and children have been scalped daily, and hundreds of thousands of dollars have been stolen.

The reports of Generals Sheridan, Augur, and Terry are accompanied by detailed tabular statements, showing that petty raids annoyed every post (none excepted), from the Missouri River, west, to Montana, and south to Arkansas, That of General Sheridan of October 24th, 1868, recapitulates distinct cases wherein an aggregate of seventy-nine white men were killed, and over five thousand head of stock had been stolen. The close of the year brought an effort to punish these outrages in that department, even at the expense of a winter campaign. This was prosecuted in spite of deep snows, and such tempests as the unprotected, treeless plains alone can furnish.

Lieutenant-Colonel A. Sully, south of the Arkansas; Captain Graham, on the Big Sandy, September 15th; Major Geo. A. Forsyth, at Beecher's Island,[1] Arickaree Fork, September 17th; Lieutenant-Colonel Bradley, with a third column, and Major E. A. Carr, 5th Cavalry, at Beaver Creek, October 18th, inflicted great loss upon the Kiowas and Comanches. Colonel Crawford, with the 19th Kansas, and Major A. W. Evans, with a portion of the 3rd Cavalry, participated in this severe campaign. On the Washita, November 27th, Lieutenant-Colonel Custer, with the 7th Cavalry, killed Black Kettle and despoiled his villages, severely punishing not only the Cheyennes, but also the Ar-

---

1. General Custer, in *Life on the Plains*, (also published by Leonaur), says, that "the Indians fought Forsyth, about seventeen to one, and the whole affair, until relieved by Colonel Carpenter's command, was a wonderful exhibition of daring courage, stubborn bravery, and heroic endurance, under circumstances of greatest peril and exposure. In all probability there will never occur, in our future hostilities with the savage tribes of the West, a struggle the equal of that in which were engaged the heroic men who so bravely defended 'Beecher's Island.'"

rapahoes under Little Raven, and the Kiowas under Santana.

During the years 1869 and 1870, the Indian forays were few and chiefly of little significance. The work of the Peace Commission began to bear fruit. The lives lost and the treasure expended had passed into the cabinet of experiences, to be looked at, wondered at, and, at last, regarded. The Indian country had nearly resumed the peaceful status which obtained before the Pandora box of frontier trouble was thrown wide open in 1866. Much still depended upon the success of Red Cloud in persuading the bands under his influence to unite with him in permanent peace. During the summer of 1870, that chief, with Spotted Tail and others, both of the Ogallalla and Brulè Sioux, visited Washington and other eastern cities.

On the 5th of October, Red Cloud, with The Man Afraid of his Horses, Red Dog, American Horse, Red Leaf, and other Sioux, met the Commission at Fort Laramie. On the 7th, Dull Knife, who visited Fort Phil Kearney in 1866 (see chapter 12 of narrative), Gray Head, Medicine Chief, and other northern Cheyennes, were present. American Horse and Medicine Chief were both afterwards killed in battle. During the summer, the first hasty expedition to the Black Hills was repressed by General Augur, and much progress toward peace was realized very early in the season, by his prudence in placing troops just where there was most danger of trespass, thus forestalling depredations in the exposed parts of Nebraska.

General Pope thus reviews the situation: "Speaking generally, there has been little trouble with the Indians in this Department this season. This result is mainly due to the fact that the Indians have been fed and furnished with nearly everything they asked for, and by this means much temptation to depredate has been removed. In General Hancock's department Major E. M. Baker destroyed a camp of Piegans north of Fort Benton, on the 24th of January, during an intensely cold period, but general quiet prevailed."

In June, 1871, Red Cloud again met the commission, and he has quite uniformly manifested friendship, in spite of some difficulty in restraining the young men of his band, and in spite of those gradual changes which are restoring the Big Horn country to the control of the whites. On the 24th of July a raid into the Gallatin valley called fresh attention to the bands of Teton Sioux who occupied a part of the line of the proposed Northern Pacific Railroad. These were largely influenced by Sitting Bull, who utterly rejected all overtures from Red Cloud, in behalf of peace with the whites. Otherwise, general peace prevailed during 1871. The Board of Indian Commissioners thus make up the record of the year:

> The remarkable spectacle seen this fall on the plains of Western Nebraska, Kansas, and Eastern Colorado, of the warlike tribes of the Sioux of Dacotah, Montana, and Wyoming hunting peacefully for buffalo, without occasioning any serious alarm among the thousands of white settlers whose cabins skirt the border on both sides of these plains, shows clearly that the efforts of the friends of peace in establishing confidence between the white people and the Indians have been eminently successful. We contrast this picture with that presented by the same tribe when, five years ago, in consequence of our government's bad faith in violating its treaties with them, they were engaged in a war made memorable by the so-called Fort Kearney massacre, in which ninety-eight of our soldiers (seventy-nine) were killed in sight of the fort (five miles from the fort), and in the course of which many of the settlers lost their lives, and so many hundreds of others were compelled to abandon their claims and flee to the larger towns for safety.

In 1872 "not a white man was killed," writes General Augur, "in the Department of the Platte." The reports of Generals Pope and Hancock were equally encouraging; Col. D. S. Stanley, of the 22nd Infantry, from Fort Rice, and Major E. M. Baker, 2nd Cavalry, from Fort Ellis, made expeditions to the Yellowstone during the summer, to protect the surveys of the Northern Pacific Railroad, without substantial opposition. Lieutenants Eben Crosby and L. D. Adair were killed by Indians while in advance of their company, and Colonel Stanley's servant was killed while hunting. Major Baker advanced as far eastward as Pompey's Pillar, and returned, mistrusting the strength of his detachment. One sergeant was killed during his march, and three soldiers were wounded.

During the year 1873 the Pawnees and Sioux again came into collision, and the infelicity of the location of the Red Cloud and Spotted Tail Agencies became apparent, and finally, in 1876, the Pawnees were removed to the Indian Territory, and their lands were purchased by the United States. Meanwhile, the Red Cloud Agency, which had been in Northern Nebraska, south of the Black Hills, at Camp Robinson, was removed to White River, greatly to the disgust of the chief. A census of his people was then taken, showing their number—mostly Ogallalla Sioux—to be 9807. The Commissioner of Indian Affairs writes:

> Until the agent was supported by a military force the Indians had been able to refuse to allow him to count them, and still to demand and draw rations.

Frank D. Appleton, clerk of the agent, was shot by an Indian, who escaped, and much anxiety prevailed as to the attempt to bring the Indians under closer subordination and the necessary restraint. The commissioner had doubts whether even Red Cloud would consent to *settling down* to a white man's work, and writes:

> After sending messengers through the Powder River and Big Horn country, Red Cloud became convinced that there was not game enough to last through a war, and at a general council (Indian) it was resolved to protect any who wished to farm.

The Spotted Tail Agency was also removed ten miles south of the Nebraska line, and their enumeration showed a population (mostly Brulè Sioux) of 7000 souls.

The Rawlings Spring massacre, Wyoming Territory, in June, growing mainly out of the uncertainty of reservation boundaries, and some inter-tribal conflicts, made the chief burden of Indian troubles for the year. The Cheyennes and Arrapahoes, in part, consented to remove to the Indian Territory, and the value of the policy finally adopted by President Grant, as the outgrowth of the work of the Peace Commission in 1868, was fully confirmed. During the month of August, Colonel Stanley, of the 22nd Infantry, conducted a military expedition, nearly fifteen hundred strong, to the Yellowstone country, in the interests of the railroad survey; Lieutenant-Colonel Custer, with eight companies of the 7th Cavalry, forming part of the column. The cavalry moved in advance of the infantry, upon reaching Powder River, and advanced as far as Pompey's Pillar. The official report of their conflict with the Sioux, near Tongue River, on the 4th of August, is in the *Army and Navy Journal* (vol. xi.), September 13th, 1873, and succeeding numbers.

The attack was made by the Indians with great vigour, lasting from half-past ten a.m., until near three o'clock p.m., "all efforts of the Indians to dislodge us," writes General Custer, "proving unsuccessful." On the day following the cavalry took the offensive and drove Sitting Bull, who was then present, eight miles, and over the Yellowstone. This fight was brought on by a decoy party of six, who "dashed boldly into the skirt of timber within which my command had halted and unsaddled, and attempted to stampede our horses," These Indians were followed, but they retired so leisurely as to excite suspicion, and finally, as they found that they were not pressed earnestly, "over three hundred well-mounted warriors dashed in perfect line from the edge of the timber, and charged down upon Captain Maylan's squadron, at the same time endeavouring to intercept the small party with me."

This fight, or succession of fights, continuing daily until the 11th of August, was sharp, and with fluctuating promise, until the entire force of the cavalry was fully engaged. The following additional extracts from the official report are important as a lesson in Indian warfare:

> Among the Indians who fought us were some of the identical warriors who committed the massacre at Fort Phil Kearney, and they, no doubt, intended a similar programme when they sent the six warriors to dash up and attempt to decoy us into a pursuit past the timber, in which the savages hoped to ambush us. Had we pursued the six warriors half a mile farther, instead of halting, the entire band of warriors would have been in our rear, and all the advantages of position and numbers would have been with them. The number of Indians opposed to us has been estimated by the various officers engaged as from eight hundred to one thousand, my command numbering four hundred and fifty officers and men. A large number of the Indians who fought us were fresh from their reservation on the Missouri River. Many of the warriors engaged in the fight, on both days, were dressed in complete suits of the clothes issued at the Agencies to Indians. The arms with which they fought us (several of which were captured in the fight) were of the latest improved pattern of breech-loading repeating rifles, and their supply of metallic rifle cartridges seemed unlimited, as they were anything but sparing in its use. [2]

---

2. Companies A, Captain Maylan, Lieutenant Varnum; B, Lieutenants T. W. Custer and B. H. Hodgson; E, Lieutenants McDougall and Aspinwall; F, Captain Gates, Lieutenant C. W. Larned; G, Lieutenants McIntosh and G. D. Wallace; K, Captain Owen Hale, Lieutenant E. S. Godfrey; L, Lieutenants Weston and Braden; M, Captain T. H. French and Lieutenant Mathey, were engaged, the two wings being commanded by Captains V. K. Hart and French. The Indian loss was large in men and material, the cavalry losing four killed and four wounded. The brilliant series of fights during the period between the 4th and the 11th were well calculated to inspire the commander with unlimited confidence in his splendid command.

The experience of General Custer on this occasion is that of all officers who have operated in that country, and the official examination as to Fetterman's massacre will indicate very clearly the success of that decoy policy to which he refers.

The Yellowstone expedition had no trouble with Indians after the battle described, and both columns returned safely to their post on the Missouri River.

The year 1873 closed with the formal demolition of old Fort Kearney. From the time that Colonel May reared its flag-staff, and his dragoons received its shelter, it has had a place in the respect of the army. Harney, Sumner, Cooke, and many other veteran Indian fighters, have their names associated with its older buildings, and in 1865 there remained old *adobe* buildings, on the door-posts of which venerated names had been cut, when the first enthusiasm of frontier life was in the soul. To hundreds of officers there are dear associations linked with those double-storied barracks, with their broad piazzas for each story, and thousands of overland travellers have still in mind that succession of ranches which are described in chapter 6 of the narrative as our own halting-places in the march from Leavenworth to Kearney, in 1865. Novel memories survive the old fort.

In those days, when military authority alone existed, the post staff were authorized to perform the marriage ceremony. A sudden summons of one staff-officer to his first professional duty of the kind compelled him to hunt the Episcopal Prayer-Book. A brother officer held a tallow-candle, and showed him, first, an appropriate prayer, and pointed to the opposite page as the next formal passage. The prayer was devoutly read; but what was the surprise of the bridal candidates and others present, when the following words followed, "Whereas it has pleased Almighty God to remove our beloved brother." Memory refuses to detail the hasty completion of the ceremony; but a marriage certificate was duly given.

On another occasion the officers went in full dress, as it was just before evening parade, accompanied by their wives, the band of thirty instruments doing its very best. Never did a frontier couple (and *this* couple was *ordered* to be married, or leave the post) unite their destinies with more enthusiastic surroundings. They went west, and the wife visited the same staff-officer at Camp Douglass, some years after, to apply for a divorce, because "her man had vagabonded to the mines." At this same old Kearney, Chambers' and Haymond's greyhounds, and Soskolski's bull-dogs, were always fighting or barking. A lady's riding-robe made of wolf-skins, and dragging on the ground, with an accompanying head-dress of like material, with wolf-tails flying, is never forgotten, nor the ejaculation of the lieutenant-general, when the figure dashed by on a fiery, snorting steed, and he rushed to the door for a better view,—"*What's that? What's that?* I thought it was an Indian, sure!"

The contest of a lad, four years old, with the same officer, as to which could shoot an arrow over the flag-staff, without lying on the back, and spreading the bow with the feet, comes, as of yesterday, fresh to mind. And from that old halting-place in life's pilgrimage comes the shadow of burials, as well as the novelty of marriages, when the dead march and solemn tread were followed by the laying away of the cold form in a desert place, where wolves roamed by night, and a quartermaster's plank was the only head-stone of record.

The old fort has been demolished, and so, in turn, will pass away other strong defences, which once were as Cities of Refuge in a boundless wilderness; but will not the incoming denizens of towns and cities, and the nation itself, forget as soon, the scores of army martyrs, who, in their establishment and defence, made possible, the succeeding civilization and safety?

CHAPTER 34

Indian Affairs on the Plains— Incidents From 1874 to 1877

The military events which distinguished the period from 1874 to 1877, either express the reluctance of the Indians to accept the treaties of 1868, in their literal force, or grew out of incidental delays and modifications, in not promptly giving to the Indian the privileges which correspond to the rights surrendered.

Let it be understood, as a historical fact, that American Indians, who have, in good faith and with a clear understanding of the terms, once formed friendship with the white man, have generally been true to obligation. The Narragansetts and Delawares of early times, and the Pawnees and Crows of later times, are examples.

The hostile operations of the period under notice had three localizations: 1st, That along Kansas, New Mexico, and Colorado; 2nd, That involved in the redemption of the Black Hills from Indian control; and 3rd, The struggle with Northern Indians who refused all terms, and claimed exclusive privileges in the Big Horn country, by virtue of ancient occupancy or old treaties.

As early as March, 1874, several persons had been killed in Southern Kansas. The treaties of 1868 had, indeed, unqualifiedly vacated the claims of the Kiowas, Cheyennes, and Comanches to hunting privileges in that region; and the operations undertaken were aggressive, and without apology, save as small parties might be ignorant of the terms or binding force of those treaties. It is but justice to the Indian that we exercise some charity, when it is known that hundreds of statutes enacted by the white man, slowly reach the people, and the most inoperative of all, are game laws, and those that relate to minor trespass upon unclosed lands. The facts in this case, however, show that with the growth of the grass, the whole south-western frontier was fretted with raids, and these gradually enlarged their scope and license until systematic warfare became inevitable.

On the 21st of July the Interior Department accepted the situation, as that of war, and applied to the War Department for "force to punish the hostile Indians wherever found." Colonel N. A. Miles, 5th Infantry, with four companies of that regiment and eight companies of the 6th Cavalry, struck the enemy a severe blow on the 30th of August, twelve miles south of Red River; and in November the campaign resulted in still more severe punishment, the capture of the principal chiefs, and the consignment of thirty-nine of the most malignant, to military custody at Fort Marion, near St. Augustine, Florida.[1] These Indians were doubly ironed, for their journey, and are described by Bishop H. B. Whipple, of Minnesota, "as desperate warriors as ever carried the tomahawk or knife." In a letter dated Savannah, Georgia, March 24th, 1876, he declares that they became Christianized "under the charge of that noble Christian soldier, Captain H. R. Pratt, seconded by every effort of Colonel Hamilton and General Dent." His testimony meets the familiar charge that Indians cannot be tamed and humanized. He writes:

> Their faces are changed. They have all lost that look of savage hate, and the light of a new life is dawning in their hearts. It was my privilege to preach to them every Sunday, and upon weekdays I told them stories from the Bible. I have never had a more attentive congregation. Captain Pratt's success is due to the fact that he has taught them to labour: he has given them, in the best sense, a Christian school. The chief Ne-min-ick said, 'When I see the white man kneel, I know that he is talking to the Great Spirit, and asking for himself and children. I try, too, to send one little breath of prayer to the Great Spirit, that he will have pity on poor me.'

Other testimony confirms Bishop Whipple's judgment as to the susceptibility of the Indian to sound religious impressions, when he has first learned to obey and accept the conditions of civilized life and usage.

On the 10th of November, 1869, a commission which had been appointed by the President, under the Act of Congress of April 10th, 1869, to co-operate with the administration in the management of

---

1. Released on good behaviour, April, 1878.

Indian Affairs, and consisting of Felix A. Brunot, Robert Campbell, Henry S. Lane, W. E. Dodge, Nathan Bishop, John V. Farwell, Vincent Collyer, George H. Stuart, and Samuel S. Tobey, thus speak of the Indians in their report:

> Paradoxical as it may seem, the white man has been the chief obstacle in the way of Indian civilization. To assert "that the Indian will not work" is as true as it would be to say that the white man will not work. In all countries there are non-working classes. The chiefs and warriors are the Indian aristocracy. They need only to be given incentives to induce them to work. Why should the Indian be expected to plant corn, fence lands, build houses, or do anything but get food from day to day, when experience has taught him that the product of his labour will be seized by the white man tomorrow? The most industrious white man would become a drone under such circumstances.

The writer has never forgotten the startling paradox presented by White Head, a Northern Cheyenne chief, whose visit to us at Fort Phil Kearney is recorded in chapter 18 of the narrative: "Why do the white men ask the Great Spirit to curse them so often?" showing that even the savage, in his blindness, revolts from that profanity which degrades and brutalizes his civilized brother. This reference to the conduct of the Cheyenne captives is in harmony with the purpose to present various phases of this frontier service, and to testify that the conduct of Captain Pratt is not exceptional, but that in all ranks, and under the most fearful trials of border exposure, there are army officers who share in General Pope's opinion, that "it is most painful to pursue and punish Indians, who, by the neglect of the white man or the progress of settlement, are compelled to steal, or starve."

During operations against Indians south of Kansas, which continued through 1874 and until February, 1875, Captain Lyman, 5th Cavalry, with one company of infantry, and a detachment of the 6th Cavalry, was corralled for three days, by four hundred Indians, south of the Washita, until relieved by Major W. R. Price, 5th Cavalry, who came in from New Mexico to co-operate with Colonel Miles, Major James Biddle, and others, thus concentrated for duty in that region.

In the Department of the Platte, Lieutenant L. H. Robinson, 14th Infantry, was killed while in charge of a lumber-train near Laramie Peak sawmill. Several parties of Arrapahoes and Cheyennes, who lodged near Pumpkin Buttes, made raids about Forts Steele and Sanders, and when Generals Sheridan and Ord were at Camp Brown, in June, Captain A. E. Bates, 2nd Cavalry, with his company, and one hundred and sixty friendly Shoshones, punished a hostile band of considerable size, and drove it back to the Buttes. On the 1st of July, Lieutenant-Colonel Custer made an exploring expedition to the Black Hills, and returned August 30th, without meeting a hostile band. On the 27th of August, General Terry broke up a proposed expedition of citizens from Sioux City, Yankton, and Bismarck, and the year 1874 closed amid substantial quiet in that region.

This state of affairs redounds to the credit of many of the Indians then at Camp Robinson, Nebraska, where "Red Cloud," "Little Wound," "Sitting Bull," "Pawnee Killer," "American Horse," and other chiefs, together with nearly thirteen thousand Indians, were gathered. Prof. O. C. Marsh, of Yale College, was at the Agency during the distribution of Indian supplies in November, 1874, *en route* for the Black Hills, where he finally obtained a large variety of fossils for the Peabody Museum of that University. Of the Indians, who gathered in great numbers about the agency, he says, "They were armed quite as well as our soldiers, with breech-loading rifles and revolvers of the most recent pattern." Of the issues of beef, blankets, etc., he complains, in a letter to the President, as of inferior quality, deficient in amount, and tardily supplied.

The opinions of Lieutenant-Colonel L. P. Bradley, and Major A. S. Burt, 9th Infantry, and Captain John Mix, Company M, 2nd Cavalry, are given in confirmation of his judgment. The result of this tardiness and insufficiency became manifest through much suffering from cold during the winter, and Lieutenant W. L. Carpenter wrote in April, 1875, that "the Indians had been compelled to eat dogs, wolves, and ponies." Professor Marsh says, "The supply of food purchased by the government, carefully and honestly delivered, would have prevented all this suffering." That Secretary Delano was in any sense privy to the malfeasance of subordinate agents or contractors, cannot be believed by any who knew him in private and professional life, as did the writer, in Ohio.

The fact is, however, to be put to the credit of those Indian chiefs who, in spite of this wrong, abstained from war and maintained good faith; while it may partially explain the large exodus of others from the agencies, during the winter and subsequent spring.

In 1875, five raids were reported by General Augur for the month of April, by which several hundred horses were run off to Pumpkin

Buttes, thence to Powder River, and up to the camp of Sitting Bull. In May, Colonel R. J. Dodge, 23rd Infantry, with six companies of cavalry and two of infantry, escorted a surveying party to the Black Hills and back again, without interruption. Mining Engineer Walter P. Jenny accompanied the expedition. In June, Lieutenant-Colonel James W. Forsyth, military secretary at General Sheridan's headquarters, and Lieutenant-Colonel F. D. Grant, A. D. C, with an escort of seven officers and one hundred men, took the steamer *Josephine*, and ascended the Yellowstone, above Pompey's Pillar, nearly two hundred and fifty miles above Powder River, or four hundred and thirty miles above Fort Buford (once Fort Union), at the mouth of the Yellowstone. Eight miles above Pryor's Fork, he met a large camp of the Crow Indians, estimated at three hundred and fifty-one lodges, but says, "No Sioux were seen at any time during the expedition."

During June and July several stock-stealing parties approached Forts Steele and Sanders, but Colonel Gibbon promptly pursued, and again urged the establishment of the two large posts already alluded to. In June, also, parties broke away from Spotted Tail and Red Cloud Agencies; the latter to punish the Shoshones who aided Captain Bates in his pursuit of the Sioux in 1874. During this time strenuous efforts were made to keep miners out of the Black Hills, pending negotiations for their surrender to the United States. On the 29th of July, General Crook ordered all miners to leave, and Captains John Mix, 2nd Cavalry, and Anson Mills, 3rd Cavalry, had already acted efficiently in the same direction. On the 15th of August, a proclamation of the President emphatically enforced this policy. The Secretary of War, in his report of November 22nd, 1875, says:

> The report of General Augur foreshadows trouble between the miners and the Indians of the country known as the Black Hills, unless something be done to obtain possession of that section; for the white miners have been strongly attracted there by the reports of rich deposits of the precious metal.

General Sherman, in his annual report of November 2nd, says:
> Generally speaking, the damage to life and property by Indians, is believed to be less during the past year than in any former year, and the prospect is that as the country settles it will be less, till all the Indians are established on small reservations. But until they acquire habits of industry, in farming and stock-raising, they will need food from the General Government, because

the game on which they have subsisted has diminished very rapidly.

Thus gradually, year by year, the country along the completed railroad began to realize rest. Just at the close of 1875, the Indian Commissioner thus alludes to the portions of the Northwest which still remained unpacified:

> It will probably be found necessary to compel the Northern, non-treaty Sioux, under the leadership of Silting Bull, who have never yet in any way acknowledged the United States Government, except by snatching rations occasionally at an agency, and such outlaws from the several agencies as have attached themselves to these same hostiles, to cease marauding.

The year 1876, the National Centennial year, and the tenth after the first military occupation of the Big Horn country and the resulting massacre of Fetterman's command, brought back the Indian war to the same field of carnage, and culminated in Custer's similar fate.

The campaign opened early. Pursuant to the proposition of the Interior Department, made December 3rd, 1875, that "runners be first sent to warn the Indians to come in by or before January 31st, 1876, or a military force would be sent to compel them," active operations were postponed, until, at the expiration of that time, the whole matter was placed in the hands of the military authorities. The first blow was struck from the south, and by reference to the map the general progress of the column can be traced.

General Sherman's annual report for 1876 states the strength of the column, which was accompanied by General Crook in person, as:

> Ten companies of the 2nd and 3rd Cavalry, under Colonel J. J. Reynolds, 3rd Cavalry; two companies of the 4th Infantry; and, with teamsters and guides, a force of eight hundred and eighty-three men.

The rendezvous was Fort Fetterman, on the North Platte, and the companies began to arrive on the 22nd of February. On the 1st of March the advance began. After reaching Crazy "Woman's Fork, the wagons were sent back to Fort Reno, now Fort McKinney, under escort of infantry, and pack-mules were used for transportation of ammunition and rations for fifteen days. Shortly after passing Crazy Woman's Fork, March 7th, the troops moved nearly north from the Old Phil Kearney road. In a telegram, dated Fort Reno, March 22nd,

General Crook says:

> We scouted the Tongue and Rosebud Rivers until satisfied that there were no Indians upon them, then struck across the country toward Powder River. General Reynolds, with part of the command, was pushed forward on a trail leading to the village of Crazy Horse, near the mouth of the Little Powder River. This he attacked and destroyed on the 17th inst., finding it a perfect magazine of ammunition, war material, and general supplies. Crazy Horse had with him the Northern Cheyennes and some of the Minneconjous,—probably, in all, one-half of the Indians off the reservation. Every evidence was found to prove these Indians in a partnership with those at the Red Cloud and Spotted Tail Agencies, and that the proceeds of these raids upon the settlements had been taken to those settlements and supplies brought back in return. I am satisfied that if Sitting Bull is on this side of the Yellowstone, that he is camped at the mouth of Powder River. We experienced severe weather during our absence from the wagon-train, snow falling every day but one, and the mercurial thermometer on several occasions failing to register.

General Sherman says:

> Colonel Reynolds moved at 5 p.m. of the 16th, and by a night march struck the camp of Crazy Horse the next morning. The Indians fled to the hills, leaving the camp in the hands of the troops, who proceeded to destroy it and its contents by fire. The Indians molested the troops during this operation by firing from rocks, bushes, and gullies, but the village was utterly destroyed, when Colonel Reynolds drew off and proceeded to make junction with General Crook at the time and place appointed. Much controversy then arose, and still continues, as to whether Colonel Reynolds accomplished all that his opportunities afforded. Nevertheless, he made junction with General Crook on the morning of the 18th, near the place agreed on, when the expedition returned to Fort Fetterman, reaching that place March 26th.

If the reader will turn to chapter 26 of the narrative, and read the public opinions given at the time concerning Fetterman's massacre, he can estimate the value of the usual newspaper speculations which immediately illustrate a military disappointment, and neither the character nor distinguished career of Colonel Reynolds exempted him from this experience. The general facts in the case are as follows:

On the 16th of March, the command then being on Tongue River, followed Red Clay Creek eastward, crossed the divide, and reached Otter Creek early in the afternoon. Two Indians had been seen by the scouts. The command was divided. Colonel Reynolds, with one day's rations, unincumbered by blankets or any superfluous impediments, was detailed with six companies,—a total force of about three hundred men,—and a small detachment of fifteen scouts, and pushed the trail of the two Indians toward Powder River; while General Crook, with four companies and the pack-train, was to move to, or near the mouth of, Lodge Pole Creek, on the same river, with view to a junction of forces the next evening. This would complete the proposed circuit, and bring the command to Fort Reno, within the fifteen days for which rations had been provided upon leaving the supply-wagons. As a matter of fact this was safely accomplished. Colonel Reynolds's command gained the vicinity of Powder River about four a. m. of the 17th.

The troops were at once secreted in a ravine until the advanced scouts could make report; and upon the discovery that a heavy trail had been struck, the forward movement was renewed. The march from Tongue River to that point, a distance of nearly fifty miles, had been made since the previous morning,—much of the time over rugged bluffs, up narrow valleys, and through a country of great exposure. At about sunrise there was partially disclosed an Indian camp of something over one hundred lodges, settled in the Canon, or basin of Powder River, at a point where it widened out, but was environed by precipitous bluffs and hills of from three hundred to six hundred feet in height. Lieutenant Morton, adjutant of the expedition, in a sketch of the surroundings, has estimated some of the hills as eight hundred feet above the river-bed.

The access to this valley, or bottom area, was by precipitous and rocky banks, requiring horses to be carefully led, and, in places, barely accessible by men on foot, and the conformation of the land, generally, was such that no impromptu combination could guarantee that different companies could equally well descend and then act, as prearranged. The details of the bluff range were not even known to the scouts, and the sole hope of success lay in an early and effective surprise. This locality was nearly, or quite, one hundred miles north of

Fort Reno, with deep snow covering foot-falls, and fissures opening here and there, to deceive the eye and step.

About eight o'clock a.m. the camp was clearly defined, and a large number of ponies and mules were seen to be in charge of Indian herders. The battalion of Captain Noyes, Companies I and K, 2nd Cavalry, descended the mountain, in order that Captain Egan, with Company K, might charge the village, pistol in hand, while Captain Noyes should cut off the herd, as the column advanced towards the village which was beyond the herd. Companies E and F, 3rd Cavalry, of Captain Morris's battalion, Lieutenant Rawolle commanding the latter, were to dismount, leave their horses with holders, and covertly approach the village to support Captain Egan when he should make his charge. Of Companies E and M, 3rd Cavalry, Captain Mills (commanding battalion), with Company M, was to dismount, descend the mountain, and support Captain Moore; while Lieutenant Johnson, with Company E, was to make the best of his way down, to also co-operate as opportunity offered. The village was on the river, pretty close to a bluff, and the attacks were made from the southwest and west, where the bluffs fell back, and where there was ample room for the Indian herds to graze.

The charge of Captain Egan was a success. The Indians, evidently surprised, gave way before his fierce assault, and abandoned their lodges for trees, ravines, and other coverts, from which to annoy the troops. About noon they made an unsuccessful attempt to regain the village, but it was already on fire, and they were promptly repulsed. The ponies and mules, estimated at about seven hundred head, were also promptly captured, and in spite of desultory attacks and continued skirmishing, the dismounted companies regained their horses, and the march to Lodge Pole Creek was accomplished that evening, with a loss of only four men killed and five wounded. The weather was intensely cold. Colonel Reynolds had his face frosted, and many suffered extremely, only being kept from freezing by enforced activity and watchful care.

The Indian ponies, which were forced along as far as Lodge Pole Creek, were herded at night in the valley, on the advice of scouts, to find their own grazing, as there was no forage. Nearly one hundred had been killed, of necessity; of the residue, the greater portion strayed away the next morning, or were drawn off by Indians, so that with some gathered up by the other column as it approached the rendezvous, probably not more than two hundred and fifty were ultimately brought to Fort Reno. The troops were nearly worn out, without rations during the night and the next morning, and, as appears from General Sherman's statement, they had much to do to keep from freezing to death.

Incidental charges were exchanged by officers of the command, and the possibilities within the reach of an adequate, well-equipped force, with fore-knowledge of the location of the village, irritated the public mind for a while, and then all was forgotten, in the real success achieved.

This attack, however, on the village of Crazy Horse, involving a march of fifty-five miles, in a little more than twenty-four hours, in such a country, thirty miles of it at night, with snow a foot deep, with ice from twelve to fourteen inches to cut through to get water, with the mercury 30° below zero; the destruction of large supplies, then of the greatest value to the Indians; the capture of seven hundred head of stock, in the teeth of an equal, or superior force, contesting every step and movement for four hours of fighting, and an additional twenty miles of marching immediately after the fight, all in thirty-six hours, is a vivid episode of frontier service, showing both how much can be done, and how much more the American people expect to be done.

If the average citizen will fancy himself a horse-holder on such an occasion, with six or eight horses to control, while rifle-shots and pistol-shots and Indian yells abound; all the time watching ravines and fissures for some scouring party of savages to emerge, with flaunting robes, to put each individual horse into a frenzy of kicking, rearing, and biting; at the same time half frozen, and half starved, on hard-tack and snow, he will then assuredly understand the difference between the appreciation of such work, by a personal experience, and the dime-novel programme of heroic deliverances, in warfare on the Plains.

General Crook reached the rendezvous during the forenoon of the 18th, with the other four companies and the supply-train, having been unexpectedly delayed on the march, and the column reached Fort Reno on the 21st, with more than a hundred horses broken down, but with the satisfaction of having accomplished an extraordinary march, with signal injury to the enemy.

On the 24th of October, at the close of the Big Horn campaign. General Crook, then at Camp Robinson, thus pays tribute to the troops:

In the campaign now closed, he (the general commanding) had

been obliged to call upon you for much hard service and many sacrifices of personal comfort. At times you have been out of reach of your base of supplies; in most inclement weather you have marched without food and slept without shelter. Indian warfare is, of all warfare, the most trying, the most dangerous, and the most thankless. In it you are required to serve without the incentive to promotion or recognition; in truth, without favour or hope of reward.

The notification, by the runners of the Indian Department, that "unless the Indians came in by January 31st, 1876, a military force would be sent to compel them," failed; and "The expedition itself," says General Sherman, "was not satisfactory or conclusive;" therefore. General Sheridan determined to proceed more systematically, by concentric movements, similar to those which in 1874-5 had proved so successful at the south against the hostile Comanches, Kiowas, and Cheyennes."

This introduces the train of events which made the year 1876 especially memorable in Indian war, and focalized public sentiment, at last, rightly to estimate the real issue in the Northwest. The initial operations were based upon the assumption that the Interior Department had approximate data as to the number of Indians who were still hostile, and that those reported at Agencies might be considered out of the reckoning. From five hundred to eight hundred Indians was the highest estimate of an anticipated resisting force to either one of the three columns about to be set in motion, and the entire number then, in open hostility, was not estimated greatly to exceed that number.

General Crook left Fort Fetterman, May 29th, with two battalions of the 2nd Cavalry, under Lieutenant-Colonel W. B. Royal; 3rd Cavalry; five companies of the 4th and 9th Infantry, under Major Alexander Chambers (now lieutenant-colonel 21st Infantry), with wagons, pack-mules, and scouts; altogether forty-seven officers and one thousand and two men present for duty. His supply camp was made at Goose Creek. The march began on the 16th, and on the 17th a large force of Indians attacked his column as it descended Rosebud Creek, fighting on both sides of the creek until night came on. The Indians left thirteen dead on the field. General Crook's loss was nine killed and twenty-one wounded. Captain Guy V. Henry, 3rd Cavalry, being of the latter number. Of this operation of the campaign, General Sherman's report says:

The ground was so rough, so covered with rocks, trees, and bushes, that it was impossible to estimate, approximately, the force of the enemy; but General Crook was satisfied that the number and quality of his enemy required more men than he had, and being already encumbered with wounded, he concluded to return to his train on Goose Creek, which he reached on the 19th, and sent back for reinforcements.

General Terry, with the 7th Cavalry, about six hundred strong, Lieutenant-Colonel Custer commanding, and four hundred infantry, left Fort Abraham Lincoln May 17th, and reached the mouth of Powder River June 9th, where steamboats met him, and a supply camp was established. He reached the mouth of Rosebud on the 21st.

The following distances are given in a report of Major George A. Forsyth, *viz.: from mouth of Powder River* to Tongue River, thirty-seven miles; to Little Porcupine River, sixty-eight miles; to Big Porcupine River, seventy-seven miles; to Rig Horn River, one hundred and sixty-four miles; to Pompey's Pillar, two hundred and three miles; to Pryor's Fork, two hundred and twenty-six miles.

Colonel John Gibbon, 7th Infantry, with four hundred and fifty men from 2nd Cavalry and 7th Infantry, marched from Ellis to a point opposite Rosebud. A glance at the map will show that if General Crook had been strong enough to have taken the offensive from Goose Creek, the army would have had the control of the rectangle, three sides of which are represented by the Big Horn, Yellowstone, and Rosebud Rivers; but at the same time the roughness of the country, and the really great distances, for a substantial combination against so mobile a foe as the Indian, made the campaign one of extraordinary difficulty.

Nor must it be forgotten that, in the operations of General Crook from the Fort Phil Kearney line, the communications with troops on the Yellowstone were cut off, requiring a circuit of two thousand miles before information could be obtained, and this was material to the highest success. Reinforcements did not reach General Crook, and an important fact, which began to be known to the people, was not known, and could not be known, to the army of the Yellowstone, and that was, the large number of Indians absent from the agencies to take the war-path.

The 2nd Cavalry scouted the Yellowstone as far up as the Big Horn River, and no Indians had crossed, although Indian pickets had approached the river and come into collision with those of Captains Ball and Wheeler's companies. Major Reno, 7th Cavalry, ascended Powder River to the mouth of Little Powder River, found a large trail, estimated as nine days old, and crossed over the divide, to Tongue River, without meeting an enemy.

At the mouth of Rosebud, General Terry, Colonel Gibbon, and Lieutenant-Colonel Custer determined upon their future action, all circumstances indicating that the Indians were between Rosebud and Little Big Horn Rivers. Colonel Gibbon's command was sent to the Big Horn, by steamer, with orders to ascend that river, at least to the Little Big Horn, while Lieutenant-Colonel Custer was ordered to ascend the Rosebud, to cross the trail reported by Major Reno, but not to follow it, then to bear to his left, farther to the south, so as to prevent the Indians slipping by to the mountains. General Terry says in his report:

> We calculated it would take Gibbon's column until the 26th to reach the mouth of the Little Big Horn, and that the wide sweep I had proposed Custer should make would require so much time that Gibbon would be able to co-operate with him in attacking any Indians that might be found on the stream. Lieutenant-Colonel Custer said his marches would be at the rate of about thirty miles a day. Measurements were made, and calculations based, on that rate of progress. I talked with him about his strength, and at one time suggested that perhaps it would be well for me to take Gibbon's Cavalry and go with him. To the latter suggestion he replied that, without reference to the command, he would prefer his own regiment alone.
> As a homogeneous body, as much could be done with it as with the two combined. He expressed the utmost confidence that he had all the force he could need, and I shared his confidence. I offered Custer the battery of Gatling guns, but he declined it, saying that it might embarrass him, and that he was strong enough without it. The movements proposed by General Gibbon's column were carried out to the letter, and had the attack been deferred until it was up, I cannot doubt that we should have been successful.
> The Indians had evidently prepared themselves for a stand; but, as I learned from Captain Benteen that, on the 22nd, the cavalry marched twelve miles; on the 23rd twenty-five miles; from 5

a.m. till 8 p.m. of the 24th, forty-five miles; and then, after night, ten miles farther, resting, but without unsaddling, twenty-three miles to the battle field, the proposed route was not taken, but as soon as the trail was struck it was followed. I do not tell you this to cast any reflections upon Custer, for whatever errors he may have committed, Custer's action is inexplicable in the case.

The reports of Major Reno, and others, substantially concur in this statement, that the trail was followed as soon as readied, and was sharply crowded, until there was developed a large Indian village, in the valley of the Little Big Horn. Like the hunter in the chase, knowing well that the discovery of his presence would disperse the objects of such long and eager pursuit, and that failure to attack, in case the game brought to bay should escape, would mortify his command, and possibly bring professional reproach, Custer seems to have been impelled, as on the Washita, to dare the risks, for a crowning victory. Assured that the enemy had not gained his left and escaped to the Big Horn mountains, and believing, as he had ground to believe, that his force was equal to fight any band which he might meet, he has closed a career of rare brilliancy and promise, only to testify of the extreme contingencies of frontier service, and to stimulate the nation to a more hearty sympathy and more appreciative regard for those who are required to meet its obligations.

The regiment approached the Little Big Horn River in three columns. Major Reno, in the centre, crossed the river by a practicable ford, with the trail, as ordered, and dashed down the valley with Companies A, G, and M. Captain Benteen, with Companies D, H, and K, then two miles above the ford, was on his march to join the command, as ordered, before Custer left; and Lieutenant-Colonel Custer, with Companies C, E, F, I, and L, moved down the bluff on the right bank, to cross three miles below. Any small band of Indians would seem to have been completely within the grasp, of this order of attack.

Reno's command found themselves confronted by superior numbers eager to take the offensive, so that, fighting now on foot and then from the saddle, it was with difficulty that he regained the ford and a defensive position on the bluff. Here, supported by Benteen's battalion and Company B, which had previously guarded the supplies, the fight continued, under cover of rifle-pits, behind heaps of saddles, and desperately, until six o'clock of the 26th, when the Indians withdrew, admonished of the approach of General Terry's command from the north. About ten o'clock that column came in sight. Of the scene of the massacre, General Terry writes, June 27th:

> It is marked by the remains of his officers and men and the bodies of his horses, some of them strewed along the path, others heaped where halts appear to have been made.

As if the veil might yet be lifted, there have been some assurances that Corporal Ryan survived, as a prisoner, and that the British authorities have been requested to apply to Sitting Bull for his surrender. A statement of Red Horse, who surrendered in February, 1877, gave substantially the same version, however, as to the movements of Major Reno, the approach of General Terry's command, and the fact, that Custer's column was so overpowered by numbers, as to offer only brief resistance.

The rescued remains have received worthy burial; but the nation mourns, too late, the necessity, which compelled a handful of fearless men to contend with a host, in a fight where victory or death was the alternative destiny of the white man.

General Sheridan at once concentrated all the available force of his division. Lieutenant-Colonel Carr and ten companies, 5th Cavalry, joined General Crook at Goose Creek, *via* Fort Laramie, and detachments of infantry were sent to the same column. Colonel Miles moved from the south of Kansas with the 5th Infantry. Lieutenant-Colonel Otis, with six companies of the 22nd Infantry and four companies of artillery from the Atlantic coast, were sent to General Terry.

As early as July 26th, General Crook was in communication with General Terry, each with a nominal command of about two thousand men; but General Sheridan thus reported, August 5th:

> General Crook's total strength is seventeen hundred and seventy-four, and Terry's eighteen hundred and seventy-eight; and to give this force to them, I have stripped every post from the line of Manitoba to Texas.

General Sherman says:

> Both columns of about the same strength, moved as agreed upon, and made junction on the Rosebud, August 10th, at a point thirty-five miles above its mouth. The Indians had, as expected, slipped out, and neither column had a chance to strike a blow. The Indians in their retreat left a broad trail leading

toward Tongue River. This was followed promptly and steadily, but it seems to be impossible to force Indians to fight at a disadvantage in their own country. Their sagacity and skill surpass that of the white race.

On the 14th of September, Captain Anson Mills, 3rd Cavalry, struck a small village, killed American Horse, before referred to as present at a friendly conference, and at Red Cloud Agency, November, 1874; and the whole autumn was signalized by hard marches, in "the most inaccessible and difficult country, east of the Rocky Mountains."

The Yellowstone River closed too early for establishment of permanent posts, and winter cantonments were established at Goose Creek and Tongue River. On the 18th of October a supply-train was attacked near Glendive Creek, not far from Tongue River, and active marching was resumed.

Meanwhile the disarming of the Indians at the Agencies, was enforced, and the small army was needed, all over Dacotah. Colonel Miles pursued and overtook Sitting Bull, on the 21st of October, to be met by the request for supplies, peace, *and* ammunition. Two days of conference was succeeded by hostilities. The Indians were pursued forty-two miles across the Yellowstone, and on the 27th of October they sued for peace, giving Red Skirt, White Bull, Black Eagle, Sun Rise, and Foolish Thunder as hostages for the others' reporting at the posts named. Crazy Horse sought refuge in the buffalo country, and escaped up Powder River.

On the 16th of November General Crook again left Fort Fetterman, and crowded Crazy Horse toward the Black Hills. Colonel Mackenzie destroyed a Cheyenne camp November 21st, on the west fork of Powder River, and the country north of the Yellowstone was so thoroughly scoured, that the remaining Indians were driven out of the region lying between the Muscle Shell and the Dry Fork of the Missouri River.

On the 17th of December, Bull Eagle, Tall Bull, Red Cloth, and another chief approached the Tongue River cantonment with a white flag, but were shot by Crow Indians, whose antipathy to the old enemies who had robbed them of the country, broke forth, before any effort could be made to arrest the attack. The best satisfaction possible was given by way of explanation and presents; but General Crook, in referring to the matter, says, "The affair was most unfortunate, as their coming in would have secured the surrender of at least one thousand fighting men."

Already, the supervision of the Lower Brulè, Cheyenne River, and Standing Rock Agencies had been turned over to the military authorities, (as early as July), so that captured Indians could be brought together and the peaceable kept from roaming; and army officers also discharged the duties of agent at Red Cloud and Spotted Tail Agencies. To all of them there came, for food and winter shelter, bands of the very Indians who participated in the fights in the Big Horn country.

CHAPTER 35

Indian Affairs on the Plains— Incidents of 1877

The period now under review is full of facts which confirm the opinion early advanced by General Sherman, that the Indian question must be settled by assuring to him a permanent reservation, sufficiently accessible for the general supervision of the government, and so restricted that he must adopt the white man's mode of living and be cut off from free roving on the plains. Already the tide of travel, if not the course of settlement, has impaired successful hunting in large bands, and the time has come when the nation demands that the attitude of all Indians shall be settled, so that the question of peace or war shall find a definite solution.

Distant and inaccessible reservations, where the Indians had arms and horses, and hunted at will over large areas of country, not only exposed them to the influence of wild and uncontrollable bands, but left open an easy method by which the young men could absent themselves, mingle with hostile parties, and then seek a place of refuge, either unsuspected or unpunished. The difficulty of finding responsible chiefs, who could, in reality, control and vouch for wandering Indians, was insurmountable.

As early as 1869, Messrs. Brunot and Campbell, and Hon. Henry S, Lane, of Indiana, with other commissioners, had advised the abandonment of the treaty system, saying:

> The legal status of the uncivilized Indian should be that of wards of the government; the duty of the latter being to protect them, to educate them in industry, the arts of civilization, and the principles of Christianity, elevate them to the rights of citi-

zenship, and to sustain them until they can support themselves.

The year 1877 was one of great unrest among the bands which were on recognized terms of friendship. The prudential reasons which led to the disarming and dismounting of some of these bands, coupled with their *third* assignment to reservations, incited distrust. Agent J. F. Cravens, particularly noticed the effect produced by news of the annihilation of General Custer's command; and military commanders clearly show, that in nearly all conflicts during the last four years in the three military departments of the plains, there have been participants, who had been fed and provided for by the United States. The partial transfer of Arrapahoes and Cheyennes to the Indian Territory, and the definite location of the Ogallalla and Brulè Sioux, until they also shall be drifted in the same direction, would seem to bring the main question to that of the disposal of Sitting Bull and the bands which still vibrate between the Yellowstone and the British possessions.

The establishment of two strong posts, both memorial in name, Fort Keogh, at the mouth of Tongue River, and Fort Custer, on the Big Horn, below the old site of Fort C. F. Smith, will realize that which Generals Pope, Hancock, and Terry long urged,—the maintenance of strong central positions, capable of outside operations, rather than the distribution of small posts, hardly self-sustaining. The latter system suits a railroad or stage-route, subject to small depredations, but is only aggravating and weak, in the midst of regions thoroughly hostile. The Secretary of War, under date of July 8th, 1876, in urging the establishment of two new posts, thus writes to the President:

> The task committed to the military authorities is one of unusual difficulty, has been anticipated for years, and must be met and accomplished.

Neither must it be overlooked that while the Yellowstone River is open from May to October, the larger number of expeditions sent to this theatre of conflict have marched by the very route on which were located the posts erected in 1866. The original orders creating the Rocky Mountain District directed Colonel Carrington to abandon Fort Reno, and, besides the post afterwards known as Fort Phil Kearney, to build posts on the Big Horn River, and on or near the upper Yellowstone.

The force was insufficient to build and protect three new posts, and Fort Reno could not be prudently abandoned, so that the third post, now Fort Ellis, which has become so important, had to be, for the time, postponed. The commanding officer of that district, Colonel Carrington, in the establishment of the two original posts, realized that they were placed where it fell heaviest upon the Indians, and, therefore, better for the emigrant, and, in October, 1866, when citizens complained of insufficiency of escort, and that the Indians were not pursued and exterminated, thus declared his policy:

> I do not regard my occupation of this line as a temporary expedition to chastise Indians, but as designed to establish a solid basis for ultimate operations, to whatever extent they may be required. I expect to be harassed, and to have constant skirmishing and minor fights; but I propose to follow up a constant, persistent purpose, to make permanent every progress, and not to hazard all, for the uncertainties attending the invasion of distant Indian villages with an inadequate force, leaving an inadequate garrison behind. Understanding well that I have to bear the responsibility, I propose respectfully to receive any communications that citizens may furnish, but to maintain the general views laid down, whether acceptable to them now or otherwise. I know it will bring some results in the end, while hot impulses and rash expeditions will only bring discredit, and make the emigration next spring doubly dangerous.

That policy has been vindicated. The instructions of the lieutenant-general, sent from Laramie during his visit at that post, were, to "discriminate carefully between Indians who honestly desired peace, and those who were hostile," with the further information that "the government is not prepared for, neither does it desire, a general Indian war."

The campaign of 1876 over-ran, into the year 1877, and there was little rest for the worn-out troops during the winter. Colonel Miles attacked Crazy Horse in the valley of Tongue River on the 8th of January, after a week of almost daily skirmishing, and routed his band, but the stock was too broken down to follow up the success, and Crazy Horse retreated to the Big Horn mountains. In a congratulatory order to his regiment, of January 31st, he notices their march of twelve hundred miles in three months, and fitly commends their merit.

In April the Sioux began to come in to the agencies in large numbers. The Indian Commissioner reports "that Spotted Tail went out with two hundred and fifty of his principal men to urge the return of his people to their agency and allegiance, adding, "His return in April with a following of one thousand one hundred, attested the remarkable success of his mission; and for this eminent service, which virtually ended the Sioux war, and his unswerving loyalty throughout the whole campaign, some suitable testimonial should be tendered him."

May 5th, Colonel Miles had a fight on Muddy Creek, a small branch of Rosebud, with Lame Deer, capturing four hundred and fifty ponies, and inflicting much loss, but narrowly saving his own life. Iron Star shook hands with him, then picking up his carbine, fired, the ball missing its mark, but killing a soldier behind him. This was after protection had been offered to all who would surrender. Ball's, Tyler's, Wheeler's, and Norwood's companies of the 2nd Cavalry were in the fight, and Dickey's, Poole's, Miner's and Casick's companies of the 22nd, as well as a detachment of the 5th Infantry.

On the 6th of May, at Camp Robinson, Crazy Horse surrendered, being introduced to Lieutenant Clark, of General Crook's staff, by Red Cloud. This surrender represented twelve hundred Indians under Crazy Horse, Little Hawk, Little Big Man, Bull Hawk, and Bad Road, and included more than two thousand ponies.

In July, Captain Kellog, of the 5th Cavalry, made a scout from Goose Creek along the Rosebud and Little Big Horn, and discovered no signs of Indians. Captain Mills also escorted two pack-trains to the mouth of Tongue River, turned over the trains to Colonel Miles, and after riding three hundred miles over the country, so infested in 1876, returned to Goose Creek without encountering an enemy.

July 25th, General Sherman dates a report,—

> Headquarters of the Army of the United States, on the Steamer *Rosebud*, Big Horn River, having steamed up the Big Horn River to the present Fort Custer, at the forks of Big Horn and Little Big Horn."

General Sheridan had just come across from Camp Stambaugh, and had seen no Indians. General Sherman writes:

> With this post, and that at the mouth of the old Tongue River, occupied by strong, enterprising garrisons, these Sioux Indians can never regain this country, and they will be forced to remain at their Agencies or take refuge in the British possessions. At this moment there are no Indians here or hereabouts; I have seen or heard of none. The country west of this is a good country, and will rapidly fill up with emigrants, and will, in the next four years, build up a community as strong and capable of self-

defence as Colorado.

On the 20th of August, Major James S. Brisbin, 2nd Cavalry, reached the mouth of Clear Creek (see map), a branch of Powder River, and found signs of a recent encampment. On the 21st he continued the pursuit through the ravines and over mountains and gullies; but the Indians lied without battle, abandoning lodge-poles, kettles, cups, and even saddle-blankets.

On the 27th of August, 1877, the following Agencies were announced, subject to a possible change, in the spring of 1878, of the first two named, for better farming lands, *viz.*:

The old Ponca Agency, sixty miles above Yankton, on the west bank of the Missouri River, for Spotted Tail; Yellow Medicine Creek, two hundred and seventy miles above Yankton, for Red Cloud; Crow Creek Agency, two hundred and thirty miles above Yankton, on the old Winnebago Reserve; Cheyenne River Agency, three hundred and sixty-five miles above Yankton; Standing Rock Agency, five hundred and twenty-nine miles above Yankton, and eighty miles below Bismark.

On the 5th of September, Crazy Horse made an attempt to escape from Camp Robinson, but was recaptured. General Crook reported him as at the bottom of the trouble at both Red Cloud and Spotted Tail Agencies, and his men were distributed among other bands. He afterwards was killed in a needless encounter.

On the 17th of October, General A. H. Terry and Hon. A. J. Lawrence had a conference with Sitting Bull at Fort Walsh, in the British possessions, at which time he refused all overtures of peace, and asserted his purpose to dwell under the sway of the white queen mother.

The year of 1877 closed with comparative peace in the three Departments of the Plains.

The record of operations in these departments is not complete, however, without some reference to another band of Indians, who have in part joined Sitting Bull in Canada, in part lurk in Montana, among the bands along the Northern border, and in part are gathered into agencies, as the result of hard-fought battles, tedious wanderings, and extreme exposure on the field.

The Nez Perces Indians belonged to Idaho, and as early as June, 1855, a treaty had been made, which allotted certain valleys to the leading chiefs, fifty-eight of whom signed the agreement. Chief Joseph occupying the Wallowa Valley. An abstract of the Indian Commissioner's report for 1877 will give the following facts. The *gold* excitement, as ever, precipitated adventurers westward, to the rescue of the gold from the lands of the Indians, and on the 10th of April, 1861, an agreement was made (not confirmed by Congress), between Superintendent Geary, Agent Cain, and Indian Chief Lawyer, with forty-seven other chiefs, opening a portion of that country to the whites, as well as the Indians, "*for mining purposes*." In October, 1861, a town was laid out and a population of twelve hundred soon settled at their ease.

In 1862 the annuities averaged only one blanket to six Indians, and two yards of calico to each person. On the 9th of June, 1863, a new treaty was made, reducing the Indian Reserve and excluding Wallowa Valley from its limits. "Chief Joseph," "Looking Glass," "Big Thunder," "White Bird," and "Eagle from the Light," ignored the treaty and roamed at will through the valley.

On the 26th of March, 1873, Hon. J. P. C. Shanks, Hon. T. W. Bennett, and Agent H. N. Reed, the first two, distinguished for service in the civil war, were appointed to investigate and report on Indian affairs in Idaho. Superintendent T. Odeneal and Agent J. B. Menteith were also appointed special commissioners to confer with Joseph as to his removal to the Lapwai Reserve. The first-named commissioners impeached the whites, for encroachments, even upon the reduced reservation, and the last-named decided it to be impracticable to effect the proposed removal. On the 16th of June, following, the President declared the Wallowa Valley, a reservation for the roving bands subject to their good behaviour; but Congress made no appropriation to buy out the settlers' claims, and as Chief Joseph would not settle down quietly, the order was revoked by President Grant, June 18th, 1875.[2]

In October, 1876, Hon. Z. Chandler, Secretary of the Interior Department, appointed D. H. Jerome, Esq., General O. H. Howard, Major H. Clay Wood, and Messrs. William Stickney and A. C. Barston, a board, to settle the troubles which were maturing toward violence and had already cost several lives. Their report was made December 1, 1876, and in May, 1877, councils were held, Chief Joseph, Looking Glass, and White Bird being present, and agreeing to go upon the reservation. On the 10th of May they had completed their examination of various localities, and the commission were satisfied that trouble was at an end.

The annual report of the Indian Commissioners says:

---

2. See note 1 at end of chapter.

One day, however, prior to the expiration of the time fixed for their removal (namely, June 14th, 1877), open hostilities by these Indians began, by the murder of twenty-one white men and women on White Bird Creek, near Mount Idaho, *in revenge for the murder of one of their tribe.*

The troops at the disposal of General Howard were few in number, and every settlement was put in peril. Company F, 1st Cavalry, was at Fort Lapwai, but far from complete in strength. The rest of the regiment was scattered through Nevada, California, Washington Territory, and Oregon. The most accessible aid was from the 7th Infantry, Colonel John Gibbon, which was distributed at Forts Shaw, Benton, Ellis, and Camp Baker, in Montana. General Howard, however, used with promptness his small force. Captain David Perry, 1st Cavalry, attacked the Indians at Hangman's Creek, near Spokane, seventy-five miles east of Lewiston, on the 17th of June, losing thirty-four men, either killed or wounded. The Lewiston volunteers, and Dayton volunteers, and other local organizations, were at once called into service.

Colonel Berry and Captain Whipple had a tight on the 4th of July, at Kamiah, near Cottonwood, on Solomon River, losing thirteen men. On the 12th of July, General Howard, commanding in person, engaged the Indians near the mouth of Cottonwood Creek, on the south side of Clearwater, losing eleven killed and twenty-six wounded. The Indians crossed the Cottonwood below Kamiah, and on the 19th of July were divided in opinion whether to prolong hostilities or surrender. A conference ensued. Red Heart and twenty-eight of his people gave themselves up, and Joseph manifested a similar purpose, but the influence of White Bird constrained him to refuse submission to the terms proposed, and the non-treaty party fled to the Bitter Root Mountains, pursued by General Howard.

On the 2nd of August, General Sherman, then at Bozeman, gave orders for all possible promptness in the effort to throw the Indians back upon General Howard, and prevent their escape to the buffalo country of Montana, in the north. On the 9th, Colonel Gibbon, of the 7th Infantry, attacked the Nez Perces at Big Hole Pass, in Montana, one hundred and twenty miles from Missoula, and nearly due west from Fort Ellis. His report of August 11th, reports his loss at seven officers and fifty-three men, killed and wounded. Among the killed were Captain Wm. Logan, 7th Infantry, and Lieutenant James H. Bradley, of the same regiment, formerly of the 18th, whose trip to Fort

Benton in 1866 is referred to in chapter 15 of the narrative. Colonel Gibbon was also wounded, and thus telegraphed to Governor Potts.

Big Hole Pass, August 9th, 1877.

Had a fight with the Nez Perces. We are here near the mouth of Big Hole Pass, with a large number of wounded men in want of everything; food, clothing, medicine, and medical attendance. Send assistance at once.

John Gibbon, Colonel Commanding.

Another despatch says: "The troops are entrenching, and the Indians are leaving." While Colonel Gibbon was thus trying to head off the retreating Nez Perces, with an original force, all told, of only one hundred and ninety-one men, including thirty-four citizens, General Howard, with a small escort, pushed ahead of his column, marching on the 10th, fifty-three miles, notwithstanding the roughness of the country, leaving his command to follow. On the 12th he reached Colonel Gibbon, and telegraphed to General McDowell's headquarters:

> Gibbon's command is in the best of spirits. The last of the Indians left last night. Shall continue the pursuit as soon as my command is up."

As the result of this battle, eighty-nine bodies of Indians were found on the field, showing that their loss was equal to half the number of whites engaged.

The retreat was southeast, nearly to Bannock City, thence southwest to Horse Prairie River, and on to old Fort Limai. Their only avenue of escape was to pass around Montana to the south, and then strike north, east of Fort Ellis, avoiding settlements and posts. Upon reaching Henry's Fork of Snake River (see map), they turned north toward Henry's Lake, which is southeast of Virginia City, and nearly at the source of Henry's Fork, with General Howard in close pursuit. At Camp Meadow, near the lake, they turned and attacked General Howard's column, inflicting a loss of one man killed and seven wounded, captured nearly a hundred horses, most of which were recovered, and on the 27th of August crossed the Yellowstone River above the falls, at the upper end of a *cañon* in the National Park, just north of the Sulphur Mountains, in the northwest part of Wyoming Territory.

They then took the Clark's Fork trail. Colonel Merritt, of the 5th Cavalry, with six companies of the 5th, and Russell's of the 3rd

Cavalry, and fifty Shoshones scouts, moved rapidly from the direction of the Goose Creek camp, to occupy the line of the Stinking River, and cut off their movement southward; and Colonel Saml. D. Sturgis, 7th Cavalry, left the New Crow Agency, at the Forks of Big and Little Rosebud, to cut off their movement to the north.

General Sheridan, in ordering the recall of Colonel Merritt, "unless his presence should be longer needed in that direction," says, that "instead of going up Clark's Fork, as was expected, Colonel Sturgis also went over to Stinking Water, and while he was doing so, the Indians came down Clark's Fork and passed him." Still, on the 13th of September, he overtook and had a fight with them on Cañon Creek, Clark's Fork, and pursued them closely on the 14th and 15th. On the latter date he reported the Indian loss at sixty, and that "nine hundred ponies had been dropped by the hostiles," and adds, "I am going ahead this morning, and propose to push them until they drop their whole herd, and I think they will abandon nearly their last horse. Today, Howard, with infantry and artillery, was north of the Yellowstone, below Clark's Fork. The 16th Infantry is moving on Muscle Shell."

At that time Colonel Sturgis had been compelled to abandon some of his own horses,—the men had lived for four days on mule meat, and very rapid pursuit was impossible.[3]

The remaining Nez Perces eluded further punishment, successively crossed the Yellowstone, Muscle Shell, and Missouri, and safely entered the Bear Paw Mountains, south of Milk River, in the country of the Blackfeet and Bloods.

On the 18th of September, Colonel Miles, having learned, on the evening of the 17th, from General Howard, then on Clark's Fork, that the Nez Perces had evaded the commands to the north of them, and were pushing northward, at once organized all the available force at his command, for a movement to intercept, or pursue. The commission sent to have an interview with fitting Bull in the British Possessions, had already left, with an escort from the 2nd and 7th Cavalry. This was overtaken, and the combined force moved on without delay.

The march led directly to the mouth of Muscle Shell, nearly northwest, there around the eastern and northern bases of the Little Rocky Mountains to Snake Creek, a fork of Milk River, the distance of two hundred and sixty-five miles being accomplished in ten days. The Missouri River, at mouth of Muscle Shell, was reached on the 23rd, and a depot was established. On the 25th Colonel Miles learned

---
3. See note 2. at end of chapter.

that the Indians actually crossed the Missouri on the 23rd, at Cow Island, (See map No. 2.) The following is the substance of Colonel Miles's official report of this extraordinary expedition, so timely in its movements and so brilliant in its success.

The train was left, to follow at leisure, and or the evening of the 29th the troops reached the northern end of Bear Paw Mountains, which the Nez Perces had approached from the south, and he was between them and Milk River. Entering the mountain range at four o'clock on the 30th, the Indian trail was struck at six a.m. near the head of Snake River. The village on Eagle Creek was immediately charged in front, by the battalion of the 7th Cavalry under Captain Owen Hale, and the 5th Infantry, Captain Simon Snyder. A battalion of the 2nd Cavalry, Captain George L. Tyler, attacked in the rear and secured the stock, to the number of seven hundred horses, mules, and ponies. The Indians took refuge in some deep ravines, and the firing was accurate and well kept up.

To avoid the loss of life incident to storming these positions, from which they could not escape, the troops remained for four days on the alert, shelling the ravines and exchanging shots, whenever it was found effective. White flags were displayed, and communications were had with the Indians several times, but on the fifth they surrendered arms and ammunition, and the contest was at an end. Looking Glass and several of the chiefs, including a brother of Joseph and twenty-five Indians, had been killed, and forty-six Indians were wounded. Colonel Miles writes:

> A severe storm of snow and wind, which set in on the 1st, added greatly to the hardships, which have been borne without murmuring.

The casualties of the command were Captain Owen Hale and Second Lieutenant Joseph W. Biddle, both of 7th Cavalry, killed; Captain Miles Moylan and Edward S. Godfrey, 7th Cavalry, First Lieutenant Geo. W. Baird, Adjutant, and Lieutenant Henry Romeyn, 5th Infantry, wounded. Enlisted men, nineteen killed and forty-two wounded.

Companies A, D, and K, 7th Cavalry, had ten sergeants among their casualties.

It is stated by the Commissioner of Indian Affairs, in his report for 1877, "That Joseph observed the rules of civilized warfare, and did not mutilate dead enemies," whereas Red Cloud and his bands, in 1866, in their first resentment of the invasion of the Big Horn country, committed atrocities upon living captives of a kind unrecorded elsewhere in human history.

The Nez Perces campaign grew out of wrongs inflicted upon their people. It is the old story; and after all due resentment is expended upon Joseph, for murders committed by his band in the immediate vicinity of their old home in Idaho, this war must be classed among the inevitable results of violated treaties and original trespass upon the red man's rights.

Note 1.—General Shanks commanded the 7th Indiana Cavalry during the civil war, and states that "Joseph's party was thoroughly disciplined; that they rode at full gallop along the mountain side in a steady formation by fours; formed twos, at a given signal, with perfect precision, to cress a narrow bridge; then galloped into line, reined in to a sudden halt, and dismounted with as much system as if regulars."

Of Joseph's character he gives these facts, as to the interview with him:

"I do not fight women," said Joseph. "It is not their fault that they are here."

Placing his hand on his breast, he said, "This is my body It came out of the earth. Do you believe it? Then the earth is my mother, and I shall return to her. Would you sell your mother? I will never sell my mother."

General Shanks put this question to Joseph: "Do you want schools and school-houses on the Wallowa Reservation?"

Answer by Joseph. "No. We do not want schools or school-houses on the Wallowa Reservation."

Question. "Why do you not want schools?"

Answer. "They will teach us to have churches."

Question. "Why do you not want churches?"

Answer. "They will teach us to quarrel about God, as the Catholics and Protestants do on the Nez Perces Reservation, and at other places. We do not want to learn that. We may quarrel with men, sometimes, about things on this earth, but we never quarrel about God. We do not want to learn that."

Note 2.—Copy of Official Report of General S. D. Sturgis (Colonel 7th Cavalry) received May 1st, too late for this edition. His command, made up largely of raw men, to supply the terrible waste of the Custer massacre, marched fifteen hundred miles during the Nez Perces campaign,[4] overtaking Colonel Miles just after the battle at Snake River. His testimony to "their patience under exposure, fatigue, hunger, and peril" is but another illustration of the character of service on the Plains.

---

4. *The Nez Percé Campaign, 1877: Two Accounts of Chief Joseph and the Defeat of the Nez Percé—The Battle of Big Hole & Chief Joseph, the Nez Percé* by G. O. Shields and Edmond Stephen Meany is also published by Leonaur.

CHAPTER 36

Honour to Whom Honour

This outline of the struggle of the Indian to retain the vast plains which the buffalo peopled, and to live as his fathers lived, has only touched the prominent facts and manifestations which from year to year demanded the serious thought of the American people. The single instances where cabins, ranches, and emigrant trains have been despoiled are not to be easily counted; but far more numerous have been the desolated lodges of the red man, whose life went out at the will of the white man's avarice, and of which wrongs history will speak as of needless robbery and cruel wrong. Many have been the marchings and thirstings, the hungerings and dyings of the obedient soldier, contending, in the name of the State, to dispossess the savage of the home of the savage, and surely there have been atrocities which demanded of the white man the punishment of the evil-doer; but far more have been the starvings and the flights and the extinguishments which have visited the Indian, for the offence of living, and loving to live, where the Great Spirit gave him breath.

And yet through all this chain of linked horrors and ceaseless conflict there is a justly-deserved tribute due to the American soldier, who, under the most painful of all pressure,—that of fighting while conscious that an inferior race is subjected to his disposal,—almost without exception, has restricted his work to the necessity of the hour, and mingled with war itself the sincere effort to secure to his savage enemy some avenue to peace. It was not traffic at one thousand *per cent*, of profit, nor the pursuit of gold, much less the glory of shooting red men as game, that took the soldier to the Plains; and aside from the protection of travel, or peaceful homes, and of legitimate traders, when such there were, he had no treasure, and little pleasure, in his mission. The succession of events already given, as the proper sequel to the personal narrative of this volume, has no more prominent fact than this assurance of history to the credit of the American Army.

Among the citizens of the Republic whose sympathies have been quick to feel for the red man, and equally earnest to labour in his rescue, few have been more sincere and unselfish than Hon. George W. Manypenny, of Columbus, Ohio, the President of the Commission appointed by President Grant to negotiate with Red Cloud, and other Indians, for the final surrender of the Black Hills and the country adjacent.

In his report of December 18th, 1876, addressed to the Hon. J. Q. Smith, Commissioner of Indian Affairs, he cites the following from the report of Generals Sherman, Harney, Terry and Augur, and Messrs. Henderson, Tappan, and Sanborn, made in connection with the treaties of 1868:

> The Indian, although a barbarian, is yet a man, susceptible to those feelings which respond to magnanimity and kindness. The injunction to do good to those that hate us is not confined to race, but is broad as humanity itself. This truth, for the practical man seeking a solution of the troubles, will serve a better purpose than whole pages of theories of Indian character.

"These words," says Colonel Manypenny, "are words which ought to be written in letters of gold, and read by every citizen."

From the same report he quotes again:

> If the lands of the white man are taken, civilization justifies him in resisting the invader. Civilization does more than this,—it brands him as a coward and a slave if he submits to the wrong. Here civilization made its own compact, and guaranteed the rights of the weaker party. It did not stand by the guarantee. The treaty was broken; but not by the savage. If the savage resists, civilization, with the Ten Commandments in one hand and the sword in the other, demands his immediate extermination. That he goes to war is not astonishing; he is often compelled to do so. Wrongs are borne by him in silence that never fail to drive civilized man to deeds of violence. Among civilized men, war generally springs from a sense of injustice. The best possible way then to avoid war is to do no act of injustice. When we learn that the same rule holds good with Indians, the chief difficulty is removed. But it is said that our wars with them have been almost constant. Have we been uniformly unjust? We answer,

unhesitatingly, "Yes."

Colonel Manypenny writes:

> These words are words wrung from brave men, who had grown gray in the service of the country. They were compelled to confess the nation's shame by the facts which they themselves had investigated.

With such sentiments of the general of the army, and of two of the department commanders, and of General Harney, generous as he is brave, and eminent above all other living men for experience in frontier war, the army of the Plains has been in substantial accord.

It would require a full volume to embody the details of the engagements referred to, and to render just tribute to detachment commanders who achieved real success in the tiresome ordeal of frontier life. That remains for future development. The immediate purpose has been realized, if substantial clearness has been given to the progress of the Indian question towards its final disposal. Of the chiefs who bore part in the campaign of 1866, Spotted Tail and Standing Elk have remained true to their first treaty obligation; and Red Cloud, who so stoutly contended for his legal rights in that opening year of the war, has vindicated his pledge to abide by contracts since made. Others have dropped out of the record as it progressed.

Of the officers of the 7th Cavalry whose career embraced active operations in each of the Departments of the Plains, it was the lot to share in the final battle with the Nez Perces at Bear Paw mountain; and there, some who had passed unscathed through the battles of the "Washita," "Beaver Creek," "The Big Horn," and "The Little Horn," laid down their lives with honour, as if the whole regiment was destined to share in the monumental record of this protracted war. As a general rule, except in quoting extracts from reports and other documents, the lineal rank has been given, so as not to confuse the reader by mingling the lineal and brevet rank in the recital. The appendix of casualties gives both, as found in the Army Register. Such legitimate material as has been accessible has been used as briefly as possible, and in equal justice to all,

It remains only to notice the faithful co-operation and unvarying integrity of the Mountain and River Crow Indians, whose home, so long since stolen by the Sioux, has been the battlefield of so many vital issues.

Ab-sa-ra-ka—the "Land that the Crow Flies Over," "The Home

of the Crows"—is to be the peaceful home of the white man, and if the end of inter-tribal conflicts shall bring with it also the earnest purpose of the American people to deserve the friendship of all the red race, and seek their enlightenment and happiness, the bloodshed, and the agony endured, will have some recompense, in justice done to the warrior race thus rescued, though the justice be tardy and the cost be vast.

Appendix

1

The following extract, from Senate Document No. 13, 1861, furnishes that portion relating to the massacre near Fort Phil Kearney in 1866, being Report of the Special Commission sent to investigate the cause of that disaster.

DISPOSITION AND CONDUCT OF THE INDIANS ABOUT FORT PHIL KEARNEY, AND THE CAUSES OF THE SAME.

The main object sought to be secured by the treaty of Laramie of July, $A.D.$ 1866, was the opening of a new route to Montana from Fort Laramie, via Bridger's Ferry and the headwaters of the Powder, Tongue, and Big Horn Rivers. This country was occupied by the Ogallalla and Minneconjoux bands of Sioux Indians and the northern Cheyenne and Arrapahoe tribes, and the mountain Crows.

The region through which the road was to pass and does pass is the most attractive and valuable to Indians. It abounds with game, flocks of mountain sheep, droves of elk and deer, and herds of buffalo range through and live in this country, and the Indians with propriety call it their last best hunting-grounds. All these Indians were reluctant to allow the proposed road to pass through these hunting-grounds, but all would reluctantly assent to this for so liberal an equivalent as the government was ready to give. The Indians were required further to stipulate that the government should have the right to establish one or more military posts on this road in their country. All the Indians occupying it refused thus to stipulate, and through the chiefs, headmen, and soldiers protested against the establishment of any military post on their hunting-grounds along that road north of Fort Reno.

While negotiations were going on with Red Cloud and their leading chiefs to induce them to yield to the government the right to peaceably establish these military posts, which right they persistently refused to yield, saying that it was asking too much of their people—asking all they had—for it would drive away all the game. Colonel H. B. Carrington, 18th United States Infantry, with about seven hundred officers and men, arrived at Laramie, *en route* to their country to establish and occupy military posts along the Montana road, pursuant to General Orders No. 33, Headquarters Department of the Missouri, March 10, 1866, Major-General Pope commanding.

The destination and purpose of Colonel Carrington and his command were communicated to their chiefs. They seemed to construe this as a determination on the part of the government to occupy their country by military posts, even without their consent or that of their people, and as soon as practicable withdrew from the council with their adherents, refusing to accept any presents from the commission, returned to their country, and with a strong force of warriors commenced a vigorous and relentless war against all whites who came into it, both citizens and soldiers.

Quite a large number of Indians, who did not occupy the country along this road, were anxious to make a treaty and remain at peace. Some of this class had for a long time resided near Fort Laramie. Others (Brulès) occupied the White Earth River valley and the Sand Hills south of that river.

The commissioners created and appointed several of the leading warriors of these Indians chiefs, *viz.*, Big Mouth, Spotted Tail, Swift Bear, and Two Strikes. A portion of these Indians have remained near Fort Laramie, and a portion of them on the Republican fork of the Kansas River, and have strictly complied with their treaty stipulations.

The number of Sioux Indians who considered themselves bound by the treaty and have remained at peace is about two thousand, while the Minneconjoux and a portion of the Ogallalla and Brulè bands, the northern Cheyennes and Arrapahoes, with a few Sans Arcs, numbering in the aggregate about six hundred lodges, remained in their old country and went to war under the auspices of their old chiefs.

We therefore report that all the Sioux Indians occupying the country about Fort Phil Kearney have been in a state of war against the whites since the 20th day of June, *A.D.* 1866, and that they have waged and carried on this war for the purpose of defending their ancient possessions and the possessions acquired by them from the Crow Indians by conquest after bloody wars, from invasion and occupation by the whites.

This war has been carried on by the Indians with most extraordinary vigour and unwonted success. During the time from July 26th, the day on which Lieutenant Wands's train was attacked, to the 21st day of December, on which Brevet Lieutenant-Colonel Fetterman, with his command of eighty officers and men, was overpowered and massacred, they killed ninety-one enlisted men and five officers of our army, and killed fifty-eight citizens and wounded twenty more, and captured and drove away three hundred and six oxen and cows, three hundred and four mules, and one hundred and sixty-one horses. During this time they appeared in front of Fort Phil Kearney, making hostile demonstrations and committing hostile acts, fifty-one different times, and attacked nearly every train and person that attempted to pass over the Montana road.

Massacre of Brevet Lieutenant-Colonel Fetterman's Party, and the Causes which led to it

General Orders No. 33, Headquarters Department of Missouri, dated March 10, 1866, directed that two new military posts should be established on this new route to Montana—one "near the base of the Big Horn Mountain," the other "on or near the Upper Yellowstone"—and designated the 2nd battalion of the 18th Infantry to garrison the three posts on this route, and created the Mountain District, Department of the Platte, and directed the colonel of the regiment (Colonel H. B. Carrington) to take post at Fort Reno and command the district, which included all the troops and garrisons on this route.

General Orders No. 7, Headquarters Department of the Platte, June 23, 1866, directed that the 2nd Battalion 18th Infantry should take post as follows: Two companies at Fort Reno, on Powder River, two companies about eighty miles nearly south of Reno, on the waters of Powder or Tongue River, which post should be known as Fort Philip Kearney, and two companies at the crossing of the Big Horn River on the same road, and about seventy miles beyond Fort Philip Kearney, to be known as Fort C. F. Smith, and directed that the colonel of the regiment should take post at Fort Philip Kearney, and command the "mountain district."

The orders above referred to were issued with the express understanding, apparently, that this road to Montana was to be opened through the Indian country by compact or treaty with the Indians occupying it, and not by conquest and the exercise of arbitrary power on the part of the government. Hence Colonel Carrington's instructions looked mainly to the duty of selecting and building the two new forts, Philip Kearney and C. F. Smith, and the command assigned was only sufficient for this purpose and properly garrisoning the posts. This command numbered in all about seven hundred men, five hundred of whom were new recruits, and twelve officers, including district commander and staff.

The commanding officer, Colonel Carrington, could not and did not fail to see at once, that although his command was entirely sufficient to erect the new forts, build the barracks, warehouses, and stables, and make preparations for winter, and properly garrison his posts, and could protect emigration from the small thieving parties of Indians, it was still entirely inadequate to carry on systematic and aggressive war against a most powerful tribe of Indians, fighting to maintain possession and control of their own country, in addition to those other duties. This officer carried the orders above referred to into effect with promptness and zeal, organizing the mountain district June 28, 1866, establishing Fort Philip Kearney on the 15th of July, and Fort C. F. Smith on the 3rd day of August, and as early as the 31st day of July informed General P. St. George Cooke, the department commander, that the status of Indians in that country was one of war, and requested reinforcements sent to him, and two days previously had telegraphed the adjutant-general of the army for Indian auxiliaries, and additional force of his own regiment.

On the 9th of August, General Cooke, commanding department of the Platte, informed Colonel Carrington that Lieutenant-General Sherman ordered the posts in his, Colonel Carrington's district, supported as much as possible, and announced a regiment coming from St. Louis.

No auxiliaries were assigned, and no reinforcements came until November, when Company C. 2nd United States Cavalry, reached Fort Kearney, sixty strong, armed with Springfield rifles and Star carbines. In December, about ninety recruits joined the battalion in the mountain district, a portion of whom were assigned to a company stationed at Fort Phil Kearney. No other reinforcements were sent to the district. Approved requisitions for ammunition were not answered. The command at Fort C. F. Smith was reduced to ten rounds per man; the command at Fort Phil Kearney to forty-five rounds per man, and the command at Fort Reno to thirty rounds per man. Recruits could not practice any in firing. Little time could be allowed from fatigue duty for drill, and with but twelve officers and three posts little could have been done in drilling recruits, if time could have been allowed.

The result of all this was that the troops were in no condition to fight successful battles with Indians or other foes, and this from no fault of Colonel Carrington; and I am astonished at the zeal with which they fought, and the damage they inflicted, December 21st.

The numerous demonstrations and attacks made by Indians prior to the 6th of December seemed to have been made for the sole purpose of capturing stock, picket posts, and small parties of soldiers who might venture beyond the cover of the garrison, and of annoying and checking the wood train constantly drawing material for the new forts.

On the morning of December 6th the wood train was attacked, a common occurrence, about two miles from the fort, and forced to corral and defend itself. Brevet Lieutenant-Colonel Fetterman, with a command of seventeen mounted infantry and thirty-five cavalry, moved out to relieve the wood train, and drive off the Indians, and Colonel Carrington, with twenty-five mounted infantry, moved out for the purpose of cutting off the Indians from retreat, and destroying them. On this day, at a point on Peno Creek, about five miles from the fort, the Indians, the second time after the fort was established, made a stand and strong resistance, and nearly surrounded Colonel Fetterman's party. The infantry obeyed orders and behaved well. The cavalry, with the exception of ten enlisted men, disobeyed the orders of Colonel Fetterman, and fled with great precipitancy from this portion of the field.

As the cavalry retreated, the Indians made a great display and every effort to create a panic with the infantry, but Colonel Fetterman, Lieutenant Wands, and Lieutenant Brown succeeded in keeping this small body of infantry cool, and by reserving their fire for proper range, rescued it from annihilation, and made a junction with Colonel Carrington's party, on the east side of Peno Creek. Lieutenant Bingham, after leaving Colonel Fetterman's party, with Lieutenant Grummond, a sergeant from Colonel Carrington's command, and two men from his own, without the knowledge or orders of any of his superiors, pursued into an ambuscade, more than two miles from the main party, a single Indian who was on foot just in front of their horses, and Lieutenant Bingham and the sergeant were there killed.

The results of this day's fighting, although not of a decidedly successful character to the Indians, were such as naturally to induce the belief on their part that by proper management and effort they could overpower and destroy any force that could be sent out from the fort to fight them, and no doubt at this time resolved to make the effort the first auspicious day, and postponed their proceedings from the new to the full moon. In the mean time everything was quiet about the fort, although they often appeared on the surrounding hills.

On the morning of December 21st the picket at the signal station signalled to the fort that the wood train was attacked by Indians, and corralled, and the escort fighting. This was not far from 11 o'clock a.m., and the train was about two miles from the fort, and moving toward the timber. Almost immediately a few Indian pickets appeared on one or two of the surrounding heights, and a party of about twenty near the Big Piney, where the Montana road crosses the same, within howitzer range of the fort. Shells were thrown among them from the artillery in the fort, and they fled.

The following detail, *viz.*, fifty men and two officers from the four different infantry companies, and twenty-six cavalrymen and one officer, was made by Colonel Carrington. The entire force formed in good order and was placed under command of Brevet Lieutenant-Colonel Fetterman, who received the following orders from Colonel Carrington:

> Support the wood train, relieve it, and report to me. Do not engage or pursue Indians at its expense; under no circumstances pursue over Lodge Trail Ridge.

These instructions were repeated by Colonel Carrington in a loud voice, to the command when in motion, and outside the fort, and again delivered in substance through Lieutenant Wands, officer of the day, to Lieutenant Grummond, commanding cavalry detachment, who was requested to communicate them again to Colonel Fetterman.

Colonel Fetterman moved out rapidly to the right of the wood road, for the purpose no doubt of cutting off the retreat of the Indians then attacking the train. As he advanced across the Piney, a few Indians appeared in his front and on his flanks, and continued flitting about him, beyond rifle range, till they disappeared beyond Lodge Trail Ridge. When he was on Lodge Trail Ridge, the picket signalled the fort that the Indians had retreated from the train; the train had broken corral and moved on toward the timber.

The train made the round trip, and was not again disturbed that day.

At about fifteen minutes before 12 o'clock Colonel Fetterman's command had reached the crest of Lodge Trail Ridge, was deployed as skirmishers, and at a halt. Without regard to orders, for reasons that the silence of Colonel Fetterman now prevents us from giving, he, with the command, in a few moments disappeared, having cleared the ridge, still moving north. Firing at once commenced, and increased in rapidity till, in about fifteen minutes and at about 12 o'clock m., it was a continuous and rapid fire of musketry, plainly audible at the fort.

Assistant Surgeon Hines, having been ordered to join Fetterman, found Indians on a part of Lodge Trail Ridge not visible from the fort, and could not reach the force there struggling to preserve its existence. As soon as the firing became rapid Colonel Carrington ordered Captain Ten Eyck, with about seventy-six men, being all the men for duty in the fort, and two wagons with ammunition, to join Colonel Fetterman immediately. He moved out and advanced rapidly toward the point from which the sound of firing proceeded, but did not move by so short a route as he might have done. The sound of firing continued to be heard during his advance, diminishing in rapidity and number of shots till he reached a high summit overlooking the battle-field, at about a quarter before 1 o'clock, when one or two shots closed all sound of conflict.

Whether he could have reached the scene of action by marching over the shortest route as rapidly as possible in time to have relieved Colonel Fetterman's command, I am unable to determine.

Immediately after Captain Ten Eyck moved out, and by orders of Colonel Carrington issued at the same time as the orders detailing that officer to join Colonel Fetterman, the quartermaster's employees, convalescents, and all others in garrison, were armed and provided with ammunition, and held in readiness to reinforce the troops fighting, or defend the garrison.

Captain Ten Eyck reported, as soon as he reached a summit commanding a view of the battle-field, that the Peno valley was full of Indians; that he could see nothing of Colonel Fetterman's party, and requested that a howitzer should be sent to him. The howitzer was not sent. The Indians, who at first beckoned him to come down, now commenced retreating, and Captain Ten Eyck, advancing to a point where the Indians had been standing in a circle, found the dead naked bodies of Brevet Lieutenant-Colonel Fetterman, Captain Brown, and about sixty-five of the soldiers of their command. At this point there were no indications of a severe struggle.

All the bodies lay in a space not exceeding thirty-five feet in diameter. No empty cartridge shells were about, and there were some full cartridges. A few American horses lay dead a short distance off, all with their heads toward the fort. This spot was by the roadside, and beyond the summit of a hill rising to the east of Peno Creek. The road, after rising this hill, follows this ridge along for about half or three-quarters of a mile, and then descends abruptly to Peno Creek.

At about half the distance from where these bodies lay to the point where the road commences to descend to Peno Creek was the dead body of Lieutenant Grummond; and still farther on, at the point where the road commences to descend to Peno Creek, were the dead bodies of the three citizens and four or five of the old, long-tried and experienced soldiers. A great number of empty cartridge shells were on the ground at this point, and more than fifty lying on the ground about one of the dead citizens, who used a Henry rifle. Within a few hundred yards in front of this position ten Indian ponies lay dead, and there were sixty-five pools of dark and clotted blood. No Indian ponies or pools of blood were found at any other point.

Our conclusion, therefore, is that the Indians were massed to resist Colonel Fetterman's advance along Peno Creek on both sides of the road; that Colonel Fetterman formed his advanced lines on the summit of the hill overlooking the creek and valley, with a reserve near where the large number of dead bodies lay; that the Indians, in force of from fifteen to eighteen hundred warriors, attacked him vigorously in this position, and were successfully resisted by him for half an hour or more; that the command then being short of ammunition, and seized with panic at this event and the great numerical superiority of the Indians, attempted to retreat toward the fort; that the mountaineers and old soldiers, who had learned that a movement from Indians, in an engagement, was equivalent to death, remained in their first position, and were killed there; that immediately upon the commencement of the retreat the Indians charged upon and surrounded the party, who could not now be formed by their officers, and were immediately killed.

Only six men of the whole command were killed by balls, and two of these Lieutenant-Colonel Fetterman and Captain Brown, no doubt inflicted this death upon themselves, or each other, by their own hands, for both were shot through the left temple, and powder burnt into the skin and flesh about the wound. These officers had also oftentimes asserted that they would not be taken alive by Indians.

In the critical examination we have given this painful and horrible affair, we do not find, of the immediate participants any officer living deserving of censure; and even if evidence justifies it, it would ill become us to speak evil of or censure those dead who sacrificed life struggling to maintain the authority and power of the government and add new lustre to our arms and fame.

Of those who have been more remotely connected with the events that led to the massacre, we have endeavoured to report so specifically as to enable yourself and the President, who have much official information that we cannot have, to determine where the censure must fall. The difficulty, "in a nutshell," was that the commanding officer of the district was furnished no more troops or supplies for this state of war than had been provided and furnished him for a state of profound peace.

In regions where all was peace, as at Laramie in November, twelve companies were stationed; while in regions where all was war, as at Phil Kearney, there were only five companies allowed.

2

Colonel Carrington's Official Report of the Phil Kearney Massacre.

Headquarters Post, Fort Philip Kearney,
Dacotah Territory, January 3rd, 1867.

Assistant Adjutant-General, Department of the Platte, Omaha, Nebraska Territory.

I respectfully state the facts of fight with Indians on the 21st ultimo. This disaster had the effect to confirm my judgment as to the hostility of Indians, and solemnly declares, by its roll of dead and the numbers engaged, that my declarations, from my arrival at Laramie in June, were not idle conjecture, but true.

It also declares that in Indian warfare there must be perfect coolness, steadiness, and judgment. This contest is in their best and almost their last hunting-grounds. They cannot be whipped or punished by some little dash after a handful, nor by mere resistance of offensive movements. They must be subjected, and made to respect and fear the whites.

It also declares with equal plainness that my letter from Fort Laramie, as to the absolute failure of the treaty, so far as related to my command, was true.

It also vindicates every report from my pen, and every measure

I have taken to secure defensive and tenable posts on this line.

It vindicates my administration of the Mountain District, Department of the Platte, and asserts that the confidence re posed in me by Lieutenant-General Sherman has been fully met.

It vindicates my application so often made, for reinforcements, and demonstrates the fact that if I had received those assured to me, by telegram and letter, I could have kept up communications, and opened a safe route for emigrants next spring.

It proves correct my report of fifteen hundred lodges of hostile Indians on Tongue River, not many hours' ride from this post.

It no less declares that while there has been partial success in impromptu dashes, the Indian, now desperate and bitter, looks upon the rash white man as a sure victim, no less than he does a coward, and that the United States must come to the deliberate resolve to send an army equal to a fight with the Indians of the Northwest.

Better to have the expense, at once, than to have a lingering, provoking war for years. It must be met, and the time is just now.

I respectfully refer to my official reports and correspondence from Department Headquarters for verification of the foregoing propositions, and proceed to the details of Fetterman's Massacre.

On the morning of the 21st *ultimo*, at about eleven o'clock, my picket on Pilot Hill reported the wood-train corralled and threatened by Indians on Sullivant Hills, about a mile and a half from the fort.

A few shots were heard. Indians also appeared in the brush at the crossing of Peney by the Virginia City road.

Upon tendering to Brevet Major Powell the command of Company C, U. S. Cavalry, then without an officer, but which he had been drilling, Brevet Lieutenant-Colonel Fetterman claimed by rank to go out. I acquiesced, giving him the men of his own company that were for duty, and a portion of Company C, 2nd Battalion. 18th U. S. Infantry. Lieutenant G. W. Grummond, who had commanded the mounted Infantry, requested to take out the cavalry. He did so.

In the previous skirmish, Lieutenant Grummond was barely saved from the disaster that befell Lieutenant Bingham by timely aid. (See chapter 23 of narrative.)

Brevet Lieutenant-Colonel Fetterman also was well admonished, as well as myself, that we were fighting brave and desperate enemies, who had sought to make up, by cunning and deceit, all the advantage which the white man gains by intelligence and better arms.

My instructions were therefore peremptory and explicit. I knew the ambition of each to win honour, but being unprepared for large aggressive action through want of adequate force, now fully demonstrated, I looked to continuance of timber supplies, to prepare for more troops, as the one practical duty; hence, two days before, Major Powell, sent out to cover the train under similar circumstances, simply did that duty, when he could have had a fight to any extent.

The day before, *viz.*, the 20th *ultimo*, I went myself to the pinery, and built a bridge of forty-five feet span, to expedite the passage of wagons from the woods into open ground. Hence my instructions to Brevet Lieutenant-Colonel Fetterman, *viz.*: "Support the wood-train, relieve it, and report to me. Do not engage or pursue Indians at its expense; under no circumstances pursue over the Ridge, *viz.*: Lodge trail Ridge, as per map in your possession." (For map, see chapter 24 narrative.)

To Lieutenant Grummond I gave orders to "report to Brevet Lieutenant-Colonel Fetterman, implicitly obey orders, and not leave him."

Before the command left, I instructed Lieutenant A. H. Wands, my regimental quartermaster and acting adjutant, to repeat these orders. He did so.

Fearing still that the spirit of ambition might over-ride prudence, as my refusal to permit sixty mounted men and forty citizens to go for several days down Tongue River valley after villages had been unfavourably regarded by Brevet Lieutenant-Colonel Fetterman and Captain Brown, I crossed the parade, and from a sentry platform halted the cavalry, and again repeated my precise orders. I knew that the Indians had, for some days, returned each time with increased numbers, to feel our strength and decoy detachments to their sacrifice, and believed that to foil their purpose was actual victory, until reinforcements should arrive and my preparations were complete. I was right.

Just as the command left, five Indians reappeared at the crossing. The glass revealed others in the thicket, having the apparent object of determining the watchfulness of the garrison, or cutting off any small party that should move out. A case shot dismounted one and developed nearly thirty, who broke for the hills and ravines to the North.

In half an hour the picket reported that the wood-train had broken corral and moved on to the pinery. No report came from the detachment. It was composed of eighty-one, officers and men, including two citizens, all well armed; the cavalry having the new carbine, while the detachment of Infantry was of choice men, the pride of their companies.

At twelve o'clock firing was heard toward Peno Creek, beyond Lodge Trail Ridge. A few shots were followed by constant shots, not to be counted. Captain Ten Eyck was immediately dispatched with Infantry, and the remaining Cavalry, and two wagons, and orders to join Colonel Fetterman at all hazards. The men moved promptly and on the run, but within little more than half an hour from the first shot, and just as the supporting party reached the hill overlooking the scene of action, all firing ceased.

Captain Ten Eyck sent a mounted orderly back with the report, that he could see or hear nothing of Fetterman, but that a body of Indians on the road below him were challenging him to come down, while larger bodies were in all the valleys for several miles around. Moving cautiously forward with the wagons (evidently supposed by the enemy to be guns, as mounted men were in advance), he rescued from the spot where the enemy had been nearest, forty-nine bodies, including those of Brevet Lieutenant-Colonel Fetterman and Captain F. H. Brown. The latter went out without my consent or knowledge, fearless to fight Indians with any adverse odds, and determined to kill one at least before joining his company.

Captain Ten Eyck fell back slowly, followed, but not pressed by the enemy, reaching the Post without loss. The following day, finding general doubt as to the success of an attempt to recover other bodies, but believing that failure to rescue them would dishearten the command and encourage the Indians, who are so particular in this regard, I took eighty men and went to the scene of action, leaving a picket to advise me of any movement in the rear, and to keep signal communication with the garrison.

The scene of action told its own story.

The road on the little ridge where the final stand took place, was strewn with arrows, arrow-heads, scalp-poles, and broken shafts of spears. The arrows that were spent harmlessly, from all directions, show that the command was suddenly overwhelmed, surrounded, and cut off while in retreat. Not an officer or man survived! A few bodies were found at the north end of the divide over which the road runs, just beyond Lodge Trail Ridge. Nearly all were heaped near four rocks, at the point nearest the fort, these rocks, enclosing a space about six feet square, having been the last refuge for defence. Here were also a few unexpended rounds of Spencer cartridge.

Fetterman and Brown had each a revolver-shot in the left temple. As Brown always declared that he would reserve a shot for himself, as a last resort, so I am convinced that these two brave men fell, each by the other's hand, rather than undergo the slow torture inflicted upon others.

Lieutenant Grummond's body was on the road between the two extremes, with a few others. This was not far from five miles from the fort, and nearly as far from the wood-train. Neither its own guard nor the detachment could by any possibility have helped each other, and the train was incidentally saved by the fierceness of the fight, in the brave but rash impulse of pursuit.

The officers, who fell, believed that no Indian force could overwhelm that number of troops, well held in hand.

Their terrible massacre bore marks of great valour, and has demonstrated the force and character of the foe; but no valour could have saved them.

Pools of blood on the road and sloping sides of the narrow divide showed where Indians bled fatally; but their bodies were carried off. I counted sixty-five such pools in the space of an acre, and three, within ten feet of Lieutenant Grummond's body. Eleven American horses and nine Indian ponies were on the road, or near the line of bodies; others, crippled, were in the valleys.

At the northwest or farther point, between two rocks, and apparently where the command first fell back from the valley, realizing their danger, I found citizens James S. Wheatley and Isaac Fisher, of Blue Springs, Nebraska, who, with "Henry Rifles," felt invincible, but fell, one having one hundred and five arrows in his naked body. The widow and family of Wheatley are here.

The cartridge shells about them told how well they fought. Before closing this report, I wish to say that every man, officer, soldier, or citizen who fell received burial, with such record as to identify each.

Fetterman, Brown, and Grummond lie in one grave; the remainder also share one tomb, buried, as they fought, together; but the cases in which they were laid are duly placed and numbered.

I ask the general commanding to give my report, in the absence of the division commander, an access to the eye and ear of the general-in-chief. The department commander must have more troops; and I declare this, my judgment, solemnly, and for the general public good, without one spark of personal ambition other than to do my duty daily as it comes; and whether I seem to speak too plainly or not, ever with the purpose to declare the whole truth, and with proper respect to my superior officers, who are entitled to the facts, as to scenes remote from their own immediate notice. I was asked to "*send all the bad news.*" I do it, so far, as far as I can.

I give some of the facts as to my men, whose bodies I found just at dark, resolved to bring all in, *viz.*:

MUTILATIONS.

Eyes torn out and laid on the rocks.
Noses cut off.
Ears cut off.
Chins hewn off.
Teeth chopped out.
Joints of fingers cut off.
Brains taken out and placed on rocks, with members of the body.
Entrails taken out and exposed.
Hands cut off.
Feet cut off.
Arms taken out from socket.
Private parts severed, and indecently placed on the person.

Eyes, ears, mouth, and arms penetrated with spear-
heads, sticks, and arrows.
Ribs slashed to separation, with knives; skulls severed in
every form, from chin to crown.
Muscles of calves, thighs, stomach, breast, back, arms,
and cheek taken out.
Punctures upon every sensitive part of the body, even to
the soles of the feet and palms of the hand.

All this does not approximate the whole truth. Every medical officer was faithful, aided by a large force of men, and all were not buried until Wednesday after the fight.

The great real fact is, that these Indians take alive when possible, and slowly torture. It is the opinion of Dr. S. M. Horton, post surgeon, that not more than six were killed by balls. Of course the whole arrows, hundreds of which were removed from naked bodies, were all used after the removal of the clothing.

I have said enough. It is a hard but absolute duty. In the establishment of this post, I designed to put it where it fell heaviest upon the Indians, and therefore the better for the emigrants. My duty will be done when I leave, as ordered, for my new Regimental Headquarters, Fort Casper. I submit herewith list of casualties, marked A.

I shall also, as soon as practicable, make full report, for the year 1866, of operations in the establishment of this new line.

    I am, very respectfully,
     Your obedient servant,
 (Signed)   Henry B. Carrington,
          Colonel 18th U. S. Infantry,
           Commanding Post.

The following note was sent to Captain Ten Eyck, in answer to message of his courier that he could see nothing of Fetterman.

      Fort Phil Kearney, Dacotah Territory,
        December 21st, 1866.

Captain T. Ten Eyck.
Forty well-armed men, with three thousand rounds, ambulances, etc., left before your courier came in. You must unite with Fetterman. Fire slowly, and keep men in hand. You would have saved two miles toward the scene of action if you had taken Lodge Trail Ridge. I order the wood-train in, which will give

fifty men to spare.

(Signed) Henry B. Carrington,
Colonel Commanding.

Note.—The reports of the Secretaries of War and the Interior to Congress in February, 1867, made up from loose private letters and speculations, without knowledge of the facts, contain one private letter dated Fort Phil Kearney, December 28, 1886, which demands correction while a deserving officer is still living.

That letter represents Captain James W. Powell as going to the relief of Fetterman and the rescue of the dead. Captain Tenodore Ten Eyck was the officer who gallantly performed that duty.

Captain Powell did not leave the stockade. Captain Ten Eyck also accompanied his colonel to the field the next morning for the rescue of the remaining dead, at the close of an officers' meeting, in which Captain Powell advised against the movement as endangering the entire garrison and post.

(See Official Report.) H. B. C.

3

SKETCH OF THE EIGHTEENTH UNITED STATES INFANTRY

The 18th Regiment United States Infantry has served on the plains since November, 1865. During the fall of that year, the 1st Battalion, under Captain and Brevet Lieutenant-Colonel R. B. Hull, occupied the lower line from Fort Leavenworth to Forts Lyon, Obree, and Dodge, marching in the depth of winter, enduring great exposure, having at one time 85 men bitten by frost, and with reduced rations, being compelled to live for weeks on buffalo and other game of the country.

The regiment was commenced in July, 1861, and the three battalions were filled in little more than a year.

In November, 1865, the 2nd Battalion, with headquarters under Colonel Henry B. Carrington, marched from Fort Leavenworth to Fort Kearney, Nebraska, where it wintered.

In May, 1866, the regiment again united, was again distributed on the frontier; and built, rebuilt, or repaired Forts McPherson, Sedgwick, Laramie, Caspar, Reno, Philip Kearney, C. F. Smith, Fetterman, Bridger, Morgan, Wardwell, Camp Douglass, and Fort Halleck, now Fort Saunders.

Up to January 1st, 1866, the regiment had received into its ranks four thousand seven hundred and seventy-three men, of whom three thousand one hundred and ninety were born in the United States. Of these, two thousand four hundred and ninety-nine were enlisted in Ohio, and of these, one thousand and forty-two were enlisted at Columbus, in that State.

Since 1866, seven hundred and ninety five recruits joined the regiment.

In 1867, the 1st, 2nd, and 3rd Battalions became, respectively, the 18th, 27th, and 36th Regiments, all of which continue on the plains in 1868.

The regiment lost in action, during the war, a total of nine hundred and sixty-eight officers and men, and has served in the States of Ohio, Kentucky, Tennessee, Georgia, Mississippi, Alabama, West Virginia, Missouri, Kansas, and Nebraska, and the Territories of Colorado, Dakota, Utah, and Montana.

The regiment participated in the following battles, besides minor engagements: *viz*.: "Siege of Corinth," "Chaplin Hill," "Murfreesboro'," "Perryville," "Jonesboro'," "Hoover's Gap," "Chickamauga," "Siege of Chattanooga," 'Mission Ridge," "Resaca," and the Atlanta campaign until the fall of that city.

One company, under Captain Ten Eyck and Lieutenant Kirtland, *en route* to join the regiment, participated in the siege of Mumfordsville, and was there captured, at the surrender of the post to overwhelming numbers,—General Bragg's entire army having laid siege to the post.

The regiment was with Colonel Robert McCook at the battle of Mill Springs, to whom Colonel Carrington turned over the command of his brigade, consisting of the 9th and 35th Ohio, the 2nd Minnesota, and 18th Infantry, under orders to return to Ohio to complete the regiment.

At "Greysville, Ga.," "Tunnel Hill, Ga.," "New Hope Chapel," "Peach Tree Creek," "Kenesaw Mountain," and "Smyrna Creek," it had spirited encounters with the enemy; and before the cedars at "Stone River," lost in less than an hour two hundred and ninety-eight men, nearly half the force engaged.

During the war it marched on foot 2447 miles; by railroad, 483 miles; by water, 1948 miles, being a total of 4878 miles.

The following is the list of officers assigned to the regiment from its first organization, with the changes that have occurred, and the present status of such as remain in the army in 1868: (*Indicates graduates at West Pont Military Academy.)

Henry B. Carrington, Colonel. May 14, 1861. Colonel 18th Infantry in 1868.
*Oliver L. Shepherd, Lieutenant-Colonel, May 14, 1861. Colonel 15th Infantry in 1868.
*Charles S. Lovell, Lieutenant-Colonel, January 7, 1863. Colonel 14th Infantry in 1868.
*Henry W. Wessells, Lieutenant-Colonel, February 16, 1865. Lieutenant-Colonel 18th Infantry in 1868.
Frederick Townsend, Major, May 14, 1861. Lieutenant-Colonel 9th Infantry in 1868.
*Henry Burton, Major, May 14, 1861. Declined promotion from 3rd Artillery.
Edmund Underwood, Major, May 14, 1861. Retired in 1862.
William A. Stokes, Major, September 7, 1861. Not confirmed.
*James N. Caldwell, Major, February 27, 1862. Retired in 1863.
*W. T. H. Brooks, Major, March 12, 1862. Resigned July 14th, 1864.
*James Van Voast, Major, December 29, 1863. Major 18th Infantry in 1808.
*Charles R. Wood, Major, April 20, 1864. Lieutenant- Colonel 33rd Infantry in 1868.
*William H. Lewis, Major, July 14, 1864. Major 36th Infantry in 1868.
*Henry Douglass, Captain, May 14, 1861. Major Infantry in 1868.
*Thomas M. Vincent,' Captain, May 14, 1861. Declined promotion from 2nd Artillery.
*Alexander Chambers, Captain, May 14, 1861. Major Infantry in 1868.
*Alexander Piper, Captain, May 14, 1861. Declined pro- motion from 3rd Artillery.
Henry R. Mizner, Captain, May 14, 1861. Captain 36th Infantry in 1868.
*Thomas C. Sullivan, Captain, May 14, 1861. Declined promotion from 1st Artillery.
Jacob W. Eyster, Captain, May 14, 1861. Out of service February 15, 1865.

William S. Thrustin, Captain, May 14, 1861. Resigned August 12, 1863.

William M. McGlaughlin, Captain, May 14, 1861. Declined appointment.

Charles E. Dennison, Captain, May 14, 1861. Wounded at Stone River. Died January 15, 1863.

*Platt J. Titus, Captain, May 14, 1861. Declined appointment.

Henry R. Belknap, Captain, May 14, 1861. Resigned May 30, 1863.

Alvah H. Bereman, Captain, May 14, 1861. Resigned July 22, 1862.

Moses M. Granger, Captain, May 14, 1861. Resigned May 30, 1862.

David L. Wood, Captain, May 14, 1861. Wholly retired September 11, 1863.

Patrick H. Breslin, Captain, May 14, 1861. Out of service November 25, 1862.

*Lymun M. Kellogg, Captain, May 14, 1861. Captain 18th Infantry in 1868.

Jacob Weidenkopf, Captain, August 5, 1861. Declined appointment.

A. B. Thompson, Captain, August 5, 1861. Retired May 6, 1864.

George W. Smith, Captain, August 5, 1861. Resigned in 1866.

John A. Thompson, Captain, October 26, 1861. Wounded at Hoover's Gap. Died June 30, 1863.

Henry Haymond. Captain, October 26, 1861. Captain 27th Infantry in 1868.

John H. Knight, Captain, August 20, 1861. Captain 36th Infantry in 1868.

Philip H. Forney, Captain, February 9, 1862. Transferred to 9th Infantry in 1866.

Tenodor Ten Eyck, Captain, February 19, 1862. Captain 18th Infantry in 1868.

Mark F. Leavenworth, Captain, February 19, 1862. Resigned April 27, 1863.

*James W. Forsyth, First Lieutenant, March 15, 1861. Major 10th Cavalry in 1868.

*William B. Hughes, First Lieutenant, April 1, 1861. Declined transfer from 9th Infantry.

*Francis J. Crilly, First Lieutenant, May 14, 1861. Declined promotion from 7th Infantry.

*Elisha E. Camp, First Lieutenant, May, 14, 1861. Declined promotion from 9th Infantry.

Robert B. Hull, First Lieutenant, May 14, 1861. Captain 18th Infantry in 1868.

William J. Fetterman, First Lieutenant, May 14, 1861. Captain, killed in action with Indians near Fort Phil Kearney, December 21, 1866.

Charles L. Kneass, First Lieutenant, May 14, 1861. Captain, killed at Stone River, December 31, 1862.

Andrew D. Cash, Jr., First Lieutenant, May 14th, 1861. Died at Louisville, Ky., March 24. 1862.

Ansel B. Denton, First Lieutenant, May 14, 1861. Resigned while Captain, September 9th, 1864.

William II. H. Taylor, First Lieutenant, May 14, 1861. Resigned September 12, 1863.

Nathanial C. Kinney, First Lieutenant, May 14, 1861. Captain, and resigned in 1867.

Richard L. Morris, Jr., First Lieutenant, May 14, 1861. Captain 18th Infantry in 1868.

Joseph L. Proctor, First Lieutenant, May 14, 1861. Captain 27th Infantry in 1868.

Anson Mills, First Lieutenant, May 14, 1861. Captain 18th Infantry in 1868.

Andrew S. Burt, First Lieutenant, May 14, 1861. Captain 27th Infantry in 1868.

Thomas B. Burrows, First Lieutenant, May 14, 1861. Captain 27th Infantry in 1868.

*Symmes Gardner, First Lieutenant, May 14, 1861. Dropped November 13, 1863.

Claudius Schmidt, First Lieutenant, May 14, 1861. Resigned June 30, 1862.

Morgan L. Ogden, First Lieutenant, May 14, 1861. Captain 18th Infantry in 1868.

Wm. W. Stevenson, First Lieutenant, May 14, 1861. Died at Louisville, Ky , February 27, 1862.

Thomas F. Brand, First Lieutenant, May 14, 1861. Retired as Captain December 31, 1864.

James P. W. Neil, First Lieutenant, May 14, 1861. Captain 36th

Infantry in 1868.

Herman G. Radcliff, First Lieutenant, May 14, 1861. Died at Murfreesboro', March 22, 1863.

John W. Hamilton, First Lieutenant, May 14, 1861. Not confirmed.

William O'Brien, First Lieutenant, May 14, 1861. Not confirmed.

Robert Sutherland, First Lieutenant, August 5, 1861. Resigned January 7, 1864.

William J. Phelps, Second Lieutenant, October 24, 1861. Declined appointment.

Horace Brown, First Lieutenant, October 26, 1861. Re- signed July 28, 1864.

Irwin J. Wallace, First Lieutenant, October 26, 1861. Died at Pittsburg, Pa., February 19, 1862.

Charles L. Truman, First Lieutenant, March 6, 1862. Killed at Chickamauga, September 30, 1863.

Charles O. Howard, Captain, May 12, 1862. Resigned in 1865.

James Simons, Second Lieutenant, May 14, 1861. First Lieutenant, died January 14, 1863, of wounds received at Stone River.

James Powell, Second Lieutenant, May 14, 1861. Captain 27th Infantry, and retired in 1808.

Wm. P. McCleery, Second Lieutenant, May 14, 186I. Captain 18th Infantry in 1808.

Daniel W, Benham, Second Lieutenant, October 24, 1861. Captain 36th Infantry in 1868.

Frederick Plasterer, Second Lieutenant. October 30, 1801. Captain 36th Infantry in 1868.

Frederick 11. Brown, Second Lieutenant, October 30, 1861. Captain, killed in action with Indians near Fort Phil Kearney, December 21, 1866.

Henry B. Freeman, Second Lieutenant, October 30, 1861. Captain 27th Infantry in 1868.

Samuel J. Dick, Second Lieutenant, October 30, 1861. Died at Nashville, December 24, 1864.

James P. Calloway, Second Lieutenant, October 30, 1861. Not confirmed.

Thaddeus S. Kirtland, Second Lieutenant, October 30, 1861. Captain 36th Infantry in 1868.

Joseph McConnell, Second Lieutenant, October 30, 1861. First

Lieutenant, died January 14, 1863, of wounds received at Stone River.

James E. Mitchel, Second Lieutenant, February 19, 1862. Died of disease.

Gilbert S. Carpenter, Second Lieutenant, June 9, 1862. Captain 45th Infantry in 1868.

William H. Bisbee, Second Lieutenant, June 9, 1862. Captain 27th Infantry in 1868.

Merrill N. Hutchinson, Second Lieutenant, Jane 9, 1862. Retired as First Lieutenant.

Ebenezer D. Harding, Second Lieutenant, June 9, 1862. Captain, and retired wholly.

John F. Hitchcock, Second Lieutenant, Juno 0, 1862. Killed at Stone River, December 31, 1802.

Augustus A. Meckling, Second Lieutenant, June 9, 1802. Resigned December 24, 1862.

Lucius F. Brown, Second Lieutenant, June 19, 1862. First Lieutenant, died October 12, 1863, of wounds received at Chicamauga.

John J. Adair, Second Lieutenant, July 14, 1862. Captain, resigned in 1867.

Henry G. Litchfield, Second Lieutenant, July 14, 1862. First Lieutenant 36th Infantry in 1868.

Alfred Townsend, Second Lieutenant, November 10, 1862. Retired as First Lieutenant.

Charles Whiteacre, Second Lieutenant, November 19, 1862 Dismissed.

Wilbur F. Arnold, Second Lieutenant, November 21, 1862. Captain 41st Infantry in 1868, and deceased.

Reuben F. Little, Second Lieutenant, February 19, 1863. Resigned in 1864.

John J. Lind, Second Lieutenant, February 19, 1863. Resigned October 12, 1864.

Edgar N. Wilcox, Second Lieutenant, February 19, 1863. Captain 18th Infantry in 1868

Samuel C. Williamson, Second Lieutenant, February 19, 1863. Retired as First Lieutenant.

James S. Ostrander, Second Lieutenant, February 19, 1863. Resigned September 30, 1864.

Rufus 0. Gates, Second Lieutenant, February 19, 1863. Resigned June 5, 1865.

George F. White, Second Lieutenant, February 19, 1863. Killed at Stone River before receiving his appointment.

William H. Madeira, Second Lieutenant, February 19, 1863. Killed at Stone River, December 31, 1862.

Frank T. Bennett, Second Lieutenant, February 19, 1863. Captain 42nd Infantry in 1868.

David D. N. Corderoy, Second Lieutenant, February 19, 1863. Died before receiving appointment.

Orrin E. Davis, Second Lieutenant, February 19, 1863. Resigned October 12, 1864.

John Lane, Second Lieutenant, June 1. 1863. Died October 15, 1863, of wounds received at Chattanooga.

Isaac D'Isay, Second Lieutenant, October 31, 1863. Captain 27th Infantry in 1868.

John U. Gill, Second Lieutenant, October 31, 1863. First Lieutenant 36th Infantry. Resigned.

Henry C. Pohlman, Second Lieutenant, August 10, 1863. Died in Libby Prison in 1863.

William W. Bell, Second Lieutenant, February 21. 1865. First Lieutenant, killed near Fort Saunders, June 7, 1868.

William A Stearns, Second Lieutenant, April 13, 1865. Resigned in 1866.

*Thomas L. Brent, Second and First Lieutenant, June 23, 1865. First Lieutenant 18th Infantry, and Quartermaster in 1868.

*Wm. S. Staning, Second and First Lieutenant, June 23, 1865. First Lieutenant 36th Infantry in 1868.

*Joseph K. Hyer, Second and First Lieutenant, June 23, 1865. First Lieutenant 18th Infantry in 1868.

E. F. Thompson, Second Lieutenant, December 14, 1865. Captain 27th Infantry in 1868.

Henry II. Link, Second Lieutenant, February 23, 1866. First Lieutenant 36th Infantry in 1868.

Oliver B. Liddell, Second Lieutenant, February 23, 1866. Resigned in 1867.

James H. Bradley, Second Lieutenant, February 23, 1866. First Lieutenant 18th Infantry in 1868.

Reuben N. Fenton, Second Lieutenant, February 23, 1866. Captain 27th Infantry in 1868.

George W. Wood, Second Lieutenant, February 23, 1866. First

Lieutenant 18th Infantry in 1868.

Alex. H. Wands, Second Lieutenant, February 23, 1866. First Lieutenant 36th Infantry in 1868.

T. H. B. Counselman, Second Lieutenant, March 30, 1866. First Lieutenant 18th Infantry in 1868.

Winfield S. Matson, Second Lieutenant, April 9, 1866. First Lieutenant 27th Infantry in 1868.

Hugh G. Brown, Second lieutenant, May 2, 1866. First Lieutenant 36th Infantry in 1868.

George W. Grummond, Second Lieutenant, May 7, 1866. Killed in action with Indians near Fort Phil Kearney, December 21, 1866.

Charles H. Warrens, Second Lieutenant, May 11, 1866. First Lieutenant 27th Infantry in 1868.

Oscar P. Hendee, Second Lieutenant, May 11, 1866. First Lieutenant 36th Infantry. Wholly retired.

Alvan S. Galbreath, Second Lieutenant, May 11, 1866. First Lieutenant 18th Infantry in 1868.

Jacob Paulus, Second Lieutenant, May 11, 1866. First Lieutenant 27th Infantry in 1868.

William F. Foulk, Second Lieutenant, May 11, 1866. First Lieutenant 36th Infantry in 1868.

E. A. True, Second Lieutenant, May 11, 1866. Declined appointment.

E. R. P. Shurley, Second Lieutenant, May 11, 1866. Second Lieutenant 27th Infantry in 1868.

William F. Davies, Second Lieutenant, May 11, 1866. Transferred to 36th Infantry and cashiered.

Jefferson P. Hibbets, Second Lieutenant, May 11, 1866. Declined appointment.

Sanford C Kellogg, Second Lieutenant, May 15, 1866. First Lieutenant 18th Infantry in 1868.

Walter F. Halleck, Second Lieutenant, May 30, 1866. First Lieutenant 27th Infantry in 1868.

Joshua W. Jacobs, Second Lieutenant, June 28, 1866. First Lieutenant 36th Infantry in 1868.

C. H. Brewer, Second Lieutenant, June 30, 1866. Re- signed 1867.

James Regan, Second Lieutenant, December 1, 1866. First Lieutenant 18th Infantry in 1868.

Wm. H. Campion, Second Lieutenant, January 22, 1867. First Lieutenant 18th Infantry in 1868.
Royal S. Carr, First Lieutenant, February 25, 1867. Resigned 18C7.
Robert P. Hughes, First Lieutenant, July 28, 1866. Captain 18th Infantry in 1868.
James Stewart, Captain, July 28, 1866. Captain 18th Infantry in 1868.
Carroll H. Potter, First Lieutenant, July 28, 1866. First Lieutenant 18th Infantry, and Adjutant, in 1868.
Frederick F. Whitehead, First Lieutenant, July 28, 1866. First Lieutenant 18th Infantry in 1868.
Henry M. Benson, Second Lieutenant, February 23, 1866. First Lieutenant 36th Infantry in 1868.
"William M. Knox, Second Lieutenant, February 23, 1866. Died *en route* to join regiment.
George M. Templeton, Second Lieutenant, February 23, 1866. Captain 27th Infantry in 1868.
Prescott M. Skinner, Second Lieutenant, February 23, 1866. Resigned 1867.
Charles E. Dibble, Second Lieutenant, February 23, 1866. Resigned 1867.
Henry E. Luther, Second Lieutenant, January 22, 1867. First Lieutenant 18th Infantry in 1868.
John A. Manley, Second Lieutenant, March 7, 1867. Lieutenant 18th Infantry in 1868.
William W. Daugherty, Second Lieutenant, March 7, 1867. Lieutenant 18th Infantry in 1868.
Robert F. Bates, Second Lieutenant, March 7, 1867. Lieutenant 18th Infantry in 1868.
George S. Hoyt, Second Lieutenant, June 18, 1867. Lieutenant 18th Infantry in 1868.
Hiram H. Benner, Second Lieutenant, June 18, 1867. Lieutenant 18th Infantry in 1868.
John H. Todd, Second Lieutenant, August 22, 1867. Lieutenant 18th Infantry in 1868.
Frederick H. E. Ebstein, Second Lieutenant, September 13, 1867. Lieutenant 18th Infantry in 1868.
The following officers have filled staff positions in the regiment, *viz.*, as Regimental Adjutant:

First Lieutenant Charles L. Kneass; First Lieutenant James P. W. Neill; First Lieutenant Frederick Phisterer; First Lieutenant John J. Adair; First Lieutenant William H. Bisbee; First Lieutenant Carroll H Potter, Adjutant from date of joining regiment, and in 1868.

The following have been Regimental Quartermasters:

First Lieutenant James Simons; First Lieutenant N. C. Kinney; First Lieutenant Frederick H. Brown; *First Lieutenant Thomas L. Brent.

The foregoing summary is gathered, by permission, from Captain Phisterer's *Regimental History,* and the supplement of Lieutenant Potter, and affords to those interested in the incidents of this volume a more complete idea of the antecedents of the regiment, which followed up an eventful war record with scarcely less active duty since its close.

NOTE TO APPENDIX 3

List of Men Killed in Action with Indians near Fort Philip Kearney, D. T., on the 21st day of December, 1866.

No.	NAMES.	RANK.	COMP'Y.	BATTALION AND REGIMENT.
1.	Augustus Lange	1st Sergt.	A	2d, 18th Inf.
2.	Hugh Murphy	Sergt.	"	"
3.	Robert Lennon	Corporal.	"	"
4.	William Dale	"	"	"
5.	Frederick Acherman	Private.	"	"
6.	William Betzler	"	"	"
7.	Thomas Burke	"	"	"
8.	Henry Buchanan	"	"	"
9.	George E. R. Goodall	"	"	"
10.	Michael Harlen	"	"	"
11.	Martin Kelley	"	"	"
12.	Patrick Shannon	"	"	"
13.	Charles N. Taylor	"	"	"
14.	Joseph D. Thomas	"	"	"
15.	David Thorey	"	"	"
16.	John Timson	"	"	"
17.	Albert H. Walter	"	"	"
18.	John M. Weaver	"	"	"
19.	Maximilian Dehring	"	"	"
20.	Francis S. Gordon	"	"	"
21.	John Woodruff	"	"	"
22.	Francis Raymond	Sergt.	C	"
23.	Patrick Rooney	"	"	"
24.	Gustave A. Bauer	Corporal.	"	"
25.	Patrick Gallagher	"	"	"
26.	Henry E. Aarons	Private.	"	"
27.	Michael O'Gara	"	"	"
28.	Jacob Rosenberg	"	"	"
29.	Frank P. Sullivan	"	"	"
30.	Patrick Smith	"	"	"

List of Men Killed in Action, etc.—Continued.

No.	NAMES.	RANK.	COMP'Y.	BATTALION AND REGIMENT.
31.	William Morgan	Sergeant.	E	2d, 18th Inf.
32.	John Quinn	Corporal.	"	"
33.	George W. Burrell	Private.	"	"
34.	Timothy Cullinans	"	"	"
35.	John Maher	"	"	"
36.	George N. Waterbury.	"	"	"
37.	Alexander Smith	1st. Sergt.	H	"
38.	Ephraim C. Bissell	Sergeant.	"	"
39.	George Philip	Corporal.	"	"
40.	Michael Sharkey	"	"	"
41.	Frank Karston	"	"	"
42.	George Davis	Private.	"	"
43.	Perrie F. Doland	"	"	"
44.	Asa H. Griffin	"	"	"
45.	Herman Keil	"	"	"
46.	James Kean	"	"	"
47.	Michael Kinney	"	"	"
48.	Delos Reed	"	"	"
49.	Thomas M. Madden	Recruit.	unas'd	"
50.	James Baker	Sergeant.	C	2d Cavalry.
51.	James Kelley	Corporal.	"	"
52.	Thomas F. Honigan	"	"	"
53.	Adolph Metzlers	Bugler.	"	"
54.	John McCarty	Artificer.	"	"
55.	Thomas Amberson	Private.	"	"
56.	Thomas Broglin	"	"	"
57.	William Bugbee	"	"	"
58.	William Cornog	"	"	"
59.	Charles Cuddy	"	"	"
60.	Patrick Clancey	"	"	"
61.	Harry S. Deming	"	"	"
62.	Hugh B. Doran	"	"	"
63.	Robert Daniel	"	"	"
64.	Nathan Foreman	"	"	"
65.	Andrew M. Fitzgerald.	"	"	"
66.	Daniel Greene	"	"	"
67.	Charles Gamford	"	"	"
68.	John Giller	"	"	"
69.	Ferdinand Houser	"	"	"

No.	NAMES.	RANK.	COMP'Y.	BATTALION AND REGIMENT.
70.	Frank Jones............	Private.	C	2d Cavalry.
71.	James B. McGuire.....	"	"	"
72.	John McColley.........	"	"	"
73.	George W. Nugent.....	"	"	"
74.	Franklin Payne.........	"	"	"
75.	James Ryan.............	"	"	"
76.	Oliver Williams........	"	"	"
77.	John Wheatley.........	Citizen.		
78.	John Fisher.............	"		

Enlisted Men 18th U. S. Infantry.....................49
   "   "   2d U. S. Cavalry..............................27
Citizens... 2
        Total 78

Names of Commissioned Officers of the 18th U. S. Infantry Killed in the same Action.

Captain William J. Fetterman, Brevet Lieutenant-Colonel U. S. Army.
Captain Frederick H. Brown.
Lieutenant George W. Grummond.

Recapitulation.

	OF'CERS.	SERG'TS.	CORP'LS.	PRIV'TES	CITIZENS	AGGREG.
18th Infantry..	3	7	8	34	....	52
2d Cavalry.....	....	1	2	24	....	27
Citizens..........	....	....	....	....	2	2
Total.........	3	8	10	58	2	81

INDIAN OPERATIONS ON THE PLAINS.

(MAP N⁰ 11.) CARRINGTONS OUTLINE

INDIAN OPERATIONS ON THE PLAINS.

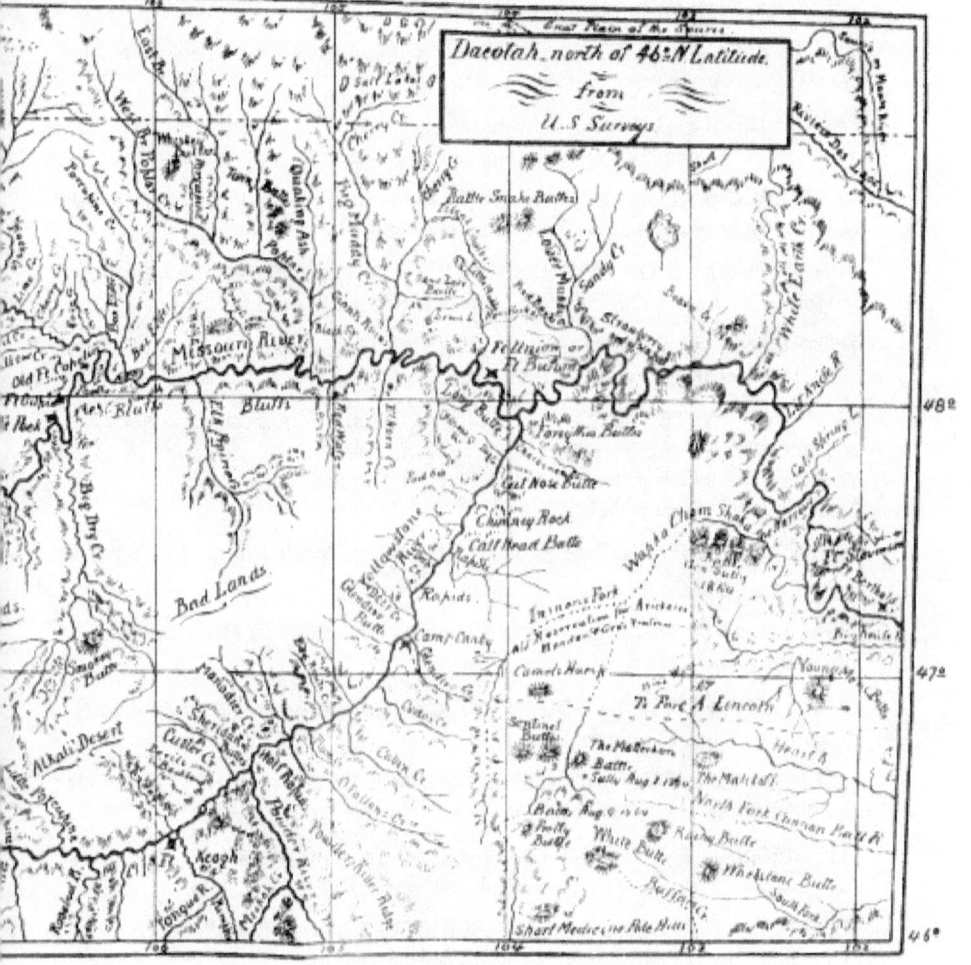

ALSO FROM LEONAUR
AVAILABLE IN SOFTCOVER OR HARDCOVER WITH DUST JACKET

THE WOMAN IN BATTLE by Loreta Janeta Velazquez—Soldier, Spy and Secret Service Agent for the Confederacy During the American Civil War.

BOOTS AND SADDLES by Elizabeth B. Custer—The experiences of General Custer's Wife on the Western Plains.

FANNIE BEERS' CIVIL WAR by Fannie A. Beers—A Confederate Lady's Experiences of Nursing During the Campaigns & Battles of the American Civil War.

LADY SALE'S AFGHANISTAN by Florentia Sale—An Indomitable Victorian Lady's Account of the Retreat from Kabul During the First Afghan War.

THE TWO WARS OF MRS DUBERLY by Frances Isabella Duberly—An Intrepid Victorian Lady's Experience of the Crimea and Indian Mutiny.

THE REBELLIOUS DUCHESS by Paul F. S. Dermoncourt—The Adventures of the Duchess of Berri and Her Attempt to Overthrow French Monarchy.

LADIES OF WATERLOO by Charlotte A. Eaton, Magdalene de Lancey & Juana Smith—The Experiences of Three Women During the Campaign of 1815: Waterloo Days by Charlotte A. Eaton, A Week at Waterloo by Magdalene de Lancey & Juana's Story by Juana Smith.

NURSE AND SPY IN THE UNION ARMY by Sarah Emma Evelyn Edmonds—During the American Civil War

WIFE NO. 19 by Ann Eliza Young—The Life & Ordeals of a Mormon Woman During the 19th Century

DIARY OF A NURSE IN SOUTH AFRICA by Alice Bron—With the Dutch-Belgian Red Cross During the Boer War

MARIE ANTOINETTE AND THE DOWNFALL OF ROYALTY by Imbert de Saint-Amand—The Queen of France and the French Revolution

THE MEMSAHIB & THE MUTINY by R. M. Coopland—An English lady's ordeals in Gwalior and Agra during the Indian Mutiny 1857

MY CAPTIVITY AMONG THE SIOUX INDIANS by Fanny Kelly—The ordeal of a pioneer woman crossing the Western Plains in 1864

WITH MAXIMILIAN IN MEXICO by Sara Yorke Stevenson—A Lady's experience of the French Adventure

AVAILABLE ONLINE AT **www.leonaur.com**
AND FROM ALL GOOD BOOK STORES

www.ingramcontent.com/pod-product-compliance
Lightning Source LLC
Chambersburg PA
CBHW030031180426
43196CB00043B/252